Jewish Life in Nazi Germany

JEWISH LIFE IN NAZI GERMANY

Dilemmas and Responses

Edited by
Francis R. Nicosia
and
David Scrase

Berghahn Books
NEW YORK • OXFORD

First published in 2010 by

Berghahn Books
www.BerghahnBooks.com

© 2010, 2012 The Miller Center for Holocaust Studies
at the University of Vermont
First paperback edition published in 2012

All rights reserved. Except for the quotation of short passages for the purposes of criticism and review, no part of this book may be reproduced in any form or by any means, electronic or mechanical, including photocopying, recording, or any information storage and retrieval system now known or to be invented, without written permission of the publisher.

Library of Congress Cataloging-in-Publication Data
Jewish life in Nazi Germany : dilemmas and responses / edited by Francis R. Nicosia and David Scrase.
   p. cm
   Includes bibliographical references and index.
   ISBN 978-1-84545-676-4 (hbk.) -- ISBN 978-0-85745-801-8 (pbk.)
   1. Jews—Germany—History—1933-1945. 2. Jews—Germany—Social conditions—20th century. 3. Jews—Government policy—Germany—History—20th century. 4. Jews—Persecutions—Germany—History—20th century. 5. Jews—Legal status, laws, etc.—Germany—History—20th century. 6. Germany—Politics and government—1933–1945. 7. Germany—Ethnic relations—History—20th century. I. Nicosia, Francis R. II. Scrase, David
   DS134.255.J495 2010
   305.892'404309043—dc22   2010011007

British Library Cataloguing in Publication Data

A catalogue record for this book is available
from the British Library.

The photograph on the cover of this book is courtesy of Yad Vashem, Jerusalem, via the United States Holocaust Memorial Museum, Washington, DC.

ISBN: 978-0-85745-801-8 (paperback)   ISBN 978-0-85745-817-9 (ebook)

"Juda verrecke"
Die Fahne spricht
"Juda lebt ewig"
Erwidert das Licht

("Death to Judah"
So the flag says
"Judah will live forever"
So the light answers)

Rachel Posner, the wife of Rabbi Dr. Akiva Posner of Kiel, wrote these words on the back of the photograph appearing on the cover of this book. She took this photograph in their apartment in Kiel at Hanukkah, 1932, just weeks before Hitler's appointment as Reich Chancellor. The window looks out on the town hall in Kiel, from which a Nazi flag is hanging. The Posners left Germany in 1933 and arrived in Palestine in 1934. Both the menorah and the photograph are featured in the new Holocaust History Museum at Yad Vashem in Jerusalem.

Contents

Preface	ix
List of Illustrations	xi
List of Abbreviations	xiii
Introduction: Jewish Life in Nazi Germany: Dilemmas and Responses *Francis R. Nicosia*	1
1. Changing Roles in Jewish Families *Marion Kaplan*	15
2. Evading Persecution: German-Jewish Behavior Patterns after 1933 *Jürgen Matthäus*	47
3. Jewish Self-Help in Nazi Germany, 1933–1939: The Dilemmas of Cooperation *Avraham Barkai*	71
4. German Zionism and Jewish Life in Nazi Berlin *Francis R. Nicosia*	89
5. Without Neighbors: Daily Living in *Judenhäuser* *Konrad Kwiet*	117
6. Between Self-Assertion and Forced Collaboration: The Reich Association of Jews in Germany, 1939–1945 *Beate Meyer*	149
7. Jewish Culture in a Modern Ghetto: Theater and Scholarship among the Jews of Nazi Germany *Michael Brenner*	170

Appendixes

A. Law for the Restoration of the Professional Civil Service,
   7 April 1933 — 185

B. Proclamation of the (New) Reichsvertretung der Deutschen
   Juden, September 1933 — 187

C. American Jewish Committee, "The Situation of the
   Jews in Germany," 1 March 1935 — 190

D. Reich Citizenship Law, 15 September 1935 — 195

E. Law for the Protection of German Blood and
   German Honor, 15 September 1935 — 197

F. American Jewish Committee, "The Jews in
   Germany Today," 1 June 1937 — 200

G. Letter from Georg Landauer to Martin Rosenblüth,
   8 February 1938 — 208

H. Law Concerning the Legal Status of the Jewish Religious
   Communities, 28 March 1938 — 209

I. Regulation for the Elimination of the Jews from the
   Economic Life of Germany, 12 November 1938 — 211

J. Establishment of the Reich Central Office for Jewish
   Emigration, 24 January 1939 — 213

K. Establishment of the Reichsvereinigung, 4 July 1939 — 215

Contributors — 221

Selected Bibliography — 223

Index — 237

Preface

FIVE OF THE ESSAYS IN this book are based on lectures delivered at the Miller Symposium on "Jewish Life in Nazi Germany," held at the University of Vermont. Organized by the Carolyn and Leonard Miller Center for Holocaust Studies at the University of Vermont, this was the fourth symposium bearing the name of Carolyn and Leonard Miller, who have been generous supporters of the Center's work and great friends of the university.

Established to honor the work of Professor Raul Hilberg, who served on the faculty of the University of Vermont for more than three decades, the Center for Holocaust Studies is committed to furthering the cause of Holocaust education and to serving as a forum for the presentation and discussion of new perspectives on the history of Nazi Germany and the Holocaust. Professor Hilberg's pioneering scholarship remains a model and a standard for scholars, and it is his work in the field that remains an inspiration for the Center's programming and also for publications such as this. The Miller Symposia have contributed significantly to the Center's efforts to explore insufficiently charted areas in the history of the Third Reich and the Holocaust. Our goal in organizing them has been to address topical, or even controversial, themes in that history, relying on the expertise of some of the most accomplished scholars and other authorities in the field.

The first Miller Symposium brought together some of the world's leading scholars in the history of eugenics and the German medical establishment during the Third Reich. It resulted in the anthology *Medicine and Medical Ethics in Nazi Germany: Origins, Practices, Legacies*, published by Berghahn Books. The second Miller Symposium focused on German business and industry under National Socialism. It brought together scholars who are among the most respected and innovative analysts of German business, industry, and finance in the years of the Third Reich. The resulting volume, *Business and Industry in Nazi*

Germany, was published by Berghahn Books. The third Miller Symposium featured some of the most important scholars in the history of the arts in Nazi Germany. Their contributions to the volume *The Arts in Nazi Germany: Continuity, Conformity, Change* address the roles of artists, writers, musicians, filmmakers, Jewish cultural institutions, US cultural influence, and German youth in the life of the Nazi state.

The fourth Miller Symposium brought to the University of Vermont some of the world's leading scholars of the history of Jews and Jewish life in Nazi Germany. Based on the authors' original scholarship, the essays assembled here serve as an introduction to some of the most current research and controversies in the tragic history of German Jews from Hitler's appointment as chancellor in January 1933 to the onset of the "final solution" in late 1941. These essays focus, for the most part, on the everyday lives of ordinary German Jews, and will be of interest to students and scholars of twentieth-century German history and the Nazi era, the history of German Jewry, and the Holocaust.

Both the fourth Miller Symposium and this volume owe a tremendous debt to Leonard Miller and his late wife Carolyn. Their support for the Center for Holocaust Studies at the University of Vermont has helped to sustain and expand its programming over the years. The editors also recognize and thank the symposium's organizing committee, which included Katherine Johnson, Jonathan Huener, and the editors of this volume. We wish to extend a special note of thanks to Dr. Robert Bernheim, Interim Director of the Miller Center from 2006 to 2007, and currently Executive Director of the Michael Klahr Holocaust and Human Rights Center at the University of Maine at Augusta, for his assistance.

ILLUSTRATIONS

2.1. Form for the authentication (by German police officials) of photographs used in conjunction with racial ancestry cases handled in 1942 by the Berlin prosecutor's office. *Courtesy*: Landesarchiv Berlin.   57

2.2. Form for the authentication (by German police officials) of photographs used in conjunction with racial ancestry cases handled in 1942 by the Berlin prosecutor's office. *Courtesy*: Landesarchiv Berlin.   58

4.1. The *Hauswegweiser* (Office Directory) at the headquarters of the Zionistische Vereinigung für Deutschland and the Jewish Agency for Palestine at Meineckestrasse 10, Berlin. *Courtesy*: Central Zionist Archives, Jerusalem.   93

4.2. An all-day seminar sponsored by the Zionistische Vereinigung für Deutschland, Berlin, 1935. *Courtesy*: Central Zionist Archives, Jerusalem.   98

4.3. Jewish Gymnasium graduates train as carpenters under the auspices of the Jewish community in Berlin. Photograph by Abraham Pisarek. *Courtesy*: Bildarchiv Preussischer Kulturbesitz, Berlin, and Art Resource, New York.   100

5.1. Jews from Hattingen, who were deported on 28 April 1942, lived for almost one year in an empty rifle factory that had served as a "Jewish House" (Judenhaus). To the right and above, one sees the Jewish star designating the building as a Judenhaus. Courtesy: Stadtarchiv Kerpen.   130

5.2. Until their deportation in 1942, the Jews of Kerpen were forced to live in a "Jewish House" (*Judenhaus*) on Hindenburgstrasse. On 18 July 1942, the last thirty-one Jews in Kerpen were deported from here. *Courtesy*: Stadtarchiv Kerpen. 130

6.1. Paul Eppstein, member of the board of the Reichsvertretung der Juden in Deutschland, ca. 1935. *Courtesy*: Stadtarchiv Mannheim, Nachlass Paul Eppstein. 156

6.2. Paul Eppstein, Elder of Jews in Theresienstadt, August/September 1944. *Courtesy*: Stadtarchiv Mannheim, Nachlass Paul Eppstein. 161

7.1. Martin Buber speaking at the "Jüdisches Lehrhaus," Berlin, 17 January 1935. Photograph by Abraham Pisarek. *Courtesy*: Bildarchiv Preussischer Kulturbesitz, Berlin, and Art Resource, New York. 177

Abbreviations

ACJ	Archiv Centrum Judaicum (Archives of the Judaica Center), Berlin
AJC	American Jewish Committee
AJDC	American Jewish Joint Distribution Committee, New York
BArch	Bundesarchiv (Federal Archives), Berlin
BJFB	Blätter des jüdischen Frauenbundes
BLHA	Brandenburgisches Landeshauptarchiv (Brandenburg Main State Archives), Potsdam
CdSuSD	Chef der Sicherheitspolizei und Sicherheitsdienst (Chief of the Security Police and Security Service)
CV	Centralverein deutscher Staatsbürger jüdischen Glaubens/ Centralverein der Juden in Deutschland (Central Association of German Citizens of the Jewish Faith/ Central Association of Jews in Germany)
CVZ	*CV-Zeitung*
CZA	Central Zionist Archives, Jerusalem
HA	Haganah Archives, Tel Aviv
HdJ	Hilfsverein der deutschen Juden (Aid Association of German Jews)
IF	Israelitisches Familienblatt
IfZ	Institut für Zeitgeschichte (Institute for Contemporary History), Munich

JVP	Jüdische Volkspartei (Jewish Peoples Party)
JWS	Jüdische Wohlfahrtspflege und Sozialpolitik
KB	Kulturbund deutscher Juden (Cultural League of German Jews)
LAB	Landesarchiv (State Archives), Berlin
LBI	Leo Baeck Institute, New York and Jerusalem
LBIJMB	Leo Baeck Institute Jewish Museum, Berlin
LG	Landesgericht Berlin (State Court of Justice) Berlin
MGWJ	*Monatsschrift für Geschichte und Wissenschaft des Judentums*
Nbg.Doc.	Nuremberg Documents
NSV	Nationalsozialistische Volkswohlfahrt (National Socialist Peoples Welfare Agency)
ORT	Obshchestvo Rasprostraneniia Truda (Organization for the Distribution of Artisanal and Agricultural Skills for the Jews of Russia)
Osb	Osobyi Secret Archives, Moscow
PA	Politisches Archiv des Auswärtigen Amts (Political Archives of the Foreign Ministry), Berlin
RjF	Reichsbund jüdischer Frontsoldaten (Reich League of Jewish War Veterans)
RSHA	Reichssicherheitshauptamt (Reich Security Main Office)
RVt	Reichsvertretung der deutschen Juden/Reichsvertretung der Juden in Deutschland (Reich Representation of German Jews/Reich Representation of Jews in Germany)
RVe	Reichsvereinigung der Juden in Deutschland (Reich Association of Jews in Germany)
SD	Sicherheitsdienst (Security Service)

USHMM	United States Holocaust Memorial Museum, Washington, D.C.
VnJ	Verband nationaldeutscher Juden (Association of National German Jews)
YVA	Yad Vashem Archives, Jerusalem
ZGJD	Zeitschrift für die Geschichte der Juden in Deutschland
ZJHA	Zentralausschuss der deutschen Juden für Hilfe und Aufbau (Central Committee of German Jews for Assistance and Construction)
ZVfD	Zionistische Vereinigung für Deutschland (Zionist Federation for Germany)

Introduction

JEWISH LIFE IN NAZI GERMANY

Dilemmas and Responses

Francis R. Nicosia

DURING A VISIT TO BERLIN and Prague in February 1939, Georg Landauer, Director of the Central Bureau for the Settlement of German Jews in Palestine in Jerusalem, wrote a long letter to Arthur Ruppin, his colleague at the Central Bureau in Palestine. Landauer, a German Zionist leader before his own emigration from Germany to Palestine in 1933, was in Berlin and Prague to assess the Jewish emigration process. In his letter, dated 17 February from Berlin (but likely sent from Prague), Landauer describes the situation as bleak for Jews in Berlin and the rest of Germany.[1] The destruction of a viable economic existence for Germany's Jews had left those remaining in Germany utterly impoverished. As a consequence, and with the increasing threat of war, the prospects for further Jewish emigration from Germany were not at all good. Landauer saw little hope of effectively moving substantially more Jews safely out of Germany. With words that were both somber and almost prophetic, he closed his 17 February letter with the following observation: "The mood of the Jews in Germany is one of indescribable dejection. They really know of no way out, and they wait to see what the government will do with them. Work camps? Other methods of liquidation?" In June of that year, with war looming and immigration opportunities to other countries likely to diminish as a result, Pino Ginzburg of the clandestine Jewish self-defense organization in Palestine, the Haganah, was in Germany working on the organization of "illegal" immigration of Jews from central Europe to Palestine. Pessimistic about the chances of Jews escaping from Greater Germany, he wrote from

Vienna to a colleague in Palestine on 5 June: "Our work becomes more difficult every day. The pressure increases steadily . . . The opportunity to leave is very small. We are helpless."[2]

The words of Landauer and Ginzburg convey a sense of despair that had come to pervade the lives of Jews in Greater Germany after six years (more than one year in Austria) of state-imposed economic deprivation, legal disenfranchisement, social and cultural segregation, intimidation, humiliation, and violence. Indeed, in the context of Marion Kaplan's description of Jewish life under National Socialism as a struggle to preserve individual and collective dignity in the face of growing despair,[3] the latter seemed to have overtaken the former by the eve of World War II. In hindsight, the process during the 1930s appears to have been steady, almost unrelenting, despite a few lulls in the intensity of Nazi persecution. Nevertheless, and in spite of the intensifying cruelty of Nazi Jewish policy in Germany from 1933 to the "final solution," German Jews went to extraordinary lengths to adapt to a steadily changing environment, one that afforded them limited and diminishing options. In the struggle to maintain their dignity and to resist the despair that would be a consequence of their disintegrating world, German Jews, individually and collectively, confronted dilemmas and fashioned responses to their changing circumstances as best they could.

In introducing his study of Nazi Germany and the Jews during the 1930s, published in 1997, Saul Friedländer observes that, notwithstanding the central role of Nazi perpetrators and their policies after 1933, "the surrounding world and the victims' attitudes, reactions, and fate are no less an integral part of this unfolding history."[4] With this in mind, this volume builds on Friedländer's approach, with its focus on the Jewish victims of Nazi persecution in Germany. The seven essays in this book consider some of the tragic dilemmas with which deteriorating circumstances in Jewish life under the Nazis confronted German Jews each day, and the complex nature of some of their responses to those dilemmas. Primo Levi's thoughts, albeit as a surviving victim of the Nazi extermination camp system, might be instructive in this regard. When describing the harsh realities of survival in the camps, he observes: "We believe, rather, that the only conclusion to be drawn is that in the face of driving necessity and physical disabilities many social habits and instincts are reduced to silence."[5] Of course, Jews in Germany before the "final solution" did not have to face the immediate life-threatening perils in their daily lives that Levi and countless others faced in the extermination camps; but beginning in 1941, many did. All had to adapt to new and, for their time and place, more dangerous circumstances, to think in terms of survival, and to face difficult dilemmas in the choices they were forced to make.

Since this is a collection of essays about the victims and the ways in which they responded to Nazi persecution, this introduction will present a brief overview of some of the policies of the perpetrators, underlining the nature and scope of the relentless Nazi assault on Jewish life in the Third Reich. Initially, Jews were not the primary targets of Nazi policy. During his first two months in office, Hitler sought total power for himself and his party by moving to destroy all political opposition, especially that of the Communists and Social Democrats and their affiliated organizations. He used the Reichstag fire of 27 February 1933 to convince President Paul von Hindenburg temporarily to suspend civil liberties in Germany. The "Decree for the Protection of the People and the State" of 28 February empowered Hitler's government to suspend basic civil liberties and to use the Nazi-controlled police to cripple the communist movement and to move swiftly against other political opponents, real and imagined.[6] On 24 March, Hitler persuaded the Reichstag to adopt an emergency measure that suspended the German parliament for four years. The "Law for Removing the Distress of the People and the Reich," also known as the "Enabling Act," empowered Hitler's government to legislate without parliamentary consent. By a vote of 444 to 94, with the Communists out of the picture and only the Social Democrats opposing the measure, effective parliamentary government was abolished in Germany by an act of parliament. Hitler was now in a position to move against any remaining opposition to his dictatorship. On 14 July 1933, the National Socialist party was declared the only legal party in Germany. A year later, with the death of President von Hindenburg on 2 August 1934 and the support of the armed forces, Hitler combined his office as chancellor with that of the presidency into the single office of "Führer and Reich Chancellor."

Notwithstanding Nazi efforts to eliminate the physically and mentally handicapped and the Gypsies from German "living space," their primary racial enemy remained the Jews. Initial Nazi intentions toward the Jews of Germany are apparent in the "Program of the National Socialist German Workers Party (NSDAP)" of February 1920, and from the speeches and writings of Hitler and other Nazis before 1933. They included the reversal of Jewish emancipation and assimilation, and the removal of all Jews from the Reich. Between 1933 and 1941, the Nazi state pursued a Jewish policy based on a two-tiered approach of enacting legislation that abolished the civil rights and economic livelihood of German Jews, forced their total separation from the non-Jewish majority, and simultaneously promoted their emigration/deportation from Germany. Throughout this process, a state-imposed environment of increasing impoverishment, intimidation, and periodic violence served to heighten the pressure on Jews to leave.[7]

When Adolf Hitler assumed power on 30 January 1933, there were about 530,000 Jews in Germany, about 100,000 of whom were foreign Jews who had in recent decades immigrated to Germany, mostly from Eastern Europe. Germany's Jewish community was comparatively small, comprising less than one percent of the total population. As a group, they were predominantly urban, with more than half living in Germany's ten largest cities, and about one-third, or more than 160,000, living in Berlin alone. Significant numbers were involved in commerce and industry, in the professions, as well as in the arts and the media. Politically, most supported democratic traditions and institutions in Germany, and the German Democratic and Social Democratic parties during the Weimar Republic. For the most part, Jews in Germany had enjoyed equal rights under the Imperial and Weimar constitutions as well as economic freedom, and most had assimilated into Germany society.[8]

Between April 1933 and end of 1935, the regime enacted laws depriving Jews of their rights as equal citizens and removing them from every facet of German life except the economy.[9] The "Law for the Restoration of the Professional Civil Service,"[10] enacted on 7 April 1933, eliminated Jews, for the most part, from the civil service. On the same day, the "Law Concerning Admission to the Legal Profession" prohibited so-called Aryan Germans from retaining Jewish lawyers, and Aryan lawyers from representing Jewish clients. The "Decree Regarding Physicians' Services with the National Health Service" of 22 April separated Jewish physicians from their non-Jewish patients by denying health insurance to Aryans who continued to see their Jewish doctors. In 1933, some 16 percent of independent lawyers in Germany were Jewish, as were about 10 percent of all practicing physicians; thus, restricting the relatively large number of Jewish lawyers and physicians to the relatively small Jewish community forced many out of their professions and eventually out of Germany. The "Law Against Overcrowding of German Schools," enacted on 25 April, was designed to drive Jewish students from German schools through the imposition of strict quotas and the incorporation of Nazi racial doctrine into the curriculum. With the "Denaturalization Law" of 14 July 1933, aimed primarily at the thousands of *Ostjuden* who had fled anti-Semitic violence in Eastern Europe after World War I, the regime could revoke the citizenship of those who had settled in Germany after November 1918. Additional legislation drove Jews out of the arts and media in German national life. It included the "Law Creating the Reich Chamber of Culture" of 29 September and the "National Press Law" of 4 October. The new Reich Chamber of Culture excluded Jewish artists, actors, and musicians, which meant that they could continue their professions only by performing the works of Jewish writers and composers in Jewish theaters and orchestras. The press law, in effect, limited Jewish writers and journalists to publishing their work only with Jewish newspapers and publishers. But the most notorious anti-Jewish legislation during the 1930s was the "Law for the Protection of German Blood and German Honor,"[11] part of the so-called Nuremberg Race Laws adopted at the annual Nazi Party rally in Nuremberg on 15 September 1935. Marriage and sexual relations between Jews and Aryans were prohibited by law. Non-Jews who socialized with Jews were often publicly ostracized, while those who were caught in sexual relationships with Jews were subject to prosecution for the crime of *Rassenschande* (race defilement). Initially, the Nazis applied the law to "full-blooded" Jews, defined as those with at least three Jewish grandparents, and later adopted complex restrictions for half-Jews (*Mischlinge*, or "mixed breeds") as well. An additional part of the Nuremberg Race Laws of September 1935, the "Reich Citizenship Law,"[12] created a greatly reduced level of citizenship for Germany's Jews. Realizing that simply revoking the citizenship of Germany's Jews would render them stateless, and thus further limit their emigration opportunities, the regime declared Aryan Germans to be the sole bearers of full rights. This confirmed the loss of civil rights that the Jews had endured since 1933, and reduced them to second-class subjects of the Reich.

By the end of 1935, Jews in Germany no longer received many of the social services that the state provided its citizens, nor were they permitted any longer to participate in the cultural and recreational life of German society, much of which was subsidized by the state.[13] They were forced to rely increasingly on their own private cultural, educational, and social welfare institutions; those that already existed were overwhelmed and had to be greatly expanded with very limited resources available, while additional social services had to be created from scratch. Jews were also forced to depend increasingly on financial support from overseas Jewish organizations.

Prior to 1938, the Nazi regime was reluctant to attack directly the Jewish position in the German economy. Fearful of compromising economic recovery and rearmament plans, Jewish businesses were generally permitted to function, albeit under the enormous pressures of organized anti-Jewish boycotts and concerted efforts to "Aryanize" Jewish businesses.[14] Moreover, Hitler's government always feared negative Jewish reactions abroad and their perceived impact on the governments of foreign powers, obsessed as the Nazis were with notions of Jewish control of foreign governments and an alleged international Jewish conspiracy.[15] But by 1938, with the German economy out of crisis, plans afoot to annex Austria and dismember Czechoslovakia, along with the strong possibility of war that those moves entailed, Hitler could undertake measures against the Jews that were meant finally to remove the Jews from the economy and thereby increase dramatically the pressure on them to emigrate. On 26 April 1938, the "Decree Regarding Registration of Jewish Property" forced Jews to register all property in Germany and abroad with a value of more than RM 5,000. This was a preliminary step to the "Law for the Elimination of Jews from the Economic Life of Germany" of 12 November, which decreed that all Jewish businesses were to close by 1 January 1939.[16]

Increased pressure on the Jews in Germany continued through 1938 in the form of arrests, with many sent to concentration camps at Dachau, Sachsenhausen, and Buchenwald. In October, the SS deported approximately 18,000 Polish Jews who had been living in Germany, even as the anti-Semitic government of Poland tried to block their return.[17] On the night of 9–10 November 1938, in response to the murder in Paris of a junior Nazi diplomat, Ernst vom Rath, by Herschel Grynszpan, a 17-year-old Jewish student from Poland, the regime unleashed the infamous *Kristallnacht* pogrom against the Jewish community throughout Germany.[18] The Jews were made liable for all of the damage that resulted from the pogrom as the regime imposed a one billion Mark fine on the Jewish community. The aftermath of *Kristallnacht* brought an acceleration of anti-Jewish measures in late 1938 and 1939, as Germany moved closer to war. Jewish communities lost their official status as corporations under public law,[19] most official Jewish organizations were dissolved, and Jewish newspapers, with few exceptions, were banned. Although religious and cultural organizations were still permitted on a private basis, the Reichsvertretung der Juden in

Deutschland (Reich Representation of Jews in Germany), established officially in September 1933 as the representative of the major Jewish organizations vis-à-vis the Nazi state, was abolished. In February 1939, it was replaced with the Reichsvereinigung der Juden in Deutschland (Reich Association of Jews in Germany), a single body representing all German Jews under the firm control of the SS.[20] Its primary functions were the administration of Jewish welfare efforts and the coordination of an all-out, SS-directed, Jewish push for emigration from Germany.

For Hitler's regime, the primary purpose of all of these actions was to pressure Jews to leave Germany, without their assets, for destinations preferably outside Europe. But the emigration process between 1933 and 1938 was slow and laborious, and did not remove Jews fast enough to satisfy Nazi wishes. During the five years between January 1933 and the beginning of 1938, about 140,000 Jews had emigrated from Germany, and by early 1938, plans were set to annex Austria and, with it, an additional almost 200,000 Austrian Jews. Despite all of the legislation, intimidation, and violence, the emigration process remained essentially voluntary, dependent on the willingness of Jews to leave and the willingness of other countries to accept them. During the 1930s, however, potential receiver countries were reluctant to admit immigrants, particularly those with little or no money. Most of an emigrant's property was declared "non-transferable" and was confiscated by the state when she or he left Germany.[21]

Nazi authorities were impressed with the brutal efficiency of the new "emigration" procedures established in Vienna by Adolf Eichmann and the SS after the annexation of Austria in March 1938, a process that is perhaps better described as "deportation."[22] As a result, those methods were adopted for the rest of Germany with the establishment, in January 1939 in Berlin, of the "Reich Central Office for Jewish Emigration." [23] Under Heinrich Müller, the head of the Gestapo, its task was to centralize the entire apparatus of Jewish emigration, including the Reichsvereinigung, under the firm control of the SS and to implement throughout Germany the forced emigration procedures that Eichmann had perfected in Vienna. But by 1941, these measures too were rendered irrelevant by Germany's conquest of most of Europe and upwards of nine million Jews. Emigration, no longer an effective mechanism for the elimination of Jewish life from German "living space," was replaced by systematic mass murder of all of the Jews in Europe.

In all of this, many German Jews, particularly older people, still found it difficult to contemplate or start the process of emigration from their native Germany.[24] As loyal and patriotic Germans, mostly integrated into German life by 1933, they found it difficult to imagine living elsewhere. Emigration for them posed its own set of dilemmas at that time, and they opted for different responses to the harsh conditions around them.

The Jewish community in Germany was as varied as any in Europe during the early decades of the twentieth century. A relatively small group, from orthodox religious to secular Zionists, identified themselves primarily, culturally and/or religiously, as Jews. Those in another minority viewed themselves strictly as Germans, families that had long since converted to Christianity, married Aryan Germans, or were simply secular or atheist citizens with no religious or cultural identity or affiliations as Jews. Most German Jews, on the other hand, were entirely secular and identified themselves as Germans by nationality and culture, while retaining some cultural and/or religious ties to their Jewish heritage and community as "German citizens of the Jewish faith."[25] Some were able to emigrate, some tried but were unable to find countries that would take them; and some survived in Germany by manipulating the often jumbled confusion of Nazi racial categorization and legislation. Others hid with or were otherwise protected by friends, or were able to pass as Aryans, while some adapted in some way to the process of Nazi persecution. About 140,000 German Jews from within the Reich's pre-March 1938 borders ultimately perished in the "final solution."[26]

Regardless of whether one belonged to any of these or other "categories" in the Third Reich, virtually all were classified as Jews after 1933 and forced to confront difficult, even life and death choices about the future. What were some of those dilemmas, and what were some of the choices made by ordinary German Jews as they confronted those dilemmas? Marion Kaplan's essay "Changing Roles in Jewish Families" looks at the impact of Nazi brutality on the traditional dynamics of gender and age in German-Jewish families. She examines the changing role of women in the family, both economically and publicly, when the men lost their jobs and careers, and their positions in public life outside of the family. Children, moreover, often differed with their parents on how to respond to the developing crisis. Adolescents and young adults not yet finished with their education or established in careers were naturally more inclined to consider emigration, while grandparents and sometimes even parents often had to be left behind. Families that in ordinary times would have remained in close contact were forced to break up so that some might be saved.

In his essay "Evading Persecution: German-Jewish Behavior Patterns after 1933," Jürgen Matthäus considers the complicated survival tactic of "evasion by compliance" as part of the spectrum of Jewish behavior during the Nazi years. This involved using the Nazi system of racial classification and family law, a reality with which all Germans in theory were required to comply, to legally deny the stigma of being classified as a Jew, and thus undermine the basis of Nazi Jewish policy, namely, the definition of who was a Jew. Matthäus brings to light the efforts of Jews who used the system and risked the necessary legal steps to secure their own racial reclassification by posing as "Aryans," *Mischlinge*, or "privileged" Jews, in order to avoid "social death" prior to 1941 or "their physical annihilation" thereafter. The system did potentially threaten Nazi efforts to establish a "racially pure" state by permitting Germans of Jewish ancestry to infiltrate the *Volksgemeinschaft* via successful reclassification applications. However, Matthäus keeps his focus on the efforts of the relatively few who were in a position to risk contesting their racial classification through established legal channels as they sought to conceal their Jewish ancestry.

Avraham Barkai's contribution, "Jewish Self-Help in Nazi Germany, 1933–1939: The Dilemmas of Cooperation," addresses one of the most sensitive and highly debated aspects of the larger question of Jewish responses to Nazi persecution, namely, the behavior of Jewish leaders in their dealings with the Nazi state. During the 1930s, did Jewish leaders in Germany have any alternatives to cooperating with Nazi officials in the process of reversing Jewish emancipation and assimilation, and pushing Jews to emigrate? Here one confronts perhaps the most fundamental dilemma faced by German Jews, namely, the necessity of working with the Nazis to achieve an outcome that was both undesirable yet tolerable given the alternatives. Barkai's focus is on the Zionists and their efforts to achieve what they had always sought to achieve, namely, an orderly and economically viable emigration of German Jews from Germany to Palestine. And this required a working relationship with the German state, both before 1933 and after the Nazis assumed power. He recognizes the dilemmas of cooperation with the perpetrators, and the fact that there were no doubt instances when cooperation "indeed turned into condemnable collaboration." But he also recognizes the inevitable "pitfalls of historical hindsight" when making judgments about the victims and their responses to the dilemmas they faced "under extremely inhuman and desperate conditions."

Francis Nicosia's "German Zionism and Jewish Life in Nazi Berlin" follows Avraham Barkai's analysis of German Zionist leaders and their relationship with the Nazi state, with an examination of the ways they sought to transform the political and cultural life of Berlin Jews between 1933 and 1941. Both as a traditional and comprehensive response to anti-Semitism in Germany, as well as an immediate political and institutional response to multi-faceted Nazi persecution after 1933, the Zionists hoped to be able to transform German-Jewish culture in preparation for an orderly and economically viable immigration to Palestine. Much of this effort was focused on Berlin, where Jewish organizations and a third of the German-Jewish population were concentrated, and on Jewish youths, the age group that had traditionally been most responsive to the Zionist message and program. In education and occupational training and retraining in particular, the Zionist movement quickly became a dominant force among Jews in Berlin in its efforts to transform the ethos of Jewish life in Berlin. But, in the end, and in spite of dramatic achievements among German-Jewish youths in Berlin and throughout the Reich, Zionist efforts soon unraveled into a scramble to secure the departure of as many Jews as possible from Berlin and the rest of Germany, as quickly as possible, regardless of their individual identities, cultural inclinations, or their commitment to Zionism and Palestine. By the outbreak of war in 1939, Nicosia concludes, the idea of rescue had replaced the ambitious goal of reeducation and orderly emigration as the imperative in the efforts of the Zionist leadership in Berlin.

In his essay "Without Neighbors: Daily Living in *Judenhäuser*," Konrad Kwiet examines those German Jews who were made homeless in Nazi Germany and were unable to emigrate after the outbreak of war in 1939. In the case of these victims, it was not a matter of facing dilemmas in making decisions about how to survive; rather, it was merely following what for them had become their only option. In describing the *Judenhäuser* (Jewish houses) and *Judensiedlungen* (Jewish settlements) in Germany, Kwiet likens the fate of the German Jews who inhabited these places inside Germany to that of Jews in the ghettos and extermination camps in the East. They were designed to separate Jews by placing them temporarily "into a new 'Jewish' place, a segregated Jewish living quarter." Comparing the *Judenhäuser* to the ghettos that the Nazis created in occupied Eastern Europe, Kwiet emphasizes that they were meant to absorb large numbers of impoverished and unemployed German Jews who would be used as forced laborers in the Nazi war economy. In likening this wartime reality for some Jews in Germany to the ghetto system established for Jews in the East, Kwiet defines them as "self-contained units, separated from the main body of workers." And, like the Jews in the ghettos in Poland, the liquidation of *Judenhäuser* and *Judensiedlungen* began when the decision was made to murder their inhabitants. These German Jews shared the fate of Jews in the East, Kwiet observes, and concludes that, "within the Nazi system, based on racial hatred and mass murder, ghettoization and forced labor were only steps along the path to genocide."

Returning to the issues raised by Avraham Barkai, Beate Meyer's contribution, "Between Self-Assertion and Forced Collaboration: The Reich Association of Jews in Germany, 1939–1945," examines the motivations and strategies of Jewish leaders who assumed the responsibility of working with the regime during the war years and the implementation of the "final solution." She takes issue with earlier assertions that a sense of responsibility, a high degree of self-confidence, and irresistible Nazi coercion explained the motivations and actions of German-Jewish leaders. Meyer uses the example of the Reichsvereinigung der Juden in Deutschland and its leadership, which was established in February 1939 as a body representing all Jews remaining in Germany and through which the regime might better force Jews to do what it expected of them. Since many of those leaders were professionals who held high positions in the German bureaucracy before 1933, they followed a more traditional style of governing with rules that they believed "would act as a counterweight to arbitrariness, violence, and murder." It did not occur to them, Meyer argues, that such methods not only would not preclude mass murder, but might in fact enhance its implementation. She concludes that preserving a Jewish administration in the Reichsvereinigung that followed the old rules "proved to be a pitifully helpless strategy for averting what Dan Diner has termed the 'rupture of civilization.'"

Finally, Michael Brenner follows, to some extent, Konrad Kwiet's theme of a "ghetto without walls" that increasingly characterized Jewish life in Germany after January 1933. In his essay "Jewish Culture in a Modern Ghetto: Theater and Scholarship among the Jews of Nazi Germany," Brenner's focus is the cultural ghettoization of German Jews that was a consequence of the spate of anti-Jewish legislation during the 1930s. While this was evident in a variety of areas, such as

Jewish adult education programs, youth movements, and Jewish publishing and media enterprises, it was most apparent in activities of the Kulturbund der deutschen Juden (Cultural League of German Jews), established just weeks after the Nazi assumption of power. Brenner refers to the debates surrounding the Kulturbund, with the positive assessment that it represented a spiritual resistance to ghettoization and the despair it would inevitably induce; and the negative conclusion that it represented compliance with the destructive intentions behind the cultural ghettoization of the Jews. Brenner also considers the work of Jewish historians who, after 1933, produced some of the most brilliant scholarship on German-Jewish history. These historians would raise questions about the efficacy of Enlightenment philosophy and Jewish emancipation, and pose questions about the failure of Jewish emancipation in German-Jewish history that have engaged historians since the end of World War II and the Holocaust.

It is hoped that these essays, along with the Appendixes at the end of this volume, will contribute to a better understanding of the tragedy of that historic failure. That German Jews at times faced paralyzing dilemmas in responding to Nazi persecution was in part the result of the nature of Nazi cruelty and brutality; but these dilemmas also stemmed from a general understanding among most German Jews of their history and rightful place in Germany, the promise of Jewish emancipation, and the meaning for most of "assimilation." The imposed separation of German Jews from the larger society and culture of their native Germany, their consequent humiliation and suffering, and the Nazi state's denial of their German nationality and national self-identity, was a bitter blow that most found agonizingly difficult to accept. That one could be both German and Jewish, regardless of the criteria used to define "Jewishness," had been a basic premise of Jewish emancipation, one that ultimately proved untenable in modern Germany between 1871 and 1945.

Notes

1. Central Zionist Archives (CZA), Jerusalem: S7–902, Central Bureau for the Settlement of German Jews in Palestine, Georg Landauer, Berlin to Arthur Ruppin, Jerusalem, 17 February 1939.
2. Haganah Archives (HA), Tel Aviv: 1/23/private/12: Private Documents of Pino Ginzburg (Ha'apala Project, Tel Aviv University), Pino Ginzburg (Vienna) to Beryl, 5 June 1939.

Introduction

3. See Marion A. Kaplan, *Between Dignity and Despair: Jewish Life in Nazi Germany* (New York: Oxford University Press, 1998).
4. See Saul Friedländer, *Nazi Germany and the Jews: The Years of Persecution, 1933–1939* (New York: HarperCollins, 1997), 2. See also his *The Years of Extermination: Nazi Germany and the Jews, 1939–1945* (New York: HarperCollins, 2007), 4ff.
5. Primo Levi, *Survival in Auschwitz* (New York: Simon & Schuster, 1996), 87.
6. Karl Dietrich Bracher, *The German Dictatorship*, trans. Jean Steinberg (New York: Holt, Rinehart & Winston, 1970), 191–214.
7. Karl Schleunes, *The Twisted Road to Auschwitz: Nazi Policy Toward German Jews, 1933–1939* (Urbana: University of Illinois Press, 1970), 62–91.
8. Donald Niewyk, *The Jews in Weimar Germany* (New Brunswick: Transaction Publishers, 2001), 11–42.
9. Schleunes, chap. 4.
10. See Appendix A.
11. See Appendix E.
12. See Appendix D.
13. Avraham Barkai, *From Boycott to Annihilation: The Economic Struggle of German Jews, 1933–1943* (Hanover: University Press of New England, 1989), 39–47.
14. See Uwe-Dietrich Adam, *Judenpolitik im Dritten Reich* (Düsseldorf: Droste Verlag, 1972), 172–203. See also Barkai, *From Boycott*, 54–85.
15. See most recently Jeffrey Herf, *The Jewish Enemy: Nazi Propaganda during World War II and the Holocaust* (Cambridge, MA: Harvard University Press, 2006), especially chap. 3.
16. See Appendix I.
17. See Sybil Milton, "The Expulsion of Polish Jews from Germany: October 1938 to July 1939—A Documentation," *Leo Baeck Institute Yearbook* XXIX (1984), 169–199. See also Schleunes, *The Twisted Road*, 236–239.
18. See most recently Alan Steinweis, *Kristallnacht 1938* (Cambridge, MA: Harvard University Press, 2009).
19. See Appendix H.
20. See Appendix K.
21. Schleunes, *The Twisted Road*, 195.
22. See Bruce Pauley, *From Prejudice to Persecution: A History of Austrian Antisemitism* (Chapel Hill: University of North Carolina Press, 1992), 284–286.
23. See Appendix J.
24. Between Hitler's appointment as Reich Chancellor in 1933 and the onset of the "final solution" at the end of 1941, some 300,000 Jews were able to emigrate from the *Altreich*, or Germany, in its pre-1938 borders. A high percentage of those emigrating were young people, leaving behind an increasingly aging population with diminishing means in the face of accelerating hardship. Between 1933 and 1939, the number of Jews in Germany between the ages of sixteen and thirty-nine decreased by about 80 percent; the number of those sixty and over decreased by only 27 percent. About 16 percent of Jews in Germany in 1933 were sixty years of age and over, while that percentage increased to almost 37 percent of the remaining Jewish population by the summer of 1941. See Herbert A. Strauss, "Jewish Emigration from Germany—Nazi Policies and Jewish Responses I," *Leo Baeck Institute Yearbook* XXV (1980): 318.

25. By far, the largest Jewish organization in Germany when the Nazis assumed power in January 1933 was the Centralverein deutscher Staatsbürger jüdischen Glaubens (Central Association of German Citizens of the Jewish Faith). Founded in 1893 in an environment of increasingly virulent anti-Semitism in Germany, the Centralverein engaged in the struggle to maintain the civic equality and economic freedom of German Jews. Its membership reflected the overwhelmingly secular, assimilated, and German character and identity of the majority of Jews in Germany, who believed that one could be both German and Jewish at the same time.
26. Estimates on the number of German Jews who perished in the Holocaust vary. See among others Raul Hilberg, *The Destruction of the European Jews*, vol. 3 (New York: Holmes & Meier, 1985), 1220; and Wolfgang Benz, *Dimension des Völkermords: Die Zahl der jüdischen Opfer des Nationalsozialismus* (Munich: Oldenbourg, 1991). More than 60,000 Jews from Austria and about 78,000 from Bohemia and Moravia also perished.

Chapter One

CHANGING ROLES IN JEWISH FAMILIES

Marion Kaplan

HAVING ACQUIRED FULL CITIZENSHIP AND middle-class status in the latter part of the nineteenth century, most of Germany's Jews felt comfortable and safe enough to consider Germany their *Heimat*, or home. They married, or intermarried, in Germany, built their businesses or careers there, sent their children to its excellent public schools, and planned their families' futures in Germany. The Nazi onslaught against their rights, their livelihoods, and their social interactions with other Germans staggered them. Their normal lives and expectations overturned, Jewish families embarked on new paths and embraced new strategies that they would never have entertained in ordinary times. For women, this meant new roles as partner, as breadwinner, as family protector, and as defender of their businesses or practices, roles that were often strange to them, but ones that they had to assume if they were to save their families and property. For children, this included growing up fast—too fast for many—in order to run the gauntlet of Nazified (Germans used the term *Gleichschaltung*) schools and to minimize the strains on their already anxious parents. Finally, the men's world as they had known it changed at a dizzying pace as they lost jobs and could no longer adequately or even barely protect or support their families or even themselves. This essay will look at several ways in which families, and the individuals in them, adjusted to extraordinary times.

Family as Haven?

Jews had, since the late nineteenth century, limited the size of their families, but they quickly reacted to their deteriorating political and financial situations by lowering their birthrate even more drastically.[1] Women underwent private and highly illegal abortions, fearful of endangering themselves and their doctors.[2] This seems to be a clear indication that Jews no longer saw a future for their children in Germany and also that, despite early hopes that the Nazi regime might fall, some planned to emigrate, waiting, perhaps, to give birth to children in places of refuge. The birth rate also tells us that the attempts of Jewish communal leaders[3] to foster a "return to the family" in this era, whether through the press, sermons, or reprints of Moritz Oppenheim's "Pictures of Old Jewish Family Life,"[4] did not resonate among harassed couples.

The family as "haven in a heartless world"[5] simply could not hold up. A teacher noted: "It would be wrong to say that the parental homes disintegrated, but in many cases home life was cheerless and full of troubles."[6] This was, perhaps, inevitable; their world was shrinking and Jews spent more and more time at home mulling over their situation[7] and getting on each other's nerves.[8] Under these circumstances, Jewish women were to take on the old/new role of what feminists have called "emotional housework," that is, making the household a more pleasant environment. Leaders urged women to preserve the "moral strength to survive" and held up Biblical heroines as role models.[9] No longer focused on Victorian notions of making the home an "island of serenity" for the bourgeois husband, spokesmen and women urged housewives to exert a calming influence on the entire family, since: "the tension that we have all been living under . . . has made people irritable; the constant struggle against attacks makes them aggressive, intolerant, impatient."[10]

The Jewish press also gave mothers the job of making their children proud of being Jews, a task that proved particularly difficult among children who simply wanted to fit in with their peers.[11] Finally, parents still tried to protect their children from worries and, accordingly, often grew silent when younger ones were in the vicinity. One woman wrote: "We knew too little. I grew up in a time when the world of children was clearly separated from that of the adults . . . Parents did not talk to children, especially not about their plans and worries."[12] Parental attempts to shelter their children may have met with only modest success. Even little Ruth Kluger knew what was going on as she pretended to sleep on the sofa in the living room: "Their secret was death, not sex. That's what the grown ups were talking about."[13]

The Job Situation for Men, Women, and Youth

As the Nazi government implemented its anti-Semitic legislation, Jewish men, in particular, lost their jobs and businesses, some as early as the "April Laws" of 1933. Suddenly, and despite limited options on the job market, many Jewish women who had never worked for pay needed employment. Some did not have to look far afield for jobs.[14] Much like their grandmothers decades earlier, they worked for husbands or fathers who had to let paid help go. By 1938, a columnist noted: "We find relatively few families in which the wife does not work in some way to earn a living."[15] In fact, as early as 1934, the Jewish feminist organization, the League of Jewish Women, noticed: "Today the woman is not only the spiritual, but, unfortunately, often the material support of the family."[16] By 1938, Hannah Karminski, an officer of the League of Jewish Women, remarked: "The picture of a woman who supports her family's basic sustenance is typical."[17] Moreover, large numbers of women and men retrained for the kinds of jobs still available in Germany or in countries of refuge, mostly in agriculture, crafts, home economics, and nursing.[18]

Did this massive change in economic conditions affect roles within the family? Yes, ever so slightly. The League of Jewish Women, for example, still regarded married women's employment as a last resort, acceptable only in times of crisis.[19] Working mothers still needed to wake their children and tuck them into bed: "The first and last look of the day must re-fuse the mother-child unit."[20] Despite new jobs and less household help, wives carried the lion's share of household work. Jewish newspapers advised housewives to consider vegetarian menus because they were cheaper, healthier, and avoided, for some, the kosher meat problem. Although meat might be easier and more time-efficient to prepare, columnists advised women that their "good will [was] an important assistant in a vegetarian kitchen,"[21] and newspapers printed vegetarian menus and recipes.[22] After the Nuremberg Race Laws of September 1935, when many Jews lost any household help they might still have retained, the *CV-Zeitung* ran articles entitled "Everyone learns to cook" and "Even Peter cooks. . ."[23] Husbands were requested to be less demanding and children, especially daughters,[24] were asked to help out. During this particularly stressful time, writers did frown upon authoritarian behavior, even that by the "head of the family." One writer asserted that such behavior stemmed from a time when "men and fathers were overvalued in comparison to women and wives."²⁵ In an era when Nazi ideology shrilly reaffirmed male privilege, with women relegated to "children, kitchen, and church," (*Kinder, Küche, Kirche*), it was being called into question—but not overtly challenged—in Jewish circles. Thus, gender roles and privileges within the family were barely modulated. Why this was so is not difficult to explain.²⁶ By proclaiming the crisis nature of women's new position, Jews, both male and female, could hope for better times and ignore the deeply unsettling challenges to traditional gender roles in the midst of turmoil.

Children and teens, too, had to reconsider the kinds of jobs they might have in the future and some had to drop out of school to assist their families. One boy dropped out of school a year before his *Abitur* in 1937. The teachers had made life miserable for him, and his family's financial problems did not allow him to continue either.²⁷ Forced to re-evaluate their options, that is, to cut back on their former hopes and plans, many Jewish teens suffered the accompanying pain and disappointment that that caused. Moreover, family dissension grew when parents and children clashed regarding the vision each had of the child's future. This seems particularly to have been the case between girls and their parents. One school survey in 1935 indicated that girls preferred jobs in offices or with children (such as a kindergarten teacher), whereas parents thought they should become seamstresses or work in some form of household setting. Parents were more likely to go along with boys' choices of crafts or agricultural training, useful, for example, in Palestine. This tension must have been greater among girls who had high school educations than those who, only attending *Volksschule*, had lower expectations from the start.²⁸ Moreover, if one excludes housework, the choices available to girls were far more limited—and hence, more frustrating—than those open to boys. Welfare organizations suggested sewing-related jobs, such as knitting, tailoring, or making clothing decorations, whereas boys could consider many more options, including becoming painters, billboard designers, upholsterers, shoe makers, dyers, tailors, or skilled industrial or agricultural workers.²⁹ To make matters worse, parents seem to have preferred keeping girls home altogether, either to shelter them from unpleasant work or to have them help out around the house as paid help was let go.³⁰ Ezra Ben Gershom described a concrete example of this kind of decision-making. With his oldest sister married, his father decided that he and his two brothers should receive vocational training and that their other sister should help their mother with housework.³¹

Women Represent the Family

Whether women had to work or not, they soon took part in public life far more than they had ever before. Increasingly, women found themselves representing or defending their men, whether husbands, fathers, or brothers. Many tales have been recorded of women who saved family members from the arbitrary demands of the state or from the secret police (the Gestapo). In these cases, it was always assumed that the Nazis would not break gender norms: they might arrest or torture Jewish men, but would not harm women. Thus women took on a more assertive public role than ever before.[32] Some actually took responsibility for the entire family's safety, a reversal of previous roles with their husbands. Liselotte Mueller traveled to Palestine to assess the situation there. Her husband, who could not leave his medical practice, simply told her: "If you decide you would like to live in Palestine, I will like it too." She chose Greece. Her husband, older and more educated than she, would in other circumstances have been the decision-maker, but he agreed.[33] Ann Lewis' mother went to England to negotiate her family's emigration with British officials and her medical colleagues. This decision was based on her fluency in English, her desire to meet members of her psychoanalytic profession, and her husband's profession; as a medical doctor, he was not welcome in Britain, but she was. She, who had always been "reserved with strangers," and for whom asking favors "did not come easily," had to ask for letters of recommendation from British psychiatrists, and to apply to the Home Office for residence and work permits.[34]

Women had to call upon assertiveness they often did not know they possessed. After traveling to the United States to convince reluctant and distant relatives to give her family an affidavit, one woman had to confront the US Embassy in Stuttgart, which insisted that there was no record of her. She showed her receipts, but the secretary just shrugged. At closing time, she refused to leave, insisting that her mother's, husband's, and children's lives depended on their chance to go to the US. She would spend as many days and nights in the waiting room as necessary until they found her documents. After much discussion, the consul ordered a search of the files and the documents were discovered. Today, her daughter refers to her mother's actions as the "first sit-in."[35]

Often facing danger and dramatic situations, women were required to have both bravery and luck. When her uncle was arrested in Düsseldorf, twenty-year-old Ruth Abraham hurried from one jail to the next until she found out where he was. Then, she appealed to a judge who seemed attracted to her. He requested that she come to his home in the evening, where he would give her a release form. Knowing that she risked a sexual demand or worse, she entered his home. The judge treated her politely and signed the release. She commented in her memoir: "I must add, that I look absolutely 'Aryan,' that I have blond hair and blue eyes, a straight nose and am tall." Later, these traits would save her life in hiding; now, she was able to gain the interest or sympathy of men who did not want to believe that she was Jewish.[36]

The judge's treatment of Abraham notwithstanding, traditional sexual conventions could be quite menacing. Despite increasing propaganda about "racial pollution" or "race defilement" (*Rassenschande*), Jewish women recorded frightening incidents in which "Aryans," even Nazis, made advances toward them.[37] One woman wrote of the perils of sexual encounters:

> During the Hitler era I had the immense burden of rejecting brazen advances from SS and SA men. They often pestered me and asked for dates. Each time I answered: "I'm sorry, that I can't accept, I'm married." If I had said I was Jewish, they would have turned the tables and insisted that I had approached them.[38]

Overcoming the stereotypes of female passivity or sexual availability meant confronting gender conventions. These new roles may have increased familial stress in some cases, but both women and men generally appreciated the importance of the new behavior. Edith Bick summed up the situation: "in the Hitler times . . . I had to take over, which I never did before. Never." Her husband "didn't like it." But, "he not only accepted it. He was thankful."[39] As conditions worsened, role reversals became ever more common.

Women forced themselves to behave in "unwomanly" ways, some putting up a strong front when the men were falling apart. For the sake of her children, one woman struggled to retain her self-control as her husband sank into a deep depression:

> He could no longer sleep. He stopped eating, as he said no one had the right to eat when he did not work and became . . . so despondent that it resulted in a deep depression . . . He feared we would all starve . . . and all his self-assurance was gone . . . These were terrible days for me, added to all the other troubles, and forever trying to keep up my chin for the children's sake.

They decided to send the children away because it was not good for them to see their father in such a state, and because they were also being constantly humiliated at school.[40]

Children and the Effects of School on the Family

Well before legislation drove them out, Jewish adolescents over the age of fourteen (after which attendance was no longer compulsory) left school in droves, the result of the insufferable atmosphere there. This occurred even in cities with large Jewish populations. In Berlin, 5,931 Jewish youths attended higher schools in May 1933; the following May, 2,777 were left; and two years later, only 1,172 remained.[41] In Württemberg, the April Laws (1933) affected only 10 percent of Jews attending higher schools, yet shortly thereafter, 58 percent left school due to the massive hostility they encountered while there.[42] University students suffered even worse discrimination. For example, they had to sit on separate "Jewish" benches, or in the back of the lecture hall. By 1934, Jewish students at the Friedrich Wilhelm University of Berlin had to come to terms with a wide yellow stripe stamped in their matriculation books. The result was that by the summer of 1934, only 656 Jewish students (485 men and 170 women) matriculated at German universities, compared with 3,950 (2,698 men and 1,252 women) in the summer of 1932.[43]

The pain of their children—who often faced anti-Semitism from classmates and teachers more immediately than their parents—disturbed both women and men profoundly as parents, but women learned of and dealt with their children's distress more directly than men. When children came home from school, their mothers were the first ones to hear the latest stories and had to respond to them.[44] Principals summoned mothers to pick up their children when they were expelled from school—and this could happen more than once—and these mothers then sought new schools for their children.[45] Teachers often telephoned mothers when children were to be excluded from class events or to receive grades beneath their actual achievement level. In a small city in Baden, the (female) teacher sent Verena Hellwig a letter regarding her daughter's grades:

> Today we were informed at a teachers' meeting that Jews or *Mischlinge* could no longer receive prizes for their achievements. Because your little daughter is the best pupil in the class, she will be

affected by these measures. I'm informing you in order that you can tell Irene, so that she won't be surprised and too hurt during tomorrow's awards ceremony.[46]

One can envision the depression and anger that would set in among children treated so badly, and the repercussions this could have in the home.

Mothers also supervised their children's homework. Imagine the contradictory feelings and thoughts of a Jewish mother who was *reassured* to learn that her son had sung patriotic songs, said "Heil Hitler" to the teacher, and received praise for his laudatory essay about Hitler: "[His] gross political miseducation at school would keep [him] out of trouble." About a year later, the same child, now enrolled in a Jewish school, wrote a story about Jewish resistance as a Mother's Day gift for his mother. Upon reading it, she was frightened: "[His] political awakening . . . could lead to trouble for the whole family."[47] Another mother, in a small south German town, commented on the lies that her children were expected to echo in their homework assignments:

> There were . . . compositions with delicate subjects, and they were not allowed to put down a contradictory opinion. Sometimes a judicious teacher gave a selection of subjects . . . but . . . all the children knew what they were expected to write. It was bad enough, that this kind of state's education taught them to hate, to despise, to be suspicious, to denounce, but worst of all perhaps was this . . . lying.[48]

Small children shared their distress openly with parents. Six-, seven-, or eight-year-olds found it agonizing not to be part of the group. One little boy, referring to his circumcision, confided to his father that he wished he were a girl, because then the other children would not know immediately that he was a Jew. When asked what he would wish for (late 1933), a seven-year-old answered, "to be a Nazi." Taken aback, his father asked what would happen to the rest of the family, and he responded that he wished they could be Nazis too. This is the same child whose teacher noted that he flinched every time the Nazi flag was raised.[49]

Older children kept more of their pain to themselves, hiding their feelings and some of the more troubling events in their daily school lives. Their already overburdened parents had "no time and too much *Angst*."[50] In a small town in Ostwestfalen-Lippe, the only Jewish girl in the school had enthusiastically participated in preparatory swimming exercises in the gym all winter long. When spring came, the class was to go to the public pool to actually swim. With sadness, her (female) teacher told her she could not join the class. "'You know why you cannot go with us to the park swimming pool?' And I said, 'yes, I know.' I did not cry. For a minute, I believe, I wanted to die . . . Curiously, I was hurt more for my parents than for myself."[51] Attempts by children to spare their parents notwithstanding, mothers, and probably fathers too (to the extent their wives did not shelter them), surmised what was happening. The Protestant mother of two *Mischling* children noted that many of her daughter's friends no longer came to their home. "Loneliness enveloped us more and more each day," she wrote.[52]

Often, children had to walk a tightrope between the demands of school and the apprehensions of parents. In one small town, the elementary school teacher insisted that Jewish children give the Nazi salute. The parents advised the children not to do so, both because it was against Judaism to exalt a human being, and because the newspapers stated that Jews were not supposed to give the salute. The teacher's response boded ill. He threatened the Jewish children with the wrath of their "Aryan" schoolmates: "'I am not responsible if the children turn against you. . . .' He goaded them, really goaded. And then, after a short time, we went along, cooperated, and didn't tell it at home."[53] Another Jewish child was simply delighted when he was forced to give the Nazi salute in school (something his parents had forbidden).[54]

Unlike Jewish adolescents, Jewish children under fourteen could not simply leave school. Why did they remain in public schools as long as they did, when, as early as 1934, the Reich Representation of German Jews (Reichsvertretung der deutschen Juden) reported that many Jewish children were showing signs of psychological disturbance?[55] There were practical reasons: the Jewish community could not build Jewish schools as quickly as they were needed. Further, the public schools had acquired reputations for educational competence. Moreover, some Jews still lived in towns in which the population of Jews was too small to support a Jewish school. A gender-specific family dimension also appears to be involved: while mothers voiced grave trepidations, fathers exhorted the children to remain in school. Toni Lessler, the founder and director of a Montessori School in Berlin, which became a Jewish school when the government forbade "Aryan" children from attending it, described the attitudes of Jewish families:

> The circumstances in the city schools became ever more difficult for the Jewish children and ever more unbearable. But there were still many parents who wanted to give children the advantage of a city

school. If the parents had only guessed what the children had to go through . . . [It] must . . . have been . . . false pride which caused the fathers in particular to keep their children in city schools.

Lessler pointed to fathers' aspirations to give their children a quality education, but also to their "stand tough" approach, since many did not believe that their children were actually suffering.[56]

Memoirs, too, attest to fathers' (unrealistic) hopes that their children would not suffer and to their insistence that their children "tough it out" and develop "thicker skin." When a sixteen-year-old, the only Jewish girl in the class, balked at participating in a class trip, aware that the class would eat at a hotel that displayed a "Jews undesired" placard, her mother supported her. The mother dreaded the anxiety and pain her daughter might experience—"she'll worry about what might happen during the entire trip"—but her father, a rabbi, insisted that she participate.[57] Another father knew the horrid details of his son's school experience, but did not seem to fathom the child's emotional state. When this man finally agreed to take his child out of school, the ten-year-old proclaimed: "Father . . . had you continued to force me to go to a school, I would have thrown myself under a train." The father confessed: "My hair stood on end with fear, cold chills ran down my spine. What must have been going on in the soul of a small, innocent child?"[58]

These and Lessler's observations are examples of gender-specific reactions in which men wished to stand firm. They are also examples of gender-specific roles in which husbands made the ultimate family decisions, although their wives had more immediate contact with their children and their children's emotional states. Also in accordance with gender socialization, wives (and children) may have kept the worst from the husbands/fathers, and boys, trying to be "manly," may have remained more silent than girls. They sought to spare their fathers yet another strain because their business or professional lives were bitter enough. One boy remembered coming home many times to his mother's admonition, "Don't talk to your father," who was very upset.[59]

Nevertheless, children also heightened family discord by confronting their parents with their desire to leave Germany behind. Children, reacting almost viscerally to present dangers at home, wanted to cut all ties with Germany, but parents feared an unknown future abroad. Many, like Ruth Eisner, had pressed for their whole families to emigrate. When her father refused, the sixteen-year-old begged: "At least let me go!"[60] Others insisted on leaving for training programs—usually agricultural—either inside or outside Germany, in the hope of eventually emigrating. By 1939, 82 percent of children aged fifteen and under and 83 percent of youths aged sixteen to twenty-four had managed to escape Germany.[61] Many of these left with their families, and many did not. In the early years, parents had tried to keep the family together, that is, to go or to stay as a unit, but as conditions worsened, some parents made the agonizing decision to send their children into safety alone, splitting the family in the hope of an uncertain reunion.

Deciding Whether to Go or to Stay

Emigration became more and more crucial as Nazi policies against Jews escalated. Women usually saw the danger signals first and urged their husbands to flee Germany.[62] Marta Appel described a discussion among friends in Dortmund about a doctor who had just fled in the spring of 1935. The men in the room, including her husband, a rabbi, condemned him:

> The women . . . found that it took more courage to go than to stay . . . "Why should we stay here and wait for our eventual ruin? Isn't it better to go and to build up a new existence somewhere else, before our strength is exhausted by the constant physical and psychic pressure? Isn't the future of our children more important than a completely senseless holding out?" All the women shared this opinion . . . while the men, more or less passionately, spoke against it. I discussed this with my husband on the way home. Like all other men, he simply couldn't imagine how one could leave one's beloved homeland and the duties that fill a man's life. "Could you really leave all this behind you to enter nothingness?" "I could," I said, without a moment's hesitation. [63]

Rural Jewish women had similar reactions. Interviews of former villagers indicate: "The role of women in the decision to emigrate was decisive . . . the women were the prescient ones . . . the ones ready to make the decision, the ones who urged their husbands to emigrate."[64] The different attitudes of men and women described here seem to reflect a gender-specific reaction remarked upon by sociologists and psychologists: in dangerous situations, men tend to "stand their ground," whereas women avoid conflict, preferring flight as a strategy.[65]

But there were more important reasons why men and women responded differently to the idea of emigration. Those men who could still earn a living felt that, as breadwinners, they could not simply leave and force their families to face poverty abroad. Women, on the other hand, claimed to be ready to become domestics if they could flee with their families. Women's subordinate status in the public world and their focus on the household probably eased their decision since they were already familiar with the kinds of work they would have to perform in places of refuge.[66] One woman described how her mother, formerly a housewife and pianist, cheerfully and successfully took on the role of maid in England, whereas her father, formerly a chief accountant in a bank, failed as a butler, barely passed as a gardener, and experienced his loss of status more intensely than his wife.[67] Even when both sexes fulfilled their refugee roles well, women seemed less status conscious than men. Perhaps women did not experience the descent from employing a servant to becoming one to the same degree as men, since women's public status had always been derivative of their father or husband anyway.

In general, women were less involved than men in the economy, even though some women had been in the job market their entire adult lives and others had entered it for the first time.[68] This had two effects. First, since Jewish men worked mostly with other Jews in traditional Jewish occupations (retail trade in specific branches of consumer goods, in the cattle trade, or in independent practices as physicians and attorneys), they may have been more isolated from non-Jewish peers (though not from non-Jewish customers—and those who continued to come gave some cause for hope).[69] A Jewish work environment spared them direct interpersonal interactions with hostile peers, but also prevented the awareness garnered from such associations. As the boycotts of Jewish concerns grew more widespread and more insistent, those Jewish men whose businesses remained intact saw their clientele become predominantly Jewish, isolating them further. Moreover, discriminatory hiring meant that Jewish blue- and white-collar workers found opportunities only within the Jewish economic sector. In 1936, Jewish voices decried a "Jewish economic ghetto" and in 1937, the Council for German Jewry in London reported that the German-Jewish community lived in a "new type of ghetto . . . cut off from economic as well as social and intellectual contact with the surrounding world."[70] Thus, Jewish men, working increasingly in a "Jewish ghetto," may have been shielded to some extent from "Aryan" hostility, whereas Jewish women (even those who worked in the same "Jewish ghetto") picked up other warning signals, as they were sensitive to their neighborhoods and their children.

Second, Jewish men had a great deal to lose. They had to tear themselves away from their life-work, whether a business or professional practice, whether patients, clients or colleagues, status or possessions. The daughter of a wealthy businessman commented, "When the Nazis appeared on the scene, he was too reluctant to consolidate everything and leave Germany. He may have been a bit too attached to his status, as well as his possessions."[71] But, even businesswomen appeared less reluctant than their spouses to emigrate. One woman, whose husband managed her inherited manufacturing business, wanted to flee immediately in 1933. He, on the other hand, refused to leave the business. Although the wife could not convince her husband to flee, she insisted that they both learn a trade that would be useful abroad.[72] In short, from women's perspectives, the family could be moved more easily than a business or profession. In light of men's deep-seated identity with their occupation, they often felt trapped into staying. Women, whose identity was more family-oriented, struggled to preserve what was central to them by fleeing with it. Summing up, Peter Wyden recalled the debates within his own and other Jewish families in Berlin:

> It was not a bit unusual in these go-or-no-go family dilemmas for the women to display more energy and enterprise than the men . . . Almost no women had a business, a law office, or a medical practice to lose. They were less status-conscious, less money-oriented than the men. They seemed to be less rigid, less cautious, more confident of their ability to flourish on new turf.[73]

Women and men also had gender-specific, distinctive connections to public organizational and political worlds. One man declared in his memoirs that he could not depart from Germany because he thought of himself as a "good democrat" whose emigration would "leave others in the lurch," and would be a "betrayal of the entire Jewish community."[74] Women's memoirs rarely use such lofty language, nor did women see themselves as so indispensable to the public.[75]

Having led relatively distinct lives, men and women often interpreted daily events differently. Whereas men focused on government pronouncements, news broadcasts, and business, women were more integrated into their community. Raised to be sensitive to interpersonal behavior and social situations, women possessed social antennae that were finely tuned and directed towards more unconventional—what men might have considered more trivial—sources of information. For example, a US Jewish couple that resided in Hamburg during the 1930s heard about the danger from their hired help.[76] Thus, women's political analyses were often more penetrating, interspersed as they were with personal observations. They registered the increasing hostility of their immediate surroundings, unmitigated by a promising business prospect, a loyal employee, a patient, or a kind customer. Their constant contacts with their own and other people's children probably also alerted them to warning signals that come through interpersonal relations—and they took those signals very seriously.

Men, on the other hand, felt as though they were more at home with culture and politics. Generally more educated than their wives, they cherished what they regarded as German culture, the culture of the German Enlightenment. This love of German *Bildung* (cultural education) gave men something to hold on to even as it "blunted their sense of impending danger."[77] In fact, one could argue that men were more "German" than women, more imbued (perhaps from their war experience) with a sense of patriotism even in a situation gone awry. When Else Gerstel fought with her husband about emigrating, he, a former judge—he'd been fired—insisted "the German people, the German judges, would not stand for much more of this madness."[78]

War veterans also refused to take their wives' warnings seriously. They had received reprieves in 1933 because of President Hindenburg's intervention after the exclusionary "April Laws" (although the reprieves proved to be temporary). The wives of these men typically could not convince their husbands that they, too, were in danger.[79] One woman, who pressed her husband to leave Germany, noted that he "constantly fell back on the argument that he had been at the front in World War I."[80] While the front argument had a deep emotional core to it—many of these men still felt the deep patriotism that the war experience invoked[81]—most men expressed it in terms of having served their country and, hence, having certain rights.[82]

A widespread assumption that women lacked political acumen—stemming from their primary role in the private and domestic sphere rather than the public and political one—gave women's warnings less credibility in the eyes of their husbands. One woman's prophecies of doom met with her husband's amusement: "He laughed at me and argued that such an insane dictatorship could not last long." Even after their seven-year-old son was beaten up at school, he was still optimistic.[83] Many men also pulled rank on their wives, insisting that they were more attuned to political realities. One husband insisted, "You mustn't take everything so seriously. Hitler used the Jews ... as propaganda to gain power—now ... you'll hear nothing more about the Jews."[84] Often, the anxious partner heard the old German adage, "nothing is ever eaten as hot as it's cooked."

Men claimed to see the "broader" picture, to maintain an "objective" stance, to scrutinize and analyze the confusing legal and economic decrees and the contradictory public utterances of the Nazis. Men mediated their experiences through newspapers and broadcasts. Politics remained more abstract to them, whereas women's "narrower" picture—the minutiae (and significance) of everyday contacts—brought politics home.[85]

Notwithstanding the gender differences in picking up signals and yearning to leave, it is crucial to recognize that these signals occurred in stages. Alice Nauen and her friends "saw it was getting worse. But until 1939 nobody in our circles believed it would lead to an end" for German Jewry.[86] And, women, too, could be confused by Nazi policies and events. When Hanna Bernheim's sister returned from France for a visit in the mid 1930s, the sister wanted to know why the Bernheims remained in their south German town. Hanna Bernheim replied:

> First of all it is so awfully hard for our old, sick father to be left by all his four children. Second there are so many dissatisfied people in all classes, professions and trades. Third there was the Röhm Purge and an army shake-up. And that makes me believe that people are right who told us 'Wait for one year longer and the Nazi government will be blown up!'[87]

Moreover, these signals were often profoundly *mixed*. Random kindnesses, the most obvious "mixed signals," gave some Jews cause for hope. One woman wrote that every Jewish person "knew a decent German" and recalled that many Jews believed "the radical Nazi laws would never be carried out because they did not match the moderate character of the German people."[88] Ultimately, confusing signals, often interpreted differently by women and men as well as attempts by the government to rob Jews of all their assets, impeded many Jews from making timely decisions to leave Germany (although as we well know, in the end, closed doors to places of refuge played a far more important role than did the timing of emigration decisions).[89]

That men and women often *assessed* the dangers differently reflected their various contacts and frames of reference. But, *decisions* seem to have been made by husbands—or, later, by circumstances. Despite some important role reversals, families generally held fast to traditional gender roles in actual decision-making unless they were overwhelmed by events. The common prejudice that women were "hysterical" in the face of danger, or exaggerated fearful situations, worked to everyone's disadvantage. Charlotte Stein-Pick had begged her father to flee in March 1933. Her husband brought her father to the train station only moments before the SS arrived to arrest the older man. Not aware of the SS visit, her husband returned home to say: "actually, it was entirely unnecessary that your parents left, but I supported you because you were worrying yourself so much."[90]

Not only were men inclined to trust their own political perceptions more than those of their wives, but their role and status as breadwinner and head of household both contributed to their hesitancy to emigrate and gave them the authority to say "no." One woman described her attempt to convince her husband to flee:

> A woman sometimes has a sixth feeling . . . I said to my husband, "we will have to leave." He said, "No, you won't have a six-room apartment and two servants if we do that." I said, "OK, then I'll have a one-room flat . . . but I want to be safe."

Despite his reluctance, she studied English and learned practical trades. His arrest forced their emigration and she supported the family in Australia.[91] Else Gerstel fought "desperately" with her husband of twenty-three years to emigrate. Fearful that he would not find a job abroad, he refused to leave, insisting: "there is as much demand for Roman law over there as the Eskimos have for freezers." "I was in constant fury," she wrote, representing their dispute as a great strain on their marriage.[92] The Berlin artist Charlotte Salomon painted this dilemma as she awaited her fate in southern France in 1941–1942. She portrayed her short grandmother looking up to her tall grandfather, whose head juts above the frame of the painting. The caption reads: "Grossmama in 1933: 'Not a minute longer will I stay here. I'm telling you let's leave this country as fast as we can; my judgment says so.' Her husband almost loses his head."[93]

A combination of events usually led to the final decision to leave and, as conditions worsened, women sometimes took the lead. In early 1938, one daughter reported that her mother "applied to the American authorities for a quota number without my father's knowledge; the hopeless number of 33,243 was allocated. It was a last desperate act and Papa did not even choke with anger anymore."[94] Yet another woman responded to narrowly escaping a battering by a Nazi mob in her small hometown by convincing her husband to "pack their things throughout the night and leave this hell . . . the next day."[95] After the November Pogrom, there were wives who broke all family conventions by taking over the decision-making when it was unequivocally clear to them that their husbands' reluctance to leave Germany would result in even worse horrors.

Sometimes the "Aryan" wives of Jewish men took the lead. Verena Hellwig, for example, feared for her two "mixed" (*Mischling*) children even as her husband, also of "mixed blood," insisted on remaining in Germany until his approaching retirement. When her teenage son could not find an apprenticeship, she spoke to a Nazi official about her children's futures. He told her that people of mixed blood "are our greatest danger. They should either return to Judaism . . . and suffer the fate of the Jews or they should be prevented from procreating like retarded people." She had reached her turning point: "her homeland was lost . . . Germany was dead [for her]." She had to find a "new home," a "future" for her children.[96]

November Pogrom: Families in Dissolution

Immediately after this cataclysm, with men imprisoned, women comprised the majority of those who remained with any possibility of action. The most crucial task confronting Jewish women was to rescue their men. Wives of prisoners were told that their husbands would be freed only if they could present emigration papers. Although there are no statistics to indicate their success, these women displayed extraordinary nerve and tenacity in saving a large number of men and in facilitating a mass exodus of married couples in 1939. Women again summoned the courage to overcome gender stereotypes of passivity in order to find any means necessary to have husbands and fathers released from camps. Charlotte Stein-Pick wrote of the November Pogrom:

> From this hour on, I tried untiringly, day in and day out, to find a connection that could lead to my husband's release. I ran to Christian acquaintances, friends, or colleagues, but everywhere people shrugged their shoulders, shook their heads and said "no." And

everyone was glad when I left. I was treated like a leper, even by people who were positively inclined towards us.⁹⁷

Undaunted, Stein-Pick entered Nazi headquarters in Munich, the notorious "Brown House," to request her husband's freedom based on his status as a war veteran. There, she was shown her husband, twenty pounds thinner, and begged repeatedly for his release The Nazis required that she explain the finances of her husband's student fraternity, of which he was still treasurer. She could do this and—upon his release—she was required to return to the Brown House monthly to do the fraternity's bookkeeping until she left Germany.⁹⁸

Some women saw not only to their husbands' releases and the necessary papers, but also to selling their joint property. Accompanying her husband home after his ordeal, one wife explained that she had just sold their house and bought tickets to Shanghai for the family. Her husband recalled that anything was fine with him, as long as they could escape from a place in which everyone had declared "open season" on them.⁹⁹

Similar expressions of thankfulness, tinged, perhaps, with a bit of surprise at women's heroism, can be found in many men's memoirs. They were indebted to women even after their ordeal when many men were too beaten in body and spirit to be of much use in the scramble to emigrate. Some men came home desperately ill, others suffered deep depression.¹⁰⁰

Many women remarked upon their own calm and self-control as an attempt to retain the families' dignity and equilibrium in the face of dishonor and persecution. Most likely, men rarely describe this kind of behavior because they took it for granted, while women, previously allowed and encouraged to be the more "emotional" sex, were particularly conscious of their own efforts at self-control and their husbands' fragility.¹⁰¹ Charlotte Stein Pick recalled her husband's counsel on the day of the pogrom: "'Just no tears and no scene. . .' But even without this warning I would have controlled myself."¹⁰² This desire to appear calm was not merely a proclamation of female stalwartness to counter the stereotype of female "frailty." Emphasis on composure also resulted from the decorum stressed in Jewish bourgeois upbringing. Moreover, it asserted Jewish pride in the face of "Aryan" savagery, human dignity in the face of general dishonor.¹⁰³ But women's perseverance is also more than the sum of its parts, suggesting a new role for women. Traditionally, men had publicly guarded the honor of the family and community; now suddenly, women found themselves in the difficult position of defending Jewish honor.

Despite their apparent calm, women's inner stress was massive as they faced the dizzying procedure of obtaining proof of immediate plans to emigrate in order to free a male relative from a concentration camp. On their own, women had to organize the papers, decide on the destination (if they had not discussed this previously with a spouse, sibling or parent), sell property, and arrange the departure. The red tape involved in emigrating was a dreadful ordeal.

Statistics from the pre-pogrom years may give the impression that a certain number of Jews smoothly managed to leave Germany and enter the country of their choice. They cover up the individual stories that describe complicated emigration attempts, failures, and new attempts. The problems encountered gave rise to gallows humor. If one studied Spanish or Portuguese to go to Latin America, sudden barriers to entry arose and one had to prepare for another country. If one turned to Hebrew, obstacles to acquiring the necessary certificates were certain to develop and one had to change to yet another language. Thus, a joke made the rounds of one town—the question was: "'what language are you learning?' The answer: 'The wrong one, of course.'"[104]

After the pogrom, women faced a critical situation. Elisabeth Freund described her and her husband's many attempts to leave Germany:

> It is really enough to drive one to despair. We've already done so many things in order to get away from Germany. We have filed applications for entry permits to Switzerland, Denmark, and Sweden. It was all in vain, though in all these countries we had good connections. In the spring of 1939, from an agent we obtained an entry permit for Mexico for 3,000 marks. But we never received the visa, because the Mexican consulate asked us to present passports that would entitle us to return to Germany, and the German authorities did not issue such passports to Jews. Then, in August 1939 we did actually get the permit for England. But it came too late, only ten days before the outbreak of war, and in this short time we were not able to take care of all the formalities with the German authorities. In the spring of 1940 we received the entry permit for Portugal. We immediately got everything ready and applied for our passports. Then came the invasion of Holland, Belgium and France by the German troops. A stream of refugees poured to Portugal, and the Portuguese government recalled by wire all of the issued permits . . . It was also good that in December 1940 we had not already paid for our Panamanian visas; for we noticed that the visas offered us did not at all entitle us to land in Panama.[105]

Freund reflected on friends who urged her and her husband to leave Germany: "As if that were not our most fervent wish." People in and outside of Germany failed to comprehend that the Freunds—like so many others—desperately wanted to get out, but that opportunities did not exist.[106]

A few opportunities to escape did exist for unaccompanied children. Zionists increased their efforts to bring children to Palestine where they lived on *kibbutzim* or in children's homes, and Quakers and other groups organized children's transports (*Kindertransporte*) that delivered children safely "into the arms of strangers," as the film on the children's transports described it. For parents, the decision to send off a child, often a very young one, was the most excruciating moment of their lives. The expression "children turned into letters" revealed their despair. Many mothers, with husbands in concentration camps or safely abroad, made the decision on their own and then suffered intensely from the loss of daily intimacy.

As just implied, families frequently had to split in order to save all or some of their members. This became clear as children escaped, often never to see their parents again. More generally, families made harsh and excruciating decisions to save the young and to leave the elderly behind. Statistics show that two-thirds of the deportees were forty-five years of age or older.[107] This meant that as the young escaped, aided by retraining programs and Jewish communal organizations, the grandparents, often the widowed grandmother, remained behind. Many felt they could no longer start anew in a place of refuge; others believed that they might join their children, once they had settled; all realized that countries of emigration did not allow in unproductive individuals unless they had secure promises of financial support, which they did not; and most thought that they would live a restricted life, but that the Nazis would not hurt them. By the time they realized the last to be untrue, the war had intervened and doors of emigration and immigration had slammed shut.

The combination of age and gender, as already intimated, was the most lethal. Fewer women than men left Germany. Why was this so? There were still compelling reasons to stay, although life became increasingly difficult. First, women, especially young women, could still find jobs as teachers in Jewish schools or in Jewish social services.[108] Dr. Martha Wertheimer, for example, worked as a journalist prior to 1933. Thereafter, she plunged into Jewish welfare. She escorted children's transports to England, worked twelve-hour days without pausing for meals in order to advise Jews on emigration and welfare procedures, and organized continuing education courses for Jewish youths who had been drafted into forced labor. Ultimately, she wrote a friend in New York that, despite efforts to emigrate, she no longer wanted to escape: "It is also worthwhile to be an officer on the sinking ship of Jewish life (*Judenheit*) in Germany, to hold out courageously and to fill the life boats, to the extent that we have some."[109]

While the employment situation of Jewish women helped keep them in Germany, that of the men helped to get them out. Some husbands or sons had business connections abroad facilitating their immediate flight, and others emigrated alone in order to establish themselves and then send for their families. Also, families believed that sons needed to establish economic futures, whereas daughters would, presumably, marry. Despite trepidations, parents sent sons into the unknown more readily than daughters.[110]

Another reason why more women remained behind was the fact that before the war, men faced more immediate physical danger than women and were forced to flee promptly.[111] After the November Pogrom, in a strange twist of fortune, the men interned in concentration camps were released only upon showing proof of their ability to leave Germany immediately. Families—mostly wives and mothers—strained every resource to provide the documentation to free these men and send them on their way while some of the women remained behind. Alice Nauen recalled how difficult these emigration decisions were for all Jews:

> Should we send the men out first? This had been the dilemma all along in my father's work . . . If you have two tickets, do you take one man out of the concentration camp and his wife who is at this moment safe? Or do you take your two men out of the concentration camp? They took two men out . . . because they said we cannot play God, but these are in immediate danger. Those had to come out.[112]

Even as women feared for their men, they believed that they would not be subjected to serious harm. The regime had, in fact, beaten, tortured, imprisoned, and shot Jewish men, but had spared women as a group[113] from the worst brutality even during the November Pogrom.[114]

Further, as more and more sons left, daughters remained as the sole caretakers for elderly parents. One female commentator noted the presence of many women "who can't think of emigration because they don't know who might care for their elderly mothers in the interim, before they could start sending them money. In the same families, the sons went their way."[115] In fact, leaving one's aging parent—as statistics indicate, usually the mother—was the most painful act imaginable. Ruth Glaser described her mother's agony as her mother realized that she had to join Ruth's father, who had been forbidden re-entry into Germany. Ruth's mother "could not sleep at night thinking of leaving her [mother] behind."[116]

As early as 1936, the League of Jewish Women saw cause for serious concern regarding the general "problem of the emigration of women which is often partly overlooked and not correctly understood."[117] Not only did the League realize that far fewer women than men were leaving, but it turned toward parents, reminding them of their "responsibility to free their daughters too."[118] As late as January 1938, the Hilfsverein, one of the main emigration organizations, announced that "up to now, Jewish emigration . . . indicates a severe surplus of men." Blaming this on the "nature" of women to feel closer to family and home and on that of men toward greater adventurousness, the Hilfsverein suggested that couples marry before emigrating, encouraged women to prepare themselves as household helpers, and promised that women's emigration would become a priority.[119] Yet, only two months later, the Hilfsverein announced it would expedite the emigration of only those young women who could prove a minimum competence in household skills and were willing to work as domestics abroad.[120] In general, fewer women than men received support from Jewish organizations in order to emigrate.[121]

Young women and their families were often reluctant to consider Palestine, and the *kibbutz*, as an alternative for daughters. Statistics for the first half of 1937 indicate, for example, that of those taking advantage of Zionist retraining programs, only 32 percent were female.[122] There was also a gender imbalance among children who went to Palestine with Youth Aliyah,[123] which required 60 percent boys and 40 percent girls because of what it considered the division of labor on the collective farms (*kibbutzim*) where the children would work.[124]

The growing disproportion of Jewish women in the German-Jewish population also came about because, to begin with, there were more Jewish women than men in Germany.[125] Thus, in order to stay even, a greater absolute number of women would have had to emigrate. In 1933, 52.3 percent of Jews were women, resulting from such factors as male casualties during World War I, greater marrying out and conversion among Jewish men, and greater longevity among women.[126] The slower rate of female than male emigration meant that the female proportion of the Jewish population rose to 57.5 percent by 1939.[127] In 1939, one woman wrote:

> Mostly we were women who had been left to ourselves. In part, our husbands had died from shock, partly they had been processed from life to death in a concentration camp and partly some wives who, aware of the greater danger to their husbands, had prevailed upon them to leave at once and alone. They were ready to take care of everything and to follow their husbands later on, but because of the war it became impossible for many to realize this intention and quite a few of my friends and acquaintances thus became martyrs of Hitler.[128]

A large proportion of these remaining women were elderly.[129] Since many of the young had emigrated, the number of aging Jews also increased proportionately, among them a large number of widows.[130] In 1939, there were over 6,000 widowed men and over 28,000 widowed women in the expanded Reich.[131] Thus, 20 percent more Jewish women than men, especially, but not only, the elderly, remained behind. When Elisabeth Freund, one of the last Jews to leave Germany legally in October 1941, went to the Gestapo for her final papers, she observed: "All old people, old women waiting in line."[132]

In conclusion, Jewish families faced the maelstrom of Nazi brutality by adjusting long-standing gender and age dynamics. Because men faced danger and often lost their jobs, women took on more assertive public and economic roles. Although parents tried to protect their children, children themselves disagreed with these strategies and urged parents to take different action, which was focused on leaving Germany. The elderly, normally cared for and protected, were unable to escape and were left behind. Families that in ordinary times would not have considered disbanding, broke up in order to save individual members. Tragically, in the end, no strategy could save them all.

Notes

1. Trude Maurer, "From Everyday Life to a State of Emergency: Jews in Weimar and Nazi Germany," in *Jewish Daily Life in Germany*, ed. Marion Kaplan (New York: Oxford University Press, 2005), 285: For example, in Königsberg in 1925: 13.1; 1933: 6.6; 1936: 6.5 births per thousand Jews. See Stefanie Schüler-Springorum,

Die jüdische Minderheit in Königsberg/Preussen, 1871–1945 (Göttingen: Vandenhoeck & Ruprecht, 1996), 369.
2. Sibylle Quack, *Zuflucht Amerika: Zur Sozialgeschichte der Emigration deutsch-jüdischer Frauen in die USA 1933–1945* (Bonn: Dietz, 1995), 58.
3. Maurer, "Everyday Life," 286, quoting *CV-Zeitung* (hereafter *CVZ*) 12, no. 12 (23 March 1933): 100.
4. Maurer, "Everyday Life," 285–286. See the painting "Sabbath Afternoon" reprinted on the High Holidays with the surrounding text (translation): "The good old days were the days of the family. Everyone was together. Tranquility and peace radiated from the rooms and the people. The family and the house were the pillars of life." (*Gemeindeblatt der Deutsch-Israelitischen Gemeinde Hamburg*, September 1936). On the ideology of the Jewish family in the Weimar Republic, which aimed to preserve a "noble past," see Sharon Gillerman, "The Crisis of the Jewish Family," in *In Search of Jewish Community: Jewish Identities in Germany and Austria, 1918–1933*, ed. Michael Brenner and Derek Penslar (Bloomington: Indiana University Press, 1998), 186–195.
5. Christopher Lasch, *Haven in a Heartless World: The Family Besieged* (New York: Basic Books, 1977).
6. Hans Gaertner, "Problems of Jewish Schools during the Hitler Regime," *Leo Baeck Institute Year Book* 1 (1956): 138.
7. Maurer, "Everyday Life," 286, citing *CVZ* 14, no. 46 (14 November 1935): 1, 2. See also: *Jüdische Rundschau*, 25 May 1937, cited in Jacob Boas, "The Shrinking World of German Jewry, 1933–1938," in *Leo Baeck Institute Yearbook* 31 (1986): 255.
8. Maurer, "Everyday Life," 286.
9. *Blätter des jüdischen Frauenbundes* (hereafter *BJFB*), February 1935: 12.
10. Maurer, "Everyday Life," 286.
11. Maurer, "Everyday Life," 286. On Jewishness as a problem for children, see also *Israelitisches Familienblatt* (hereafter *IF*) 36, no. 36, 7 September 1934: 9, and Ernst Loewenberg, memoirs, Leo Baeck Institute, New York (hereafter LBI), 78.
12. Maurer, "Everyday Life," 287, citing from Ruth Weiss, *Wege im harten Gras: Erinnerungen an Deutschland, Südafrika und England* (Wuppertal: P. Hammer, 1995), 20.
13. Ruth Kluger, *Still Alive: A Holocaust Girlhood Remembered* (New York: Feminist Press, 2001), 15.
14. Elisabeth Drexler sought employment in a department store in Magdeburg. Ms. in Collection BMS GER 91, Houghton Library, Harvard University (hereafter Harvard).
15. *IF*, 13 January 1938: 13–14. See also *IF*, 14 July 1938: 12.
16. *BJFB* 10, no. 1 (1934): 11.
17. *CVZ*, 25 August 1938. See also *IF*, 13 January 1938: 13–14, and *IF*, 14 July 1938: 12.
18. Nevertheless, the employment and economic situation of all Jews was bleak. Whereas in the census of 1933, 46 percent of Jews were registered as "independent" in the Occupation Status section, by 1939, only 15 percent came under that heading. Conversely, only 8 percent of Jews were manual workers in 1933, but 56 percent fell into that category by 1939. As unemployment increased, so too did poverty. Berlin saw concentrated poverty. In 1937, the Jewish community there supported fifteen soup kitchens and provided used clothing for 42,900. By 1939, in Germany

as a whole, Jewish Winter Relief would subsidize 26 percent of a greatly diminished and aging population.
19. *IF,* 36, no. 29 (19 July 1934): 20.
20. *BJFB* 10, no. 1 (1934): 11. See also: *BJFB,* 10, no. 10 (1934): 5.
21. *IF,* 25 June 1936.
22. *IF,* 27 February 1936; *CVZ,* 24 February 1938: 17.
23. *CVZ,* 27 February 1936, see also *IF,* 19 March 1936.
24. *IF,* 21 May 1936.
25. *IF,* 21 May 1936. See also *Frankfurter Israelisches Gemeindeblatt,* January 1936: 137.
26. *IF,* 14 July 1938: 12.
27. Helmut Krueger, memoirs, LBI: 5, 16, 24, 41.
28. *Jüdische Wohlfahrtspflege und Sozialpolitik* (hereafter *JWS*), Berlin, 1935: 185–189.
29. *JWS,* 1937: 140–143.
30. In early 1937, one report on vocational training for youth suggested that 70 percent of girls leaving school refused any sort of training. Parents kept them at home to assist with household chores. The report noted that in 1936, the proportion of girls at training sites was only 25 percent. Clemens Vollnhals, "Jüdische Selbsthilfe bis 1938," in *Die Juden in Deutschland 1933–1945,* ed. Wolfgang Benz (Munich: Beck Verlag, 1989), 391.
31. Ezra Ben Gershom, *David: The Testimony of a Holocaust Survivor* (Oxford and New York: Berg, 1988), 56.
32. See for examples: Jacob Ball-Kaduri, memoirs, LBI: 30; Lisa Brauer, memoirs, LBI: 43, 57.
33. Liselotte Kahn, memoirs, LBI: 23.
34. Ann Lewis, memoirs, LBI: 26.
35. Lore Steinitz about her mother, Irma Baum. Note to the author entitled "The first 'sit in'." 7 January 1995, also deposited at the LBI.
36. Ruth Abraham, memoirs, LBI: 2.
37. Gerta Pfeffer in *Sie durften nicht mehr Deutsche sein; Jüdischer Alltag in Selbstzeugnissen 1933–1938,* ed. Margarete Limberg and Hubert Rübsaat (Frankfurt and New York: Campus, 1990), 141.
38. Rosy Geiger-Kullmann, memoirs, LBI: 72. Echoing these fears, the League of Jewish Women worried about the prohibition of its railroad station shelters for young women who might be accosted by men who would take advantage of their situation. Bundesarchiv, Coswig: 75C Jüd. Frauenbund Verband Berlin, folder 37—"Protokoll der Arbeitskreistagung vom 2. November 1936 re. Gefährdung der Jugendlichen." The records of the former Coswig branch of the Bundesarchiv are now housed at the Centrum Judaicum Archiv, Stiftung Neue Synagoge, in Berlin.
39. Edith Bick interview (born 1900, interviewed 1972), 18. Research Foundation for Jewish Immigration, New York (hereafter Research Foundation).
40. Hilde Honnet-Sichel, ms., Harvard: 72–73.
41. Vollnhals, "Jüdische Selbsthilfe bis 1938," 332.
42. Ibid., 333.
43. See: Claudia Huerkamp, "Jüdische Akademikerinnen in Deutschland, 1900–1938," *Geschichte und Gesellschaft,* 19 (1993): 327. See example of matriculation book at the US Holocaust Memorial Museum, Washington, DC.
44. Aralk in Limberg and Rübsaat, *Sie durften nicht mehr Deutsche sein,* 230.

45. Erna Segal, memoirs, LBI: 78–79. Some children were forced out of schools as often as three times even before the war. See Aralk in Limberg and Rübsaat, *Sie durften nicht mehr Deutsche sein*, 230.
46. Verena Hellwig, ms., Harvard: 29–30. See also Monika Richarz, ed., *Jüdisches Leben in Deutschland: Selbstzeugnisse zur Sozialgeschichte 1918–1945* (Stuttgart: Deutsche Verlags-Anstalt, 1982), 234.
47. Steve J. Heims, ed., *Passages from Berlin: Recollections of the Goldschmidt Schule, 1935–1939* (South Berwick, MA: Atlantic Printing, 1987), 73, 76.
48. Hanna Bernheim, ms., Harvard: 50–51. Eventually, they decided to send their son to a Jewish school in Berlin and their daughter to England.
49. Ernst Loewenberg in Limberg and Rübsaat, *Sie durften nicht mehr Deutsche sein*, 217–218.
50. Paula Salomon-Lindberg, quoted by Mary Felstiner, *To Paint Her Life: Charlotte Salomon in the Nazi Era* (New York: HarperCollins, 1994), 52.
51. Joachim Meynert, "'Das hat mir sehr weh getan!' Jüdische Jugend in Ostwestfalen-Lippe," in *Opfer und Täter: Zum nationalsozialistischen und antijüdischen Alltag in Ostwestfalen-Lippe*, ed. Hubert Frankemölle (Bielefeld: Verlag für Regionalgeschichte, 1990), 63. The pastry that the Jewish child ate was a *Mohrenkopf*, a racist term, still used in Germany today: "a Moor's head," referring to a chocolate pastry. In addition, see Margot Littauer, ms., Harvard: 14–15.
52. Verena Hellwig, ms., Harvard: 30.
53. Joachim Meynert, "'Das hat mir sehr weh getan!'" in Frankemölle, *Opfer und Täter*, 62.
54. Ernst Loewenberg in Limberg and Rübsaat, *Sie durften nicht mehr Deutsche sein*, 217–218.
55. Limberg and Rübsaat, *Sie durften nicht mehr Deutsche sein*, 208.
56. Toni Lessler, memoirs, LBI: 22.
57. Mally Dienemann, ms., Harvard: 23a.
58. Limberg and Rübsaat, *Sie durften nicht mehr Deutsche sein*, 210–211.
59. Werner A. Stein, chair of the *Aufbau* newspaper, in *New York Times*, 10 November 1992, B3 (a story on the Kaliski School in Berlin).
60. She left in January, 1939. Ruth Eisner, *Nicht wir allein: Aus dem Tagebuch einer Berliner Jüdin* (Berlin: Arani Verlags-GmbH, 1971), 8.
61. Herbert Strauss, "Jewish Emigration from Germany I," *Leo Baeck Institute Yearbook* XXV (1980): 318; *JWS*, 1937: 163.
62. See also Martina Kliner-Fruck, whose interviews support this point: *"Es ging ja ums Überleben": Jüdische Frauen zwischen Nazi-Deutschland, Emigration nach Palästina und ihrer Rückkehr* (New York and Frankfurt am Main: Campus, 1995), 79.
63. Richarz, *Jüdisches Leben*, 237.
64. Ulrich Baumann, "Jüdische Frauen auf dem Land" (referring to Baden-Württemberg), University of Freiburg, 1992, unpublished manuscript, 40.
65. Of course, there were also women who were too fearful to move, as Peter Gay describes his own mother, but in all of the memoirs and interviews I have read, they are in the miniscule minority. Peter Gay, "Epilogue: The First Sex," in *Between Sorrow and Strength: Women Refugees of the Nazi Period*, ed. Sibylle Quack (Cambridge: Cambridge University Press, 1995), 364.
66. Quack, *Zuflucht Amerika*, chs. IV and VI.

67. Lore Segal, *Other People's Houses* (New York: Harcourt, Brace & World, 1964). See also Quack, *Between Sorrow and Strength*.
68. Claudia Koonz, "Courage and Choice among German-Jewish Women and Men," in *Die Juden im nationalsozialistischen Deutschland / The Jews in Nazi Germany, 1933–1945*, ed. Arnold Paucker (Tübingen: Mohr/Siebeck, 1986), 285. Also, see Claudia Koonz, *Mothers in the Fatherland: Women, the Family, and Nazi Politics* (New York: St. Martin's Press, 1987), chap. 10.
69. Avraham Barkai, *From Boycott to Annihilation: the Economic Struggle of German Jews 1933–1945* (Hanover and London: University Press of New England, 1989), 2–3, 6–7.
70. Quoted by Barkai, *From Boycott*, 80–83.
71. Marianne Berel, "Family Fragments," memoirs, LBI: 16.
72. After his arrest and release from a concentration camp in November 1938, they managed to escape to Shanghai, where their new skills helped them survive. Lecture by Evelyn Rubin, their daughter, at Queens College, December 1988. See also: *The Long Island Jewish Week*, 188, no. 25 (19 November 1978). This article points in a different direction from Claudia Koonz, who argued that women with strong business ties judged the situation much as men did. Koonz, *Mothers*, 364.
73. Peter Wyden, *Stella* (New York: Simon and Schuster, 1992), 47.
74. Leo Gompertz, memoirs, LBI: 7.
75. Even women who remained in Germany in order to work in the Jewish community rarely used this kind of argumentation.
76. Elsie Axelrath, ms., Harvard: 37. She and her husband spent twelve years (1927–1939) in Hamburg. They were the only Jews in the US colony.
77. Claudia Koonz, "Courage and Choice among German-Jewish Women and Men," in Paucker, *The Jews in Nazi Germany*, 287.
78. Else Gerstel, memoirs, LBI: 7l.
79. Elisabeth Drexler, Harvard, no ms., just summary. Her husband remained optimistic because of President Hindenburg; Charlotte Hamburger, memoirs, LBI: 40–41; Marga Spiegel, *Retter in der Nacht: Wie eine jüdische Familie überlebte* (Cologne: Pahl-Rugenstein Verlag, 1987), 15. Spiegel's husband insisted that "no one will lay a hand on me" because he had been decorated in the war.
80. Erna Segal, memoirs, LBI: 45–46, 61.
81. Hilda Branch recalled that her father, who had been an officer in the Prussian army, was "more nationalistic" than she or her mother and wanted to remain in Germany, whereas the women were prepared to leave in January 1933. Sylvia Rothchild, ed., *Voices from the Holocaust* (New York: New American Library, 1981). Ruth Eisner also reported that her father, a World War I veteran, insisted on staying. See Eisner, *Nicht wir allein*, 8.
82. Ruth Fleischer in Douglas Morris, "The Lives of Some Jewish Germans Who Lived in Nazi Germany and Live in Germany Today: An Oral History," BA thesis, Wesleyan University, 1976, 93; Carol Gilligan, *In a Different Voice: Psychological Theory and Women's Development* (Cambridge: Harvard University Press, 1982).
83. Erna Segal, memoirs, LBI: 45–47, 61.
84. G.W. Allport, J.S. Bruner, and E.M. Jandorf, "Personality under Social Catastrophe: Ninety Life-Histories of the Nazi Revolution," *Character and Personality: An International Psychological Quarterly*, 10 (September 1941): 3.

85. Carol Gilligan's psychological theories may apply again here: men tend to view and express their situation in terms of abstract rights, women in terms of actual affiliations and relationships. Gilligan, *In a Different Voice*. See also: Elizabeth Bamberger, memoirs, LBI: 21.
86. Alice Nauen interview, 8, Research Foundation.
87. Hanna Bernheim, ms., Harvard: 53.
88. Charlotte Hamburger, memoirs, LBI: 41, 46. She decided to flee after her husband and children faced public abuse.
89. Hilde Honnet-Sichel in *Sie durften nicht mehr Deutsche sein*, 184. For example, on 26 July 1933, the government demanded the *Reichsfluchtsteuer*. On 11 September 1935, Jews were issued passports valid only within Germany, making their flight more difficult. On 11 October 1935, Jews could take foreign securities with them only if they could prove that they had them before 1 January 1933. This was intended to prevent Jews from taking their money with them. On 2 April 1936, emigrés had to place their money in blocked accounts and were not given the use of their own cash to take information trips abroad. On 1 December 1936, the Law against Economic Sabotage declared the death penalty for anyone caught sending money abroad or leaving it there, thereby hurting the German economy. In May and June of 1938, Jews had to inform the government of everything they took with them and requests from Jews to bring valuables abroad were to be denied. Laws listed in: Joseph Walk, ed., *Das Sonderrecht für die Juden im NS-Staat: Eine Sammlung der gesetzlichen Massnahmen und Richtlinien—Inhalt und Bedeutung* (Heidelberg: Müller Juristischer Verlag, 1981).
90. Charlotte Stein-Pick, memoirs, LBI: 2 and 38. Elizabeth Bamberger, memoirs, LBI: 5. See also, Vera Deutsch [only reader's comments, no ms.], Harvard.
91. John Foster, ed., *Community of Fate: Memoirs of German Jews in Melbourne* (Sydney and Boston: Allen & Unwin, 1986), 28–30. See also, Elizabeth Bab, memoirs, LBI: 180. In the rare cases in which husbands followed their wives' assessment and emigrated, the wives either brought in other male friends to help convince the husbands or were themselves professionals whose acumen in the public world was difficult to deny. Marie Bloch, who had read Hitler's *Mein Kampf* in 1929 and insisted on sending her children out of the country in 1933, constantly urged her husband to emigrate. After the Nuremberg Race Laws, she knelt in front of his bed, begging him to leave. He said he could not leave his factory and could not "give up the thought that the Germans would see in time what kind of a man Hitler was." Driven to despair, she asked him whose opinion he would respect and invited that friend to consult with them. The friend told them to flee to the United States where he, himself, was heading. Only then did her husband agree to go. Marie Bloch interview (born 1890, interviewed 1971), 6, 8. Research Foundation.
92. Else Gerstel, memoirs, LBI: 71.
93. Felstiner, *To Paint Her Life*, 74.
94. Ilse Strauss, memoirs, LBI: chap. 8, 44. (Her parents and young brother were deported and killed).
95. Hanna Bernheim, ms., Harvard: 45.
96. Verena Hellwig, ms., Harvard: 25–26. A Protestant, she was 43 years old in 1940. She had married in 1920 and lived in a town of 150,000 in Baden. Peter Edel's "Aryan" mother also took the lead, attempting to rescue him and her Jewish husband. But the war broke out and she was expelled from England. See Peter

Edel, *Wenn es ans Leben geht: meine Geschichte* (Berlin: Verlag der Nation, 1979), 149–150.
97. Charlotte Stein-Pick, memoirs, LBI: 41.
98. Ibid., 43–45. See also Ruth Abraham, memoirs, LBI: 3–5.
99. Limberg and Rübsaat, *Sie durften nicht mehr Deutsche sein*, 325.
100. Charlotte Stein-Pick, memoirs, LBI: 45. See also Gerdy Stoppleman, memoirs, LBI: 5. Stoppleman's husband left Sachsenhausen in March 1939. "More than his body, my husband's mind was deeply affected. Almost every night he experienced Sachsenhausen Concentration camp anew in nightmares so alarming that I feared for his sanity."
101. An extreme example of this happened during the deportations, when a nurse walked into a double suicide. Terribly upset, she wanted to share her feelings with her husband but could not "because of his own depressions." She did confide in her girlfriend. Frieda Cohn, Yad Vashem, Ball Kaduri Collection, 01/291, 5. See also Leo Gompertz, memoirs, LBI: 10.
102. Charlotte Stein-Pick, memoirs, LBI: 39.
103. Erna Albersheim, ms., Harvard: 33.
104. Mally Dienemann, ms., Harvard: 25.
105. Elisabeth Freund, in Monika Richarz, ed., *Jewish Life in Germany: Memoirs from Three Centuries* (Bloomington: Indiana University Press, 1991), 413.
106. Elisabeth Freund in Richarz, *Jewish Life*, 414–415.
107. Richarz, *Jüdisches Leben*, vol. 3: 61. Richarz writes that of the deportees (of about167,000), the proportion of women was 20 percent higher than that of men. Also, 28,077 Austrian Jewish women, almost twice the number (15,344) of Jewish men, were deported from Vienna. Josef Fraenkel, *The Jews of Austria* (London: Vallentine, Mitchell, 1970), 526.
108. *JWS*, 1937: 7–13; 27. Home care assistants (*Pflegerinnen*) were recruited from among women who were previously sales personnel, independent business people, nurses' aides, artists, kindergarten teachers, and housewives. *JWS*, 1937: 78–81. Avraham Barkai has discovered that some Jews protested against Jewish women who worked in the social service sector of the Jewish communities as "double earners" (women whose husbands also had jobs). Also, he has found letters to the editor of the *CVZ*—the newspaper of the Central Association of German Citizens of the Jewish Faith—proposing that these women should become domestics in order to let older and more experienced men who needed jobs take their places. Avraham Barkai, "Der wirtschaftliche Existenzkampf der Juden im Dritten Reich, 1933–38," in Paucker, *The Jews in Nazi Germany*, 163.
109. Hanno Loewy, ed., *In mich ist die grosse dunkle Ruhe gekommen, Martha Wertheimer Briefe an Siegfried Guggenheim (1939–1941)* (Frankfurt am Main: Frankfurt Lern- und Dokumentationszentrum des Holocaust, 1993), 6, 9, 13, 15, 22, 37.
110. "Laura Pelz" in Morris, "The Lives of some Jewish Germans," 43.
111. Ruth Eisner recalled that her male cousin left in 1936, three years before she did, because his parents did not want him to face more beatings from neighborhood bullies. See her *Nicht wir allein*, 8.
112. Alice Nauen interview, 15. Research Foundation. Her father was secretary of the Hilfsverein in Hamburg.
113. Attacks on individual women seem to have occurred mostly in small towns, although, for examples from Nuremberg and Düsseldorf, see Rita Thalmann and

Emmanuel Feinermann, *Crystal Night* (London: Thames and Hudson, 1974), 70 and 8l. If one collected all of these tales, it would be noticed that women were not "exempt" from violence even as early as 1938.

Erna Albersheim reported on a small town in East Prussia where some women and girls were imprisoned for about two weeks. Ms., Harvard: 63. Alice Baerwald described the same town, reporting that the fourteen women had to march through town saying "we have betrayed Germany." People ran alongside them crying "beat them to death, why are you still feeding them!" Ms., Harvard: 58.

For examples of women who were beaten in small towns, see "Lest We Forget!" by Anonymous, memoirs, LBI: 5. Also, see Frances Henry, *Victims and Neighbors: A Small Town in Nazi Germany Remembered* (South Hadley, MA: Bergin and Garvey, 1984), 11–17, describing a Jewish woman, blood dripping down her face as she ran down the street in "Sonderburg," and another elderly couple forced to run through the town's streets followed by SA throwing stones at them.

In Eberstadt, the local Nazi party leader murdered an 81-year-old Jewish woman, shooting her three times, when she resisted his orders to march to the city hall. Ulrich Baumann, "Jüdische Frauen auf dem Land," (referring to Baden-Württemberg), University of Freiburg, unpublished paper, 1992, 38. In Breisach, a Jewish woman was badly beaten in her home on 10 November. Günther Haseler, *Geschichte der Stadt Breisach am Rhein* (Breisach: Stadt[verwaltung], 1985), 450.

In Arheilgen (later part of Darmstadt), about a dozen SA men cornered a young woman and her father in their home. When one of them shouted for a "long knife," Johanna Reinhard jumped out of the window. She died of her injuries the following day and her father killed himself a few days later. Klaus Moritz and Ernst Noam, eds., *NS Verbrechen vor Gericht, 1945–55: Justiz und Judenverfolgung*, vol. 2 (Wiesbaden: *Kommission für die Geschichte der Juden in Hessen*, 1978), 94–97.

In Usingen, a town of about 2,000 people in 1933, the November Pogrom involved the beating of at least two Jewish couples. Moritz and Noam, *NS Verbrechen*, 232–233. Reports from the cities of Nuremberg and Fürth describe Jews being driven from their homes with leather straps and Jewish women with evidence of strap marks on their faces. *Deutschland-Berichte, 1939*, 920.

For three more instances of violence against women in small towns, see Heinz Lauber, *Judenpogrom: Reichskristallnacht November 1938 in Grossdeutschland* (Gerlingen: Bleicher, 1981), 110–114, 221–233. In addition, some women were also taken hostage for husbands who had hidden. In Frankfurt, for example, they were taken hostage, but a few were released after a day in jail in order to care for their children at home. Andreas Lixl-Purcell, *Women of Exile* (Westport: Greenwood, 1988), 71. In Dresden, women were taken hostage until their husbands turned themselves in. *Deutschland-Berichte, 1939*, 922.

Finally, the elderly, female and male, were not spared physical brutality either. On the edges of Berlin, rioters set the tiny shack (*Laube*) of an elderly couple aflame. When the couple tried to escape in their nightshirts, the band tried to force them back into the house. The man died of a heart attack and the woman needed to be institutionalized thereafter. *Deutschland-Berichte der Sozialdemokratischen Partei Deutschlands, 1938* (Frankfurt am Main: Verlag Petra Nettelbeck, 1980), 1340.

114. This was not true for Eastern European Jews who had been deported *before* the pogrom. There, men, women, children, and the aged were swept up and deported.
115. *BJFB*, April 1937: 5. See also, Erika Guetermann, "Das Photographien Album," memoirs, LBI, for another example of a woman who would not leave her parents and was later killed by the Nazis.
116. Ruth Glaser, memoirs, LBI: 26, 7l.
117. *BJFB*, December 1936: l.
118. *BJFB*, April 1937: 10; *BJFB*, December 1936: 1.
119. *CVZ*, 20 January 1938: 5.
120. *CVZ*, 3 March 1938: 6. The article was written by Hannah Karminski, who also encouraged women to take household preparation seriously.
121. For example, in 1937, *the number of emigrés supported by the emigration section* (Wanderungsausschuss) of the Reichsvertretung der Juden in Deutschland was 7,313 [the Hilfsverein supported 5,762 and the Palestine Office of the Jewish Agency—Palästina-Amt—supported 1,551]. This broke down to approximately 4,161 men and 3,041 women. January/February 1938: 6–7. The Hilfsverein supported 3,250 men and 2,512 women (that is, 56.4 percent of the people it supported were male and 43.5 percent were female). The Palestine Office supported 911 men and 529 women. There were 111 people not categorized as male or female. (If one ignores these 111 people, the other figures of 911 and 529 result in: 63 percent men and 36.7 percent women).

These are all approximate figures since about 16 percent of the Hilfsverein emigrés and 16 percent of those heading for Palestine did not require financial support, but are included in the overall statistics.
122. These programs included: Hechaluz, Habonim, and Makkabi Hazair.
123. Pioneered by Recha Freier in Berlin in 1932, Youth Aliyah was officially begun in 1934 and supported financially by Hadassah, the Zionist women's organization in the United States. Its purpose was to rescue children by sending them to Palestine.
124. Until April 1939, Youth Aliyah sent 3,229 children from Germany to Palestine, saving them from Nazi terror. Thank you to Sara Kadosh of the Joint Distribution Committee Archives (Jerusalem) for the figures from Germany. Other figures for Youth Aliyah, claiming 7,000 children brought into Palestine, are cited by Norman Bentwich, *Jewish Youth Comes Home: the Story of the Youth Aliyah, 1933–1943* (London: V. Gollancz Ltd., 1944), 62, 82. In the pamphlet *Ten Years Children and Youth Aliyah* (London: Children and Youth Aliyah, 1944), 2, it is claimed that 10,000 children were brought to Palestine in the ten years of YA. See also Report of the Central Bureau for the Settlement of German Jews in Palestine prepared for the 21st Zionist Congress (1939) for statistics and sum total of Youth Aliyah.
125. Women were a majority in the Jewish population of German-dominated Europe. In Poland (1931), 52.08 percent of the Jews were female. In Hungary (1930), 52.08 percent were female; in the Netherlands (1919), 51.9 percent were female, in Lithuania (1923), 52.08 percent were female. Raul Hilberg, *Perpetrators, Victims, Bystanders: The Jewish Catastrophe, 1933–1945* (New York, Aaron Asher Books, 1992), 127.
126. *IF*, no. 9 (27 February 1936).

127. Sybil Milton, "Women and the Holocaust," in *When Biology Became Destiny: Women in Weimar and Nazi Germany*, ed. Renate Bridenthal, Atina Grossmann, and Marion Kaplan (New York: Monthly Review Press, 1984), 301. Bruno Blau set up the following table to show the disparity between males and females in 1939 (figures include Austria, exclusive of Vienna and the Sudetenland.)

	Male	Female	Total
Single	32,254	43,222	75,476
Married	50,746	49,563	100,309
Widowed	6,674	28,347	35,021
Divorced	2,700	3,982	6,682
TOTAL	92 374	125,114	217,488

See Bruno Blau, "The Jewish Population of Germany, 1939–1946," *Jewish Social Studies* 12 (1950): 165.
128. Lixl-Purcell, *Women of Exile*, 92.
129. Erich Rosenthal, "Trends of the Jewish Population in Germany, 1910–39," *Jewish Social Studies* 6 (1944): 248.
130. About 22 percent of women were widowed in 1939. Bruno Blau, "Die Juden in Deutschland von 1939 bis 1945, " *Judaica* 7 (1951): 271. Of the total number of widows, 16,117 (56.8 percent) were 65 or over. See Blau, "The Jewish Population," 165.
131. These figures include Austria (exclusive of Vienna) and the Sudetenland. Blau, "The Jewish Population," 165. In Berlin alone, the number of old age homes grew from five in 1933 to thirteen in 1939 with 1,683 occupants. In 1939, 3,000 people waited for accommodations in the community's thirteen old age homes. By 1942, the number of such institutions had grown to 21. See Wolf Gruner, "Die Reichshauptstadt und die Verfolgung der Berliner Juden 1933–1945," in *Jüdische Geschichte in Berlin*, ed. Reinhard Rürup (Berlin: Edition Hentrich, 1995), 242, 251.
132. "Alles alte Leute, alte Frauen," Elisabeth Freund, memoirs, LBI: 146.

Chapter Two

EVADING PERSECUTION

German-Jewish Behavior Patterns after 1933

Jürgen Matthäus

The Setting

AFTER THE HOLOCAUST, THE QUESTION of Jewish agency has been more the subject of public debate than of in-depth analysis.¹ In the past, the extremes dominated this debate. After her idea of the "banality of evil," Hannah Arendt is best known for her polemic against leaders of the German-Jewish community, especially Rabbi Leo Baeck, going so far as calling him "the Jewish *Führer*"—a charge she later withdrew.² Dozens of books have been written to refute the stereotypical yet persistent assumption that Jews had gone "like sheep to the slaughter."³ However, the more these works focus on one aspect, usually armed resistance, the less they explore other, more subtle and less visible, forms of Jewish reactions to persecution. For the assessment of Jewish history in Nazi Germany, this rigid frame of reference has an especially negative effect. Compared to the Warsaw ghetto uprising or the revolt of the Sonderkommando in Birkenau, attempts at counteracting the effects of *Judenpolitik* by German Jews seem to pale into insignificance, irrespective of the fact that there is ample proof for a multitude of behavior patterns from private reactions via organized efforts to militant opposition thereafter, or as Marion Kaplan has written, when "social death" had set in.⁴ The publications by Konrad Kwiet and Francis Nicosia as well as the other contributions to this volume attest to the broad range of this spectrum.⁵

Raul Hilberg, the doyen of Holocaust studies, has presented the most systematic interpretation of collective Jewish behavior patterns during the Holocaust, based on his analysis of a long tradition of Jewish reactions to earlier forms of persecution. Hilberg's schema stretches from resistance and alleviation via evasion and paralysis to compliance. Of these categories, alleviation—defined as "activities to avert danger or, in the event that force has already been used, to diminish its effects"—and compliance are identified as the ones most frequently adopted by Jews in reaction to Nazi persecution; cases of armed resistance, on the other hand, were, in Hilberg's view, "small and few" as well as "actions of last (never first) resort."[6] Other scholars have applied a similar interpretation. Marion Kaplan notes that the "desire of Jews to find some workable agreement" increased their tendency to accommodate and go on with their lives despite the danger signals gradually building up around them.[7]

Little attention has been paid so far to the subject of this chapter, the actions of those who tried to evade becoming targets of anti-Jewish policies. One reason for the relative neglect is that evasion is difficult to separate from other forms of Jewish reactions. Hilberg defines it as "flight, concealment, and hiding," terms that denote the physical withdrawal of Jews from their places of residence in reaction to or in anticipation of persecution.[8] Emigration and hiding during the Holocaust are—even if restricted to German Jews—indeed important phenomena. By May 1939, roughly a quarter million—half the Jewish population in Germany in 1933—had managed to leave the country; by the end of the war, an estimated 10,000 Jews in Germany and Austria had taken the illegal route, but most of them did not survive.[9]

Yet there are other, so far largely neglected aspects of evasion that do not necessarily imply physical retreat. I cannot cover here the whole spectrum of evasive Jewish behavior stretching beyond emigration and hiding, from the private into the political sphere. The focus of this chapter will be on the question of how persons targeted by anti-Jewish measures applied legal means of undermining the cornerstone in the edifice of persecution—the definition of who a Jew was in the eyes of the regime. I define "evasion" here as active rejection of "out-group" definition, or more precisely: the attempt by those whom Nazi agencies labeled as Jews to escape this designation and be treated as members of either the "in-group" or a less contentious minority (in the eyes of the rulers), such as *Mischlinge* (mixed breeds) or otherwise "privileged" Jews.[10]

The regulations enacted after 1933 on who was to be perceived and treated as a Jew reflected two different, though not necessarily opposing, tendencies: on the one hand, they expanded the definition of Jewishness by including persons who had never, no longer, or only partly, identified themselves as being Jewish, such as the roughly 40,000 Jews of Christian faith and the approximately 50,000 *Mischlinge*.[11] On the other hand, they restricted the range of those earmarked for persecution by providing exemptions. These exemptions reflected both the randomness of categorizing human beings along seemingly scientific, but in reality social, categories and the inherent problems of racial profiling. During the Third Reich, the discussions about how to define Jewishness were bizarre in the arguments made, yet potent in their consequences for the persons affected. "Clear segregation," the catchword of the Nazi racial revolution, required intricate methods of data gathering, evaluation, and decision-making, and involved deliberations within and between a multitude of agencies, often resulting in conflict or compromise.[12]

The interests of the state added to the problem, as did popular perceptions according to which Jews at least to some extent "looked Jewish." This helped those who came close to the "Aryan" ideal type, and made life more difficult for those who did not.[13] Public opinion mattered, if only in the minds of those in power; their key concern was to avoid discontent on the home front that could lead to the erosion of support for the regime. We know now that the persecution of the Jews never created enough unrest among German elites or the population at large to become politically dangerous for Nazi rulers; in fact, only the tacit compliance of, and active support by, important strata of German society can explain why the Holocaust happened. Yet, at the time, not only the victims, but also their persecutors lacked the ability to clearly foresee the "final solution" in its genocidal dimensions. It is here, in the murky area of racial definition and stigmatization within the Reich, that the prospective victims could become active, over time with increasing personal risk and decreasing chances of success, to attain reprieve from persecution, be it only a partial or temporary reprieve.

Rejecting the Yellow Badge

Concrete manifestations of how those targeted tried to evade being hit by anti-Jewish measures are anything but rare. The basis for evasion was built into the earliest regulations. The "Aryan paragraph" of the "Law for the Restoration of the Professional Civil Service," enacted on 7 April 1933, contained an exemption for civil servants who had joined the public service before the beginning of World War I. The

Nuremberg Race Laws and their supplementary decrees enacted in November 1935 allowed so-called *Mischlinge* to apply to the Reich Ministry of the Interior and the office of the Deputy of the Führer for special permission for marriages with persons of "German and related blood."[14] More importantly, both the Reich Citizenship Law and the "Law for the Protection of German Blood and Honor" contained provisions for the granting of exemptions by Hitler for anyone whom the Führer, for whatever reason, saw fit to exclude from discriminatory measures.[15]

From the time of Hitler's coming to power, those trying to escape Nazi policy argued—without necessarily denying either their Jewishness or the existence of a "Jewish question," however defined—that anti-Jewish measures should not apply to them due to their convictions, achievements or status. Examples abound, especially for the early phase after the Nazi takeover; they range from invoking privileges for Jewish war veterans to the claim that one was a staunch supporter of the "national revolution."[16] In view of the preceding history, these calls for exemptions are not surprising. German Jewry at the time of Hitler's takeover was—even if one leaves out *Mischlinge* and other fringe groups—a highly diverse minority lacking, beyond strong, but often diffuse ties to shared traditions, a collective mentality, and unified organizational infrastructure. While the latter would emerge over time, the former remained an abstraction more in tune with anti-Semitic stereotypes about "the Jews" than with the reality of Jewish life in Nazi Germany.

Historians still have not fully investigated the interrelationship between those who, using the powerful imagery introduced symbolically by Robert Weltsch in the Zionist newspaper, the *Jüdische Rundschau* in April 1933, were willing to "wear the yellow badge with pride," and those who rejected it as an unacceptable stigma. The prevailing perception, with its emphasis on collective victimhood, not only limits our understanding of Jewish fate and agency during the Nazi era; it also tends to exclude aspects of historical reality that contradict our current image of how Jews behaved.[17] To overcome the tendency of defining Jewish behavior in static, collective terms, we have to acknowledge the diversity of the target group of persecution in the context of the changes that took place over time. In the course of the nineteenth century, the relinquishing of community affiliations and the estrangement from traditional ties became a *fait accompli*, so much so that those representing the majority of German Jews became branded as "assimilationists."[18] In the everyday life of Jews, this development could express itself in a number of ways, including conscious acts, such as conversion, as well as in a gradual blurring of ties to the surrounding majority with its cultural or political values, e.g., by embracing German nationalism or adaptations like the "Jewish Christmas tree."[19] Simultaneously, German Jews developed an increasing awareness of their specific identity, which led them for the most part toward embracing more assertive means of defending their rights and status; a minority went farther in the direction of what Kurt Blumenfeld called "post-assimilatory Zionism."[20] The escalating dynamics created by the Nazi onslaught had a centripetal as well as centrifugal effect: most Jews were, as the leading German Zionist Franz Meyer pointed out after the war, "forced back into their Jewishness."[21] At the same time, mounting outside pressure increased the desire to escape the straitjacket of German *Judenpolitik*.

After 1933, for those who did not or could not emigrate, there were various ways to make use of the fuzziness of the Nazi definition of who was a Jew. In many cases, desperation led those affected to pursue more than one of the available options at the same time or consecutively. Renouncing one's membership in the Jewish community was one alternative, although not one that many pursued.[22] This is hardly surprising given the Nazi state's insistence that what mattered was race, not religion, as well as the assertive tradition within German Jewry. Even representatives of converted Jews who felt as Christians and staunch German nationalists reminded the members of their group that "nothing could be more dishonorable or contemptible than for one of us to dare deny the existence of our ancestors or to besmirch the homes of our parents."[23] For some, the way to sidestep the classification trap involved petitions to Hitler or the use of prominent helpers—an escape route that, over time, fewer and fewer victims of racial persecution could pursue with any realistic hope for success; in total, between 1,300 and 3,000 petitions achieved the desired goal.[24]

More important was the attempt to receive formal decisions by the Reichssippenamt (Reich Kinship Office) or by German courts as further elaborated below. A significant number of those who found themselves labeled as Jews or *Mischlinge* claimed that they represented a case of mistaken identity as their family history was wrongly documented. For the most part, they argued that their father-of-record was not the Jewish husband of their mother, but an "Aryan" man. It is important to note that claims like these threatened the Nuremberg classification system to the core, unless a workable procedure could be found to clarify the question of ancestry. To dismiss these claims summarily would have collided with the racial state's declared aim of separating the bad apples from the good. Thus, in addition to the granting of exemptions by Hitler and other forms of protection based on favor, mechanisms and procedures had to be created that would ensure the proper designation of human beings according to racial principles.

The Reich Kinship Office (part of the Reich Ministry of the Interior, and until October 1940, called the Reichsstelle für *Sippenforschung*, or Reich Office for Kinship Research) was one of the most important agencies deciding in matters of racial identity and status. It would investigate cases of doubt on the basis of genealogical, biometrical, and other documentation before it issued authoritative decisions in the form of so-called certificates of ancestry (*Abstammungsbescheide*).[25] The officials of the Reichssippenamt and its regional offices were aware of their role as gatekeepers of the racial state: their ruling meant inclusion in or exclusion from discriminatory measures, depending on whether a person was classified as a Jew, a *Mischling* or as *deutschblütig* ("of German blood"). One of the key pieces of evidence used to clarify ancestry was expert advice provided by designated anthropologists and racial scientists. Applying what was then regarded as cutting-edge science, these experts would evaluate genealogy, blood composition, and phenotypical traits. In other words, they provided the methods and the material for drawing the line between the in-group and the out-group. Overall, the Reich Kinship Office processed more than 52,000 requests during the war; the number of persons who received a "racial upgrade" from Jewish to non-Jewish by way of an administrative decision probably exceeded 4,000.[26]

Many historians have noted the absence of a uniform, linear pattern in the process of persecution, and the persistence of the semblance of normalcy in matters of *Judenpolitik*. Indeed, despite a gradual tightening of anti-Jewish measures, those targeted could still pursue their own interests in a number of ways. What is more, on occasion new methods adopted to streamline racial segregation opened new avenues to escape the full impact of persecution. I am referring here particularly to a piece of legislation inserted into the German civil code on 12 April 1938 that introduced, in addition to a certificate of ancestry issued by the Reich Kinship Office, another way of formally deciding on a person's racial affiliation. With the notable exception of Beate Meyer, historians have so far largely ignored this law, less because of the fact that its long title, *Gesetz über die Änderung und Ergänzung familienrechtlicher Vorschriften und über die Rechtsstellung der Staatenlosen* ("Law to

Amend and Supplement Family-Related Regulations and to Regulate the Status of Stateless Persons"), subsequently family law novella, did not make any reference to Jews, than because of the scarcity of documentation on its application and meaning for those affected.[27] This law codified racial policy in its dual function by separating members of the in-group from those of the out-group. For the latter, the novella's importance as the last exit on the road to destruction grew with the ferocity of anti-Jewish policy. Yet, given the intentions of the authors of this piece of legislation, the actual effect of invoking it was anything but risk-free. Let us look at this law and its application more closely as it reflects an under-researched aspect of behavior by those threatened with falling victim to anti-Jewish measures after 1938. I will focus on Berlin, with its more than 80,000 Jews in the spring of 1939, one-third of the Jewish population left in Germany.[28]

Escape Route and Dead End: The Dual Effect of Judicial Proof of Ancestry

The revision of the German civil code in early 1938, as embodied in the new law, enabled state prosecutors to bring charges for the purpose of deciding if paternity for the person in question was with the husband—the father-of-record—or with another man—the biological father. The aim of the family law novella was to leave the clarification of a person's ancestry, especially in terms of race, no longer to the parents alone, but to involve the courts and make them custodians of ethnic cleansing. One of the authors of the new law, state prosecutor Rexroth from the Reich Ministry of Justice, stressed in his commentaries the state's "interest in the clarification of blood-related genealogy" (*Interesse an der Klarstellung der blutmäßigen Abstammung*), which transformed every case of unclear ancestry involving Jews and "Aryans" into a matter of public concern that trumped both the child's and the parents' interest.[29] At the time of its passing, some Jewish observers understood the novella as one of many discriminatory measures enacted in early 1938 that would further erode the living conditions of Jews in Germany.[30] Yet the more the situation in the Reich worsened, the more they grasped the life-saving potential inherent in changing their racial status under the Nuremberg definitions.

It took more than the will to survive for someone targeted by anti-Jewish measures to turn this piece of Nazi legislation around and attempt to use it for his or her benefit. First, either the person in question or someone else, often one of the parents, had to approach a state prosecutor with the request to open a paternity case. In view of the highly Nazified German judiciary and the dangers of taking legal action as a Jew, this was not an appealing idea. Second, to create a convincing case, evidence had to be presented to the effect that the father-of-record was in fact not the biological father, but that the child had been conceived in an adulterous affair—an argument that, even in cases where it was true, went against some of the most basic tenets of conventional morality, especially when the parents were still alive. Third, German prosecutors did not consider evidence provided by Jews or *Mischlinge* as reliable.[31] Thus, each applicant had to agree to (and pay for) a full-scale genealogical and racial investigation. It goes without saying that these investigations by "experts" such as Professor Dr. Otmar Freiherr von Verschuer, Josef Mengele's mentor at the Kaiser-Wilhelm-Institut für Anthropologie, menschliche Erblehre und Eugenik (Kaiser-Wilhelm Institute for Anthropology, Genetics, and Eugenics) in Berlin-Dahlem, involved a high risk and invaded privacy in more than one respect.[32] Fourth, the judicial procedure, even when successful, could endanger family members and other witnesses, e.g., by revoking the "privileged" status of a Jewish man married to an "Aryan" woman once their child had been declared illegitimate and fathered by an "Aryan" man. Finally, persons who approached the prosecutor's office with the claim of being fully "Aryan" abandoned whatever safety the Jewish community, with its shielding social relief and communal identity, could offer. This became an issue for those who failed in their efforts at court; although we have no reliable data, one can assume that being thrown back into enforced Jewishness after the judiciary had thrown out one's case made a person's standing in the community and its agencies even more precarious than before.

    Despite all of these odds, between the spring of 1938 and 1945, in Berlin alone, about 700 persons—mostly *Mischlinge*—used the family law novella for the purpose of evading the full force of anti-Jewish persecution. As racial reclassification had consequences for the status not only of the person in question, but also for his or her children, the minimum of those in Berlin directly involved in cases under this law can be estimated at roughly one thousand. The available data do not offer a coherent picture for Germany as a whole; yet it is not unrealistic to assume that the fate of several thousand persons in the Reich and in Austria was decided, directly or indirectly, by courts applying the family law novella.³³ In the context of the Holocaust, this is doubtless not a insignificant number. Yet, this law and its application are crucial for a better understanding of how Jews not only used loopholes in the fabric of German *Judenpolitik*, but also actively went against the thrust of Nazi measures to evade being persecuted.

Not surprisingly, then, most cases involving Jews or *Mischlinge* were opened on the basis of testimonies presented by them; the prosecutor would then look at the evidence—witness statements and, most importantly, the expert opinions by racial scientists. If satisfied that there was a case, the prosecutor opened proceedings at the Landgericht (state court), which, as a rule, decided in favor of the prosecutor's application while the defendant offered no objection.³⁴ The bizarre legal constellation implied that the accused had no interest in refuting the prosecutor's evidence, as he or she depended on it in order to be racially upgraded. The increase in the number of applications under the family law novella reflects the actual threat posed by the ensuing "final solution." The more imminent the prospect of being deported, the greater was the willingness by those affected, in their desperation, to overcome inhibitions of presenting intimate personal and family affairs for judicial scrutiny. Roughly half of all Berlin cases involving Jews or *Mischlinge* were opened in the years 1941 and 1942, at the height of the deportations to the death camps and ghettos in the East.³⁵

The hopes of the applicants were often unfounded. In Berlin, the sample selected from a total of 700 cases involving Jews comprises 64 cases on 61 persons, almost equally divided according to gender, but much younger than the average age of the remaining Jewish population in the Reich.³⁶ Less than half of them (26) ended with a verdict that improved the applicant's racial status. Of those who were successful, two-thirds had applied as *Mischlinge ersten Grades* (mixed breeds of the first degree)³⁷ and became *deutschblütig* as a result of the court verdict. Only five *Volljuden* (full Jews) managed to be reclassified as *Mischlinge*. The remaining cases (38) brought no improvement in racial status; they were either rejected by the prosecutor (13), were pending until the end of the war (11), cannot be retraced on the basis of the remaining documents (7), or were terminated as a result of the deportation of the applicants (5). In two cases, the applicants were downgraded from "Aryan" to the status of *Mischling ersten Grades*. Though the number of family members deported cannot be established, it seems to have been considerably higher than that of the applicants sent to the East. In short, the family law novella turned out to be less a means of escape for those desperate to evade German anti-Jewish policy than a tool in the hands of the state to make that very policy more efficient.[38]

For the guardians of the nation's purity as a *Volk*, the dual aim of the racial state—to exclude the bad and to include the good—offered *one* set of problems, the application of the law *another*. Formally independent in their decisions, German judges received mixed guidelines on how to decide in matters of ancestral proof: on the one hand, the Reich Justice Ministry demanded "[that judges] . . . integrate *Volksgenossen* wrongly regarded as *Mischlinge* or Jews into the community," and on the other hand, it called for "energetically refusing intruders whose German blood qualities (*Deutschblütigkeit*) could not be proven without doubt."[39] "Expert" opinions provided by racial scientists were as crucial to the administrative decisions of the Reich Kinship Office as they were to the working of the family law novella, yet in practice, they presented serious problems to the courts. The few institutions qualified to perform the investigations were sitting on a rising number of requests, which created backlog and delay.

Moreover, in most cases, the expert opinions offered varying degrees of likelihood and probability as opposed to the certainty desired by jurists to reach a decision. For believers in racial theory and Nazi propaganda, it was difficult to accept the fact that Jews had no distinct, hereditarily ingrained phenotypical traits.[40] Ideology was not supported by empirical evidence; thus, the measurements, charts, and tables produced in the course of the racial investigations said more about the mindset of their scientific originators than about the ancestry of their objects of study. In 1939, in an official party publication, Otto Reche, one of the founders of *Erb- und Rassenbiologie* (Hereditary and Race Biology), refuted the judicial demand for unequivocal proof with the hardly convincing argument that racial biologists were aware of the "general imperfection of human knowledge" (*der allgemeinen Unvollkommenheit der menschlichen Erkenntnis bewußt*).[41]

Cases and Context

Let us take a closer look at some of the ancestry cases handled by Berlin prosecutors in the broader context of racial policy as well as in their consequences for those affected. Having to administer the family law novella, despite its inherent problems, the Berlin prosecutors eagerly defended their territory against rival institutions while paying little attention to the fate of the persons for whom a court decision could mean life or death. By the time the new law took effect, anyone who had experienced German *Judenpolitik* directly or indirectly knew that the judiciary represented but one institution involved in the execution of the "final solution." Himmler's security police and SD insisted on upholding its prerogative vis-à-vis the courts; its dislike of legal procedures grew with the pace of genocide. In late summer 1942, the SD, in its *Meldungen aus dem Reich*, criticized state agencies for slowing down the executive process by bothering themselves and expert racial scientists with ancestry cases.[42] After the Reichssippenamt had come under the control of Ernst Kaltenbrunner's Reich Security Main Office in late 1943, the family law novella appeared as one of very few loopholes left in the attempt to evade being caught up in the "final solution." One year before the end of the war, the chief of the security police and SD complained at the Reich Justice Ministry that Jews used the courts to hide their true ancestry so that they could escape "security police measures planned and already implemented against them" (*für sie vorgesehenen bzw. bereits durchgeführten sicherheitspolizeilichen Maßnahmen zu entziehen*).[43]

FIGURE 2.1.: Form for the authentication (by German police officials) of photographs used in conjunction with racial ancestry cases handled in 1942 by the Berlin prosecutor's office. *Courtesy*: Landesarchiv Berlin.

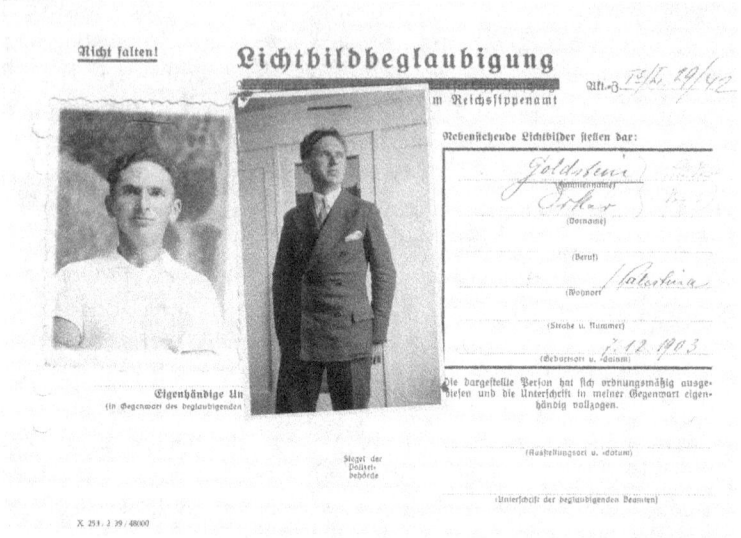

FIGURE 2.2.: Form for the authentication (by German police officials) of photographs used in conjunction with racial ancestry cases handled in 1942 by the Berlin prosecutor's office. *Courtesy*: Landesarchiv Berlin.

The Gestapo and SD kept up their criticism of the judiciary, while those looking to the courts for help had all the more reason to fear for their future. It is clear from the files of the Berlin Landgericht that the prosecutors in the Reich capital would rarely go ahead with a case against the advice of Himmler's officers.[44] Where they did, a positive outcome for the claimant was anything but guaranteed. The following is one such exceptional case: Julius K., a Jew according to the Nuremberg Race Laws, who was fifty-years old and was married to a non-Jewish woman. In March 1942, his lawyer filed a case at the Berlin prosecutor's office for racial reclassification based on the claim that K.'s mother had had an affair with an "Aryan" man. The alleged biological father as well as both his parents had died in the early 1930s; K.'s siblings had already been, as his lawyer called it, "evacuated." Before K. filed his case in Berlin, a regional version of the Reich Kinship Office, the Landesamt für Rassewesen (State Office for Race Affairs) in the state of Thuringia, had ruled that he was a Jew and that his children were *Mischlinge*. Bernhard Lösener, Judenreferent in the Reich Ministry of the Interior, had looked into the case, agreed, and threatened "further measures" (*weitere Maßnahmen*) against K. and his wife for still pursuing the matter. Prosecutors in Berlin were not impressed by interventions from the outside, and demanded an additional investigation, which, in view of the backlog of work facing the relevant institutes, was not forthcoming. The director of the Thuringian Landesamt called for short shrift (*kürzeren Prozeß*) and voiced his consternation that in early 1945, one should have more important things to do than to "hatch a half-Jew" (*einen Halbjuden auszubrüten*). The delay caused by the prosecutor's insistence on ancestral proof worked in K.'s favor; the end of the war seems to have saved him and his children from the fate of his siblings.[45]

Exceptions proved the rule. The aim of the state's jurists was not to undermine the effects of executive *Judenpolitik*, but to assist it by making the Nuremberg definition work. Indeed, there were cases under the family law novella in which the Berlin prosecutor brought charges against "Aryans" whose ancestry was doubted and who, in the process, became downgraded.[46] Where rivalries between both agencies ensued, it was the applicant and his or her family members who had to bear the consequences.

A case in point is that of the forty-five-year-old Dr. Hans L., who approached the Berlin prosecutors in February 1942 after his father-of-record had told him on his deathbed that Hans and his two siblings were illegitimate children. According to the application for opening an ancestry case, Hans L.'s mother Alma had confirmed the paternity by her "Aryan" friend and explained her long silence with a promise to her husband; prior to his death, she had seen no reason to share the secret as her other two children were living in the USA, while Hans, married to an "Aryan" woman, father of a baptized daughter, war veteran, and an established doctor, seemed not threatened. As the danger for her family was mounting, Alma L. decided to disclose the embarrassing truth, as she put it to the Staatsanwalt, "in the interest of the living" (*im Interesse der Lebenden*).

The expert opinion, as usual, did not prove anything regarding Hans L.'s ancestry, nor did it quantify his "Jewish race component." Shortly after the prosecutor, Staatsanwalt Horn, who worked on many of the Berlin cases, had sent the file on to the Gestapo office for their comment, L.'s mother must have received her deportation order to Theresienstadt. The file contains a note that Hans L. called the prosecutor's office on 2 October 1942 expressing his deep anxiety and urging the postponement of her impending deportation. That same day, Horn asked at the Gestapo whether "the evacuation of Alma Sara L. can be suspended until the closing of the case as she is needed as witness." On 8 October 1942, Alma L. signed a notarized statement confirming that all three of her children had an "Aryan" man as their biological father; she added that she was about to be deported, and thus in all probability could not attend any future court proceedings in her son's case. The statement also mentioned that the advice to testify before a notary had been provided to Hans L.'s wife by a Gestapo officer.

For her son, Alma L.'s statement must have been a ray of hope; for the Gestapo, it made no difference. Having sat on the case file for almost four months, the Gestapo office sent it back to the prosecutor in January 1943 with the remark that the "evacuation" of Alma L. settled the matter. Indeed, shortly thereafter, Staatsanwalt Horn informed Hans L. that his case could not go to court due to lack of evidence. Despite L.'s insistence that the *Gutachten* (expert opinions) by the racial experts had not ruled out his partly "Aryan" descent, and despite his plea that the case was "for me and my child of vital importance" (*für mich und mein Kind von lebenswichtiger Bedeutung*), Horn turned him down. Hans L. was deported to an unknown place, his fate unknown. Whether his mother Alma survived the war also remains unclear.[47]

Being privileged did not mean much after the "final solution" had started. Like Hans L. who lived in a *Mischehe* (mixed marriage) and had a baptized daughter, Gertrud Elisabeth H. belonged to a fringe group outside the core of German anti-Jewish policy. Born in 1887 as the daughter of a Jewish father and an "Aryan" mother, Gertrud H. was a *Mischling* who faced deportation in late 1941, the time when she applied at the Berlin prosecutor's office. Hers was typical for the majority of cases: both of her parents as well as the alleged "Aryan" father were already dead. Gertrud H. claimed to have been told about her true father on her mother's deathbed, but had remained silent to avoid embarrassment for her late parents. Only the imminent deportation made her approach the prosecutor's office, but it was too late. Though Staatsanwalt Horn acted promptly, the case got stuck in the queue of racial expert opinion. When Gertrud H. received an appointment for a racial examination, she was already gone. In January 1942, she had been deported to Riga.[48]

The Berlin court files show only to a certain degree how members of the target group made use of the narrow opportunities at their disposal to evade being labeled under the Nuremberg definitions, especially after the beginning of deportations from the Reich to the killing centers in the East. We do not know how many of the cases were based on claims fabricated by the applicants or their relatives. Standard arguments according to which the Jewish husband, at the time of conception, had been absent, had health problems that prevented him from fathering a child, or had already broken with his wife, seem highly unreal, especially under the circumstances. Postwar testimony by those who survived can help here, as Beate Meyer has shown for Hamburg.[49] To rule out completely the possibility of illegitimate paternity among Jewish couples or those in a mixed marriage implies too rigid an interpretation of bourgeois sexual morals; yet the truth can rarely be established. An exception from this rule is the case of Günter B., born in June 1939, whose "Aryan" mother was married to a Jew. The application filed one year later by the state custodian (Jugendamt) passed all legal hurdles without any problems, despite the fact that no racial expert opinion was produced to back up the claim by the Jewish husband, Willi B., that he was not the child's father. Willi B., however, easily convinced the prosecutor as he had been incarcerated since the middle of 1938 without interruption in the Buchenwald concentration camp.[50]

As indicated already, the expert opinions produced by racial scientists, despite the key role they played in determining whether the prosecutor would open a case under the family law novella as requested by the applicant, rarely helped in clarifying ancestry to the extent hoped for by the applicants or desired by state jurists. Given the inherent deficiencies of their approach, the experts stayed within the narrow confines of self-referential guesswork and racial astrology, only occasionally challenged by criticism from the outside or from members of their own profession. Applicants had not only to overcome high stakes in convincing race experts and prosecutors; they also faced additional risks involved in the bureaucratic process. As just one example of the tangled web of persecution, in December 1938, Luise W., a Jewish woman, approached the Berlin Staatsanwaltschaft with the claim that the biological father of her son Heinz Georg C., born in 1911, was not her Jewish husband whom she had divorced in 1923, but an "Aryan" man. As the racial examination of this "Aryan" man, at the time a prisoner in the Sachsenhausen concentration camp, neither confirmed nor refuted this claim, prosecutor Horn decided not to proceed with the case. Yet Luise W. pleaded for a reassessment, until the senior prosecutor (Oberstaatsanwalt) at the Berlin Kammergericht started an investigation against her because she had failed to use her forced name "Sara" when signing her letter of appeal. It is not clear from the file what happened to Luise W. After the case had lapsed, her son Heinz

Georg C. was classified by the Reich Kinship Office in August 1942 as a "full Jew" and was deported to Auschwitz in March 1943, like his sister before him. Both perished.[51]

An applicant had the best chance whenever he or she found a strong ally in one of the German agencies involved, even if—and especially when—their reasons for embracing the cause of the claimant were entirely selfish. An exceptional case in the Berlin archive exemplifies this strange interaction within an already strange legal framework. In February 1942, the certified genealogist (*Sippenforscher*) Karl Unger approached the Berlin prosecutor on behalf of his client, Ernst K., a middle-ranking civil servant, with the request to open a paternity case against his former Jewish wife, 45-year-old Hanna K., "in the interest of his two children." Both parents of his former wife as well as her alleged biological father were already dead; the application lost further in credibility as a result of Unger's claim that Hanna K.'s mother had been sexually abstinent vis-à-vis her Jewish husband while having an affair with an "Aryan" man. As the "expert" opinion by Dr. Dubitscher of the Poliklinik für Erb- und Rassenpflege (Polyclinic for Hereditary and Race Care)—one of the busiest court-approved institutes in Berlin—merely stated that paternity from both fathers was equally likely, the case seemed stillborn. Yet, Ernst K. did not give in and solicited an expert psychological opinion on his former wife's "mental characteristics" (*seelische Eigenschaften*).[52]

In early March 1943, Professor Dr. Matthias H. Göring's Deutsches Institut (since early 1944, Reichsinstitut) für Forschung und Psychotherapie (German/Reich Institute for Research and Psychotherapy) in Berlin presented a twenty-page case analysis (*charakterologisches Gutachten*) based on comparative graphological, literary, and physiognomic analysis in combination with interrogations of Hanna K. The result deviated as drastically from the earlier expert opinion by Dubitscher's institute as it mirrored the randomness of racial categories and the prevalence of anti-Semitic stereotypes. K.'s Jewish father-of-record was described as a "serious and established man strongly bound in Jewish tradition and thus mentally confined" with a "penetrating mind in typically Jewish manifestation," while devoid of any "open-minded and relaxed life-affirming spontaneity" (*aufgeschlossener und gelöster Lebensunmittelbarkeit*)—all of which represented "characteristics of Jewishness in a somewhat 'old-testamentarian' form" (*Grundzüge jüdischer Wesensart von einer gewissen 'alttestamentarischen' Ausprägung*). Compare this to the ruling by Göring's institute on the "Aryan" lover of Hanna K.'s mother: "Affable personality" combined with "a happy mind, humane attitude and developed love of nature," in addition to his most prominent features of "Prussian patriotism and national consciousness," were clearly a result of his "Nordic type." In terms of paternity, the psychologists had no doubt about the high, almost certain likelihood that the "Aryan" man, and not the Jewish husband of K.'s mother, was the biological father.[53]

This case is rare not only due to the involvement of psychological expertise in the legal process, but also in regard to the remarkable and, for the applicant, positive momentum it gathered in the course of internecine rivalry, as well as the insight it provides behind the façade of the scientific Potemkin village. Trying to avoid a clash of related approaches, Dr. Dubitscher, himself a psychiatrist, had positive things to say on the meticulousness of the rival "expert" opinion. Yet he stuck to his conclusion and pointed to the relative novelty of psychological analysis that could be used as evidence only "with great reservation" (*mit großer Zurückhaltung*).[54] Coming from a racial scientist who habitually provided hazy conclusions himself, this argument seems hardly convincing; nevertheless, Staatsanwalt Horn bought into it in his rejection of K.'s appeal to open the case. However, neither kinship researcher Unger nor Göring's institute gave in; instead, they solicited a decisive racial-biological opinion by a leading expert, Professor Verschuer. While K. had the welfare of his children, perhaps also that of his former wife, in mind, Göring was aware of the precedence inherent in "a general decision on the evidence-value of scientifically sound psychological expert opinions," and of the tempting prospect of being involved, particularly during the war, in legal work.[55]

As it turned out, Göring could regard Verschuer's assessment that came down in July 1944 as confirmation. While the application of expert psychological opinions for the purpose of establishing paternity had to be restricted to special cases and handled with special care, Verschuer attested to the professional nature of the work Göring's institute had conducted. Dubitscher's Polyclinic, on the other hand, fared less well. It had been sloppy in its investigation and analysis to the extent that the conclusion that Hanna K. bore "characteristically Jewish traits" and no similarity to her mother's "Aryan" lover appeared "most certainly wrong."[56] In the struggle between the scientists, the judiciary backed the one with the greatest prestige. On 11 September 1944, Horn applied to the Landgericht (state court) to bring charges based on the validity of the psychological expertise and asked for

Gestapo agreement to proceed with the case. In its verdict passed in early November, the court ruled in favor of the applicant, presumably saving Hanna K. and her children from further persecution as objects of German *Judenpolitik*.[57]

Insights and Open Questions

In administering the family law novella as part of a racial policy, the state could not lose: it would either weed out a member of an undesirable out-group, or gain an "Aryan" for the *Volksgemeinschaft* (racial community). Cases that seemed too weak, that is to say, claims by those whose Jewish ancestry seemed obvious or in which applicants could not produce sufficient evidence, were turned down by the prosecutor and never made it to court. Successful claimants knew they could beat the system only if they were lucky; yet luck was not enough. Claimants depended on the support of their parents, especially those who relinquished their Jewish identity by claiming to be "Aryan," and thus reaffirming the crucial importance of family bonds even in situations where their mothers or fathers were facing deportation. Like Luise W., many women dared to get involved with the German justice system and agreed to a dangerous and degrading procedure not for their own sake, but for that of their children and grandchildren. Their motives are but dimly reflected in the surviving prosecutor files with their formalistic language; yet it is clear that claimants and their supporters hoped to cut through the close-knit web of persecution by wielding the double-edged Nazi family law against the intentions of its originators, administrators, and executors.

If one wants to apply a descriptive label to the kind of Jewish behavior exemplified by the Berlin prosecutorial cases, it could be called "evasion by compliance." The applicants used the existing system to undermine the basis of the "final solution," the definition of who was a Jew, and turned Nazi racial policy on its head. By posing as members of the in-group, they defied "social death" as well as their physical annihilation. As a result of the family law novella's prime purpose as a mainstay, and not a loophole in the structure of persecution, this form of evasion was not possible for the majority of Jews in Germany and in German-dominated Western Europe, and clearly out of the question in Eastern Europe where Germans cared little about keeping up the appearance of legality and clear-cut definitions. Yet, denying the stigma of being labeled as a member of the out-group forms part of the spectrum of Jewish behavior during the Third Reich—a spectrum much broader than commonly acknowledged.

In assessing the historical importance of this kind of evasion, one should not forget that it worked only as long as those administering German *Judenpolitik* did not perceive it as a threat to the system of persecution—a caveat that applies also to other forms of Jewish reactions within the limits of what was deemed legal at the time. Further studies are necessary to clarify how far these specific contingencies add up to form a consistent pattern beyond the individual case. Who pursued the legal route toward racial reclassification, what background—socially, economically, and in terms of orientation—did these people have? How important were access to money, privileged information or to non-Jews with "connections"? Were lower-class or otherwise underprivileged Jews less inhibited than their bourgeois brethren in revealing intimate details about themselves and their family history to state functionaries and racial experts? What other means were applied by them at the same time, earlier, or later? Did those who pursued the legal path first end up further down the road of potentially life-saving, but even more risky clandestine or illegal action, such as going into hiding? While offering a flat, selective, and, to some extent, distorted picture of the applicants and their relatives, the case files of the Berlin prosecutor's office provide a basis for further research. Combined with other wartime and postwar sources, they have the potential to broaden our so far remarkably limited understanding of the full range of Jewish responses to Nazi persecution.

From looking at the persecutors, in this case the authors and administrators of the family law novella of 1938, it is clear that despite a multitude of publications on German *Judenpolitik* during the Third Reich, its mechanisms to determine who belonged to the in-group and who had to be treated as a Jew require more in-depth study. Functionaries of the racial state could easily interpret the family law novella as a tool that had more potential for doing harm by infiltrating the *Volksgemeinschaft* with persons of Jewish ancestry than strengthening it. The practical ambiguity of the law worked both ways: after the war, state jurists pointed to successful cases in which "upgraded" Jews or *Mischlinge* escaped annihilation in order to bolster the claim that German courts had contributed decisively to the "containment of Nazi racial politics" (*eindeutigen Beitrag der Justiz zur Einengung nationalsozialistischer Rassenpolitik*) and "most generously used the principle '*in dubio pro reo'* (*von dem Grundsatz 'in dubio pro reo' in weitherzigster Weise Gebrauch gemacht haben*)."[58] At the same time, survivors in a way "re-privatized" what had been dragged into the spotlight of Nazi courts and interpreted the family law novella as an important means of their rescue and survival. Similarly, the few historians who have dealt with the subject come to more positive conclusions than the ones presented here.[59] Irrespective of current interpretations, within the overall history of the Holocaust, the reaction of Jewish victims calls for more in-depth research before we can properly understand its aspects in all of their complexity and nuance.

Notes

1. This chapter addresses one of the conceptual issues that have come up in the course of the source edition project on "Jewish Responses to Persecution, 1933–1946," conducted by the Center for Advanced Holocaust Studies at the United States Holocaust Memorial Museum (USHMM), especially volume 1 (1933–1938) edited by Mark Roseman and myself. For an analysis that focuses more on the perpetrator-related aspects of the topic, see my "'... im öffentlichen Interesse.' Staatsanwaltliche Abstammungsklagen im Kontext der NS-Judenpolitik," in *Deutsche, Juden, Völkermord. Der Holocaust als Geschichte und Gegenwart*, ed. Jürgen Matthäus and Klaus-Michael Mallmann (Darmstadt: Wissenschaftliche Buchgemeinschaft, 2006), 123–140. I thank the participants of the Miller Symposium at the University of Vermont, especially Beate Meyer, for their valuable comments. The views presented here are those of the author and do not reflect the opinion of the USHMM.
2. See Jürgen Matthäus, "Between fragmented memory and 'real history': The LBI's perception of Jewish Self-Defence, 1955–1970," in *Preserving the Legacy of German Jewry: A History of the Leo Baeck Institute, 1955–2005*, ed. Christhard Hoffmann (Tübingen: Mohr/Siebeck, 2005), 375–408; here, 394–395.
3. For a concise introduction to the debate, see Nechama Tec, *Jewish Resistance: Facts, Omissions, and Distortions* (Washington: USHMM Occasional Paper, 1997).
4. Marion Kaplan, *Between Dignity and Despair: Jewish Life in Nazi Germany* (New York: Oxford University Press, 1998), 5, 229, 239n2. The term "social death" was coined by Orlando Patterson to describe the distinctive features of the slave condition (ibid., 239n2).
5. See especially Konrad Kwiet and Helmut Eschwege, *Selbstbehauptung und Widerstand. Deutsche Juden im Kampf um Existenz und Menschenwürde 1933–1945* (Hamburg: Christians, 1984); Francis R. Nicosia, "Resistance and Self-Defence. Zionism and Antisemitism in Inter-War Germany," *Leo Baeck Institute Yearbook* XLIV (1997): 123–134. For different manifestations of Jewish reactions, see also Arnold Paucker, *German Jews in the Resistance 1933–1945: The Facts and the Problems* (Berlin: Gedenkstätte deutscher Widerstand, 2005), and "Changing Perceptions: Reflections on the Historiography of Jewish Self-Defense and Jewish Resistance, 1890–2000," in *Jüdische*

Welten. Juden in Deutschland vom 18. Jahrhundert bis in die Gegenwart, ed. Marion Kaplan and Beate Meyer (Göttingen: Wallstein Verlag, 2005), 440–456.
6. Raul Hilberg, *The Destruction of the European Jews*, 3rd ed. (New Haven: Yale University Press, 2003), 20–27, 1104–1118. See also Hilberg's *Perpetrators, Victims, Bystanders: The Jewish Catastrophe, 1933–1945* (New York: Aaron Asher, 1992).
7. Kaplan, *Dignity*, 230. Detlev Peukert, *Inside Nazi Germany: Conformity, Opposition, and Racism in Everyday Life* (New Haven: Yale University Press, 1987), 82–85. Peukert describes dissident behavior of German non-Jews in terms of a scale ranging from nonconformity via refusal and protest to resistance.
8. Hilberg, *Destruction*, 24.
9. Avraham Barkai, Paul Mendes-Flohr, and Steven Lowenstein, *Deutsch-Jüdische Geschichte der Neuzeit. Aufbruch und Zerstörung 1918–1945*, vol. 4 (Munich: C.H. Beck. 1997), 226, 363.
10. See the pioneering study by Beate Meyer, *"Jüdische Mischlinge." Rassenpolitik und Verfolgungserfahrung 1933–1945* (Hamburg: Dölling und Galitz Verlag, 1999).
11. Meyer, *"Jüdische Mischlinge,"* 465 (figures on *Mischlinge* for 1939).
12. See Cornelia Essner, *Die "Nürnberger Gesetze" oder die Verwaltung des Rassenwahns 1933–1945* (Paderborn: Schöningh, 2002).
13. Kaplan, *Dignity*, 35, 60.
14. For the law of 7 April 1933, the Nuremberg Race Laws, and their first supplementary decrees, see Karl A. Schleunes, ed., *Legislating the Holocaust: The Bernhard Loesener Memoirs and Supporting Documents* (Boulder: Westview, 2001), 154–157, 173–177. The Nuremberg Race Laws, passed on 15 September 1935, defined Jews as persons who were descended from three or four Jewish grandparents, or persons with two Jewish grandparents who either belonged to the Jewish religion or were married to a Jew at the time of the enactment of the Nuremberg laws. A *"Mischling* of the first degree" was a person with two Jewish grandparents who did not belong to the Jewish religion and was not married to a Jew; a *"Mischling* of the second degree" was a person with one Jewish grandparent.
15. See John M. Steiner and Jobst Freiherr von Cornberg, "Willkür in der Willkür. Befreiungen von den antisemitischen Nürnberger Gesetzen," *Vierteljahrshefte für Zeitgeschichte* 46 (1998): 143–187; Jeremy Noakes, "The Development of Nazi Policy Towards the German-Jewish 'Mischlinge' 1933–1945," *Leo Baeck Institute Yearbook* XXXIV (1989): 291–354.
16. For the rightwing fringe of the Jewish political spectrum in the Weimar Republic and the early Nazi era, see Matthias Hambrock, *Die Etablierung der Außenseiter. Der Verband nationaldeutscher Juden 1921–1935* (Cologne, Weimar, Vienna: Böhlau Verlag, 2003), 567–699; Carl J. Rheins, "The Schwarzes Fähnlein, Jungenschaft, 1932–1934," *Leo Baeck Institute Yearbook* XXIII (1978): 173–197; "The Verband nationaldeutscher Juden, 1921–1933," *Leo Baeck Institute Yearbook* XXV (1980): 243–268; and "Deutscher Vortrupp, Gefolgschaft deutscher Juden, 1933–1935," *Leo Baeck Institute Yearbook* XXVI (1981): 207–229.
17. For an excellent case study of German-Jewish behavior during the Weimar period, see Frank Bajohr, "'Nur deutsch will ich sein.' Jüdische Populärkünstler, antijüdische Stereotype und heutige Erinnerungskultur. Das Beispiel der Hamburger Volkssänger 'Gebrüder Wolf'," in *Jüdische Welten. Juden in Deutschland vom 18. Jahrhundert bis in die Gegenwart*, ed. Marion Kaplan and Beate Meyer (Göttingen: Wallstein Verlag, 2005), 373–396.

18. See Avraham Barkai, *"Wehr Dich!" Der Centralverein deutscher Staatsbürger jüdischen Glaubens 1893–1938* (Munich: Verlag C.H. Beck, 2002), 369–371.
19. Monika Richarz, "Der jüdische Weihnachtsbaum—Familie und Säkularisierung im deutschen Judentum des 19. Jahrhunderts," in *Geschichte und Emanzipation, Festschrift für Reinhard Rürup*, ed. Michael Grüttner, Rüdiger Hachtmann, and Heinz-Gerhard Haupt (Frankfurt am Main: Campus, 1999), 275–289. For a compelling overview, see Marion Kaplan, ed., *Jewish Daily Life in Germany, 1618–1945* (New York: Oxford University Press, 2005).
20. See Barkai, *Centralverein*; Nicosia, "Resistance"; Jehuda Reinharz, "The Zionist Response to Antisemitism in Germany," *Leo Baeck Institute Yearbook* XXX (1985): 105–140.
21. *"Es war keine Blüte, aus dem Untergang herausgewachsen! Der größte Teil der Juden ist zwangsläufig auf sein Judesein hingewiesen worden, und es wurde der Versuch gemacht, Judentum zu begreifen und lebendig zu machen."*; Franz Meyer (1897–1972), at the Leo Baeck Institute working session, 14 May 1961, LBIJMB, MF 491, reel 26, folder 8/2 (meeting minutes). Meyer was a member of the Reichsvertretung board from 1933 to 1939, and president of the Zionist Federation for Germany (*Zionistische Vereinigung für Deutschland*), between 1937 and 1939.
22. For statistical aspects of relinquishing the Jewish faith, see Peter Honigmann, *Die Austritte aus der jüdischen Gemeinde Berlin 1873–1941* (Frankfurt am Main, New York: Peter Lang, 1988).
23. "Aims and tasks of the Reichsverband," speech by Richard Wolff to members of the *Reichsverband der nichtarischen Christen*, 21 February 1934, in Richard Wolff, *Wir nichtarische Christen. Drei Reden vom Vorsitzenden des Reichsverbandes der nichtarischen Christen* (Frankfurt an der Oder: no publisher, 1934), 11.
24. According to Noakes, "Development," 319, until May 1941, there were only 263 successful petitions out of a total of 9,636 by persons requesting to be reclassified as *Mischlinge* or "Aryans." See also Meyer, *Jüdische Mischlinge*, 108; Alexandra Przyrembel, *Reinheitsmythos und Vernichtungslegitimation im Nationalsozialismus* (Göttingen: Vandenhoeck & Ruprecht, 2003), 101–120.
25. See Thomas Pegelow, "Determining 'People of German Blood,' 'Jews' and 'Mischlinge': The Reich Kinship Office and the Competing Discourses and Powers of Nazism, 1941–1943," *Contemporary European History* 15 (2006): 43–65; Eric Ehrenreich, *The Nazi Ancestral Proof: Genealogy, Racial Science and the Final Solution* (Bloomington: Indiana University Press, 2007). For an organizational history, see Diana Schulle, *Das Reichssippenamt. Eine Institution nationalsozialistischer Rassenpolitik* (Berlin: Logos, 2001).
26. Pegelow, "Determining," 64.
27. Meyer, *Jüdische Mischlinge*, 113–131. See also Kaplan, *Dignity*, 83; Anke Schnabel, "Im Schatten der Nürnberger Gesetze. Statusklagen jüdischer Kinder am Berliner Landgericht 1938–1945," MA thesis, TU Berlin 2004. I thank Anke Schnabel for providing me with a copy of her thesis.
28. Of the approximately 4,000 cases under the family law novella that form part of the existing collection "Staatsanwaltschaft beim Landgericht (LG) Berlin" held at the Landesarchiv Berlin (hereafter, LAB A Rep. 358-02), roughly 700 have been identified as involving Jews or *Mischlinge*, of which sixty-four cases involving sixty-one persons form the basis for this chapter. For the wider context, see Matthäus, "Interesse." For Jewish population figures, see Wolf Gruner, *Judenverfolgung in Berlin 1933–1945*.

Eine Chronologie der Behördenmaßnahmen in der Reichshauptstadt (Berlin: Edition Hentrich, 1996).

29. Staatsanwalt Rexroth, "Die Familienrechtsnovelle vom 12. April 1938 (Teil 1)," *Deutsche Justiz* 18/1938 (6. Mai 1938): 707–716.
30. See "Übersicht über die Verfolgungen gegen die Juden in den zentraleuropäischen Ländern (18.–24. Mai 1938)," World Jewish Congress Office Paris, USHMM Archive RG 11.001.M36 (Osobyi Archive Moscow 674-1-109), reel 106.
31. See regulation by *Reichsstelle für Sippenforschung*, 16 November 1939 (Przymbel, *Reinheitsmythos*, 114–115); regulation by *Reichsinnenministerium* (Ie 176 III/42), 2 November 1942, BArch R 3001/488, 404.
32. Examples in Meyer, *Jüdische Mischlinge*, 117–131; Matthäus, "Interesse."
33. In most cases, the prosecutor files and the court files pertaining to the family law novella seem to have been destroyed and only fragments remain. See Essner, *Verwaltung*, 204n124. No systematic search in German and Austrian archives for relevant case files has yet been undertaken. Meyer, *Jüdische Mischlinge*, traced sixty-six cases for Hamburg, the remainder of a larger collection of files.
34. For the only Berlin cases involving Jews in which the courts did not follow the argument of the prosecution, see LAB A-Rep. 358–02 Nr. 55119 and 55245.
35. Based on a list produced by the LAB of all 712 *Anfechtungsfälle* involving Jews or *Mischlinge*, the following numbers reflect the cases opened by the prosecutor (court verdict often followed one or even two years later): 1938: 47 cases opened; 1939: 51; 1940: 47; 1941: 144; 1942: 218; 1943: 117; 1944: 71; 1945: 17.
36. Of the 61 persons represented in the case files surveyed, 32 were male and 29 were female. Age distribution is as follows: 1–5 years, 5 persons; 6–10 years, 3 persons; 11–15 years, 2 persons; 16–21 years, 5 persons; (total minors: 15 persons); 22–25 years, 12 persons; 26–30 years, 6 persons; 31–35 years, 4 persons; 36–40 years, 5 persons; 41–45 years, 5 persons; 46–50 years, 6 persons; 51–55 years, 4 persons; 56–60 years, 1 person; 61–63 years (maximum age of applicants), 3 persons. Accumulated for the years 1938 to 1945, the age group up to 50 thus included 86 percent of the applicants in Berlin; in the summer of 1939, the same age group comprised only 48 percent of all Jews in the *Altreich*. See "Zur Situation der Juden in Deutschland (Altreich)," World Jewish Congress Paris office, USHMM RG 11.001M.36 (Osobyi Archive Moscow 1190–3-7).
37. *Mischlinge ersten Grades*, or "Mixed Breeds of the First Degree," were people with just two Jewish grandparents, also referred to as "half-Jews."
38. From the Berlin case files, it is not clear how many *Volljuden* were among the applicants; the available data suggest a ratio of roughly 20 percent. The 66 cases in Hamburg investigated by Beate Meyer produced 54 positive verdicts, including 10 *Volljuden* (Meyer, *Jüdische Mischlinge*, 114–115, 463). This high success rate could be the result of selective destruction of justice files after the war.
39. "Richterbrief Nr. 5," 1 February 1943, in *Richterbriefe. Dokumente zur Beeinflussung der deutschen Rechtssprechung 1942–1944*, ed. Heinz Boberach (Boppard: Boldt, 1975), 78.
40. See Annegret Kiefer, *Das Problem einer "jüdischen Rasse." Eine Diskussion zwischen Wissenschaft und Ideologie, 1870–1930* (Frankfurt am Main: Peter Lang, 1991); for the inner-Jewish discourse on this issue, see John M. Efron, *Defenders of the Race: Jewish Doctors and Race Science in fin-de-siecle Europe* (New Haven: Yale University Press, 1994).

41. Otto Reche, "Der Wert des Abstammungsnachweises für die richterliche Praxis. Eine amtliche Stellungnahme des rassenpolitischen Amtes der NSDAP," *Deutsches Recht* 9 (1939): 1606–1612 (quotation on 1610).
42. "Meldungen aus dem Reich," 10 August (Nr. 307), 25 September 1942 (Nr. 321), BArch: R 58/174, 175; printed in Heinz Boberach, ed., *Meldungen aus dem Reich 1938–1945. Die geheimen Lageberichte des Sicherheitsdienstes der SS* (Herrsching: Pawlak, 1984), 4058–4060, 4252–4254. The *Meldungen* are the secret "situation reports" of the Security Service (*Sicherheitsdienst*) of the SS, published in seventeen volumes in 1984.
43. CdSuSD 4 b (I)a 4647/43 to RJM, 3 May 1944, BArch R 3001/489, 110.
44. In the Berlin sample presented here, the only case is LAB A Rep. 358–02 Nr. 55543.
45. LAB A Rep. 358–02 Nr. 59650, 21, 268. Here and subsequently in the text, I anonymized the names of applicants and family members.
46. For two cases in my Berlin sample in which "Aryans" were reclassified as *Mischlinge ersten Grades*, see LAB A Rep. 358–02 Nr. 55000, 55125.
47. LAB A Rep. 358–02 Nr. 55753.
48. LAB A Rep. 358–02 Nr. 55695.
49. Meyer, *Jüdische Mischlinge*, 137–143.
50. LAB A-Rep. 358–02 no number (90a Hs 506/40). For a similar case see LAB A-Rep. 358–02 Nr. 55922 (90a Hs 171/42).
51. LAB A-Rep. 358–02 Nr. 55004.
52. Karl Unger to Generalstaatsanwaltschaft Berlin, 19 February 1942; expert opinion by Poliklinik für Erb- und Rassenpflege e.V. (Dr. Dubitscher), 30 July 1942; note prosecutor's office 25 August 1942; Unger to Generalstaatsanwaltschaft, 10 November 1942, LAB A Rep. 358–02, Nr. 61995, 1, 9–14, 17.
53. "Charakterologisches Gutachten Deutsches Institut für psychologische Forschung und Psychotherapie (Leiter Prof. Dr. med. et jur. M.H. Göring)," 1 March 1943, ibid., 25–44. Matthias Göring was a cousin of Reichsmarschall Hermann Göring and since 1940, president of the German Allgemeinen Ärztlichen Gesellschaft für Psychotherapie. See Brigitte Spillmann, "Die Wirklichkeit des Schattens. Kritische Überlegungen zu C.G. Jungs Haltung während des Nationalsozialismus und zur Analytischen Psychologie," *Analytische Psychologie* 29 (1998): 272–295.
54. Expert statement Dr. Dubitscher to Generalstaatsanwaltschaft, 29 March 1943, LAB A Rep. 358–02, Nr. 61995, 23–24.
55. Decisions Horn, 1 April and 25 June 1943, with copies to Unger, Deutsches Institut; Reichsinstitut (Göring) to Unger, 23 February 1944, with expert opinion by Prof. Dr. Pfahler, Universität Tübingen, 11 December 1943, ibid., 45, 48, 51–52.
56. Expert advice ("Obergutachten") KWI für Anthropologie, menschliche Erblehre und Eugenik, 17 July 1944, ibid., no page number.
57. Decision Horn, 11 September 1944; verdict Landgericht Berlin, 3 November 1944, ibid., 58–59, 63.
58. Statement of Dr. Hinrichs in Case 3 ("Jurists' case") at the subsequent US trials at Nuremberg (Essner, *Verwaltung*, 203); statement by Bernhard Lösener's colleague in the Reich Ministry of the Interior, Culmsee, in Bernhard Lösener, "Als Rassereferent im Reichsministerium des Innern," *Vierteljahrshefte für Zeitgeschichte* 9 (1961): 309.
59. See Przyrembel, *Rassenmythos*, 109–110, 162; Meyer, *Jüdische Mischlinge*, 110–114; Schnabel, *Schatten*, 4–5, 74–77, 87–88.

Chapter Three

JEWISH SELF-HELP IN NAZI GERMANY, 1933–1939
The Dilemmas of Cooperation

Avraham Barkai

THE ACCENT ON COOPERATION is almost self-evident for a symposium at the Carolyn and Leonard Miller Center for Holocaust Studies of the University of Vermont. The Center was established to honor Raul Hilberg, one of the earliest and most outstanding scholars of the Holocaust. In his opus magnum of 1961, as well as in its revised and enlarged later editions, Hilberg describes the role of Jewish leadership, including that occurring in prewar Germany, in quite critical terms. He carefully traces the central body of Jewish leadership in Germany and its changing structure and functions between 1933 and 1939, as it changed from a freely established and generally respected Jewish representation, the Reichsvertretung der deutschen Juden (Reich Representation of German Jews), to become the mandatory association of all persons who were regarded as Jews by the definitions of the Nuremberg Race Laws, the Reichsvereinigung der Juden in Deutschland (Reich Association of Jews in Germany), which was created and controlled by the Gestapo.[1] Hilberg concludes:

> The Germans had not created the Reichsvereinigung, and they had not appointed its leaders. Rabbi Leo Baeck, Dr. Otto Hirsch, Direktor Heinrich Stahl, and all the others *were* the Jewish leaders. Because these men were not puppets, they retained their status and identity in the Jewish community throughout their participation in the process of destruction, and because they did not lessen their diligence, they contributed the same ability that they had once

marshaled for Jewish well-being to assist their German supervisors in operations that had become lethal. The Reichsvereinigung . . . was the prototype of an institution—the Jewish Council—that was to appear in Poland and other occupied countries, and that was to be employed in activities resulting in disaster.[2]

In fact, most of the men and women of the Reichsvereinigung were convinced, in my opinion rightly so, that they still worked for the subsistence of the Jews who remained in Germany before the start of the deportations, at a level of life that was little more than wretched, and that they tried to lessen the misery of the deportees afterwards.

It was Hannah Arendt, however, and not Raul Hilberg himself, who derived from his work "the whole truth that, if the Jewish people had really been unorganized and leaderless, there would have been chaos and plenty of misery, but the total number of victims would hardly have been between four and a half and six million people."[3] Of course, nobody can be blamed for the way in which his or her work is used by others. Still, Hilberg's unsympathetic attitude, to say the least—toward the Jewish Councils, starting not only with the Reichsvereinigung, but also with its predecessor, the Reichsvertretung and Rabbi Leo Baeck, who stood at the head of both organizations, is undeniable. I do not know if Hilberg ever softened his judgment. He may have been convinced to do so by a host of later publications based on internal Jewish sources. However, our evaluation of the various Jewish leaderships under Nazi rule has today generally become far subtler than, in comparison, the harsh judgment that was implied in the term "Judenrat," which was invented by the Nazis. We have learned to refine the distinction between cooperation and collaboration postulated by Isaiah Trunk in his classic book on the subject published in 1972.[4]

Since I began working in the field of Holocaust Studies, I have sought primarily to understand the Jews and their communities during the period of their persecution and destruction, rather than focus on the perpetrators. Relying as much as possible on the saved original sources of Jewish provenance, I have tried to explore Jewish life during those horrible times, rather than focus on the fate of Jews as victims, to find out how they coped for as long as they possibly could with the changing conditions and stages of persecution as individuals and as an organized community.[5] What I learned from this "paper trail" and from postwar testimonies has led me to conclude that as long as Jews were allowed to live, cooperation with the ruling powers was unavoidable everywhere, and continued up until the bitter end. In Germany, it naturally lasted the longest and, at least until 1937–1938, Jews had more freedom of decision and room for maneuver than was possible later during the war and in the occupied countries. Therefore, the changing patterns of organized cooperation are probably easier to distinguish in the actions of the Jews in Germany than in other countries.

The Framework of Jewish Self-Help

Despite its quite advanced state of assimilation, German Jewry was, in some respects, well equipped to react as an organized community to the events that occurred after 1933. Unlike in Western European countries or the United States, membership in, and paying taxes for, the local Jewish community in Germany had been mandatory for every Jewish resident. Since the nineteenth century, this requirement had been based on specific "Jew-laws," only slightly adjusted in the Weimar period. The German Reich, founded in 1871, remained a federation of eighteen *Länder* (states) after World War I. These laws were somewhat different from one state to the other, but in all of them, individual membership in the community could be cancelled only by a personal declaration in court. Even where community taxes were quite substantial, a surprisingly low percentage of assimilated or non-religious Jews took this legal step of separation both before and after World War I. As a result, most Jewish communities, especially those in mid-sized and large towns and cities, could rely on quite considerable means to finance their activities. Taxes and voluntary contributions enabled the Jewish communities to establish a remarkable network of welfare institutions for their needy members. In larger cities, this was the task of dedicated officials versed in advanced methods of social work. In 1917, all communal welfare departments were united in the Central Welfare Organization of German Jews (Zentralwohlfahrtsstelle der deutschen Juden), officially recognized by the authorities of the Reich and the individual states as a member of their welfare networks.[6] This cooperation continued for some time even after the Nazis' rise to power. We will return later in this chapter to some aspects of this cooperation, which appear problematic only in hindsight.

In this regard, therefore, German Jews were not unprepared when the Nazis came to power. The deterioration of the economic, social, and political situation of the Jews in Germany had in fact started earlier. The post-World War I inflation had hit middle-class trade especially hard in the "traditionally Jewish" branches of clothing and other long-term consumer goods, and erased the savings of their owners. During the economic crisis that started in 1929, Jewish employees were hit harder than their gentile colleagues by unemployment. Accordingly, Jewish welfare organizations were forced to expand their activities. Initially, their main task had been to meet the needs of immigrants from Eastern Europe; but as the economic crisis affected more and more German Jews, they were compelled to join their often despised co-religionists from Galicia and Russian-Poland as applicants to Jewish welfare institutions.

On the political level, aggressive anti-Semitism in the years of the Weimar Republic had alerted German Jews to the dangers they faced. Individual Jews as well as their organizations financially supported the Democratic and Social Democratic parties in the center and on the left of the political spectrum, and a growing number of Jews were active in their ranks. Most outstanding on the political front was the Centralverein deutscher Staatsbürger jüdischen Glaubens (Central Association of German Citizens of the Jewish Faith, or CV). Founded in 1893 to fight anti-Semitism, it became the largest and most important Jewish political organization in the Weimar Republic. Besides over twenty regional and 500 local chapters, hundreds of so-called "trust-persons" kept in contact with the CV in places with small numbers of Jewish residents. Over 70,000 tax-paying members received weekly, and at least some of them even read, the organization's newspaper, the *CV-Zeitung*. In comparison, the membership of its main ideological opponent, the Zionistische Vereinigung für Deutschland (Zionist Federation for Germany, or ZVfD) never exceeded 10,000 to 15,000 members before 1933. Under the impact of the Shoah and the establishment of the state of Israel, the Centralverein has appeared in many memoirs and historical studies as the tragic victim of an alleged assimilationist utopia. In my book on the Centralverein,[7] I have tried to prove that, in fact, it did not propagate assimilation, at least not in the extreme sense of shedding Judaism in order to be fully absorbed into German society. True, the term *Assimilation* often appeared in the discourse and publications of the CV, but what the organization meant by it was the symbiosis of Deutschtum and Judentum, the assimilation of German culture while keeping a Jewish religious or cultural identity intact. This is what today we call acculturation, a term that did not exist at the time, at least not in German.

There were, of course, some German Jews who did aim at total assimilation. They either converted or had their children baptized, or tried to become what Isaac Deutscher has termed the freethinking "non-Jewish Jew."[8] But neither the totally assimilated nor the "non-Jewish Jew" belonged to the CV. To do the CV justice, we have to admit that Eugen Fuchs, the outstanding thinker among its "founding fathers," was justified when he stated at the end of his life: "Our defense efforts led us to the knowledge of our tradition, and only in this way did we gain our most important weapon: our pride in our Jewishness, our Jewish self-confidence. [It is to the] merit of the Centralverein that German Jewry has regained its self-confidence, its self-respect and self-criticism, and that conversion returned to be considered as a breach of honor and as desertion."[9] Still, the political situation after World War I caused the CV to devote most of its activities and its financial means to fighting anti-Semitic propaganda and the rise of the Nazi party. One single effort to unite with other Jewish organizations in an ad hoc committee for the elections of September 1930 was aborted mainly because of the reluctant support and half-hearted participation of the Zionists.[10] The Nazis' sensational success in winning 107 seats in the Reichstag enabled the NSDAP (Nazi Party) to become the second largest party in parliament. But even this did not lead to a further attempt to close Jewish ranks, and the CV continued the fight virtually alone. We know today that these efforts were in vain. In historical hindsight, they had no chance to be effective. However, none of the statutory or voluntary Jewish organizations of the time exposed itself to the same extent as the CV in the struggle against the Nazis.

The Reichsvertretung 1933–1938

The local Jewish communities had no adequate or effective instruments to fight the Nazis. Since they were officially recognized as juridical institutions, their rules and governing bodies were confirmed and controlled by the local or regional authorities. In most of the *Länder*, most importantly in Prussia where approximately two-thirds of the Jewish population of Germany lived, a similar legal standing was denied the regional or national associations (Landesverbände) of the Jewish communities. Attempts to create a nationwide, officially recognized Jewish representative body like, for example, the Board of Deputies of British Jews, had failed in Imperial Germany as well as in the Weimar Republic. Only under the pressure of Nazi rule did the first and only such body representing German Jews come to life. It was the

Reichsvertretung der deutschen Juden (Reich Representation of German Jews), founded with almost general agreement among German Jews in September 1933.

We cannot deal here with the details of the internal Jewish debates that accompanied the establishment of the Reichsvertretung. Some earlier works have criticized the Reichsvertretung because of its cooperation with the Nazi government and bureaucracy. Some have even labeled it the "first Judenrat." In fact, it was an authentic Jewish representative organization, established by democratically elected representatives, and it functioned through democratic decisions within the larger context of a dictatorship based on the *Führerprinzip* (leader principle). Until 1938, the Reichsvertretung tried to cope with the economic, political, and personal persecution of the Jews in Germany, and it did so with impressive, though diminishing, success. The compulsory Reichsvereinigung, formally established by order of the Gestapo in July 1939 to replace the Reichsvertretung, was an entirely different body. While the Reichsvertretung was a voluntary umbrella organization that represented the major Jewish organizations in Germany, the Reichsvereinigung represented all Jews in Germany and membership was compulsory. It is true that, in the eyes of some contemporaries and some later historians, this replacement appeared more as a change of name than a change of function. Work went on under the same leadership, headed by Rabbi Leo Baeck, in the same offices and with the same staff that had run the Reichsvertretung. However, the different terms of the Reichsvereinigung's authority and functions indeed are clear and are expertly outlined in the contribution of Beate Meyer to this volume.

The Reichsvertretung was founded in a kind of peaceful coup d'état, by which the main Jewish political organizations took over the leadership role from the traditional heads of the Jewish communities. Some of those organizations, mainly in large towns and especially in Berlin, joined only under considerable public pressure and never completely abandoned their initial opposition. Officially, however, only two small minority groups, the separatist Orthodox organization and the rightwing German-nationalist Jews, the Verband nationaldeutscher Juden (Association of National German Jews), led by Max Naumann, refused to acknowledge the authority of the Reichsvertretung. Never recognized *de jure* by the Nazi authorities, it stood de facto at the head of almost all organized Jewish activities, except in strictly religious affairs. Its success in supervising and coordinating the institutions of Jewish self-help in welfare, education, and emigration depended solely on the general cooperation of the traditional establishment of German Jewry.

This is all the more impressive as the Reichsvertretung had no financial resources of its own. It was totally dependent on contributions from the Jewish communities throughout Germany, and increasingly dependent on the support of Jewish funds from abroad. Its annual budget never exceeded about 5 million Reichsmark, while the combined outlays of the Jewish communities gradually declined from 40 to 25 million Reichsmark per year. Jewish self-help was organized and coordinated by the Reichsvertretung, but it was essentially financed by the German Jews themselves, and it was run by the officials and unpaid volunteers of their communities and organizations who continued their former work under its guidelines. The communities kept up their religious institutions and cemeteries, educational institutions and activities, and their expanding welfare and health systems. The Zionists fostered and regulated Jewish emigration to Palestine as well as almost all of the occupational and educational training of the emigrants. They also negotiated (outside but not behind the back of the Reichsvertretung) the transfer of some Jewish capital, namely, the still controversial Haavara Transfer Agreement, to which we will return later. The Centralverein concentrated its efforts on providing legal advice and support to those Jews who wanted, or were compelled, to continue their lives in Germany, and to a large extent the CV also helped to finance them. In a silently agreed division of labor, each partner performed the work that most accorded to its ideological identity and goals. Previous differences did not disappear overnight; however, the Reichsvertretung did succeed in uniting these different parties and views under one roof, and in committing the communities to mobilize their still considerable financial resources for all of its activities, despite their ideological differences.

Welfare and Economic Self-Help

Let me turn first to the efforts of Jewish organizations to deal with the impact of Nazi rule on the material existence of the Jews in Germany. The welfare departments of the communities and the Zentralwohlfahrtsstelle (Central Welfare Office) cooperated in April 1933 with other Jewish institutions in the establishment of the Zentralausschuss für Hilfe und Aufbau (Central Office for Help and Construction), which was to become the nucleus of the future Reichsvertretung. The Zentralausschuss was officially integrated into the Reichsvertretung in 1935. Even after 1933, however, the Zentralwohlfahrtsstelle remained recognized by the central and municipal welfare departments as representing and coordinating all Jewish welfare and charity. As long as Jews in need were entitled to public welfare, the subsidies from Jewish welfare agencies were an additional support mechanism. It did not take the Nazis long to discover this "advantage" and to find ways to eliminate it. Jewish welfare offices were consistently harassed to disclose the names of their applicants and the amounts of their payments, which were then deducted from their public welfare payments. What had previously been a reasonably friendly cooperation to care for the needy turned into a daily struggle over legal rights. Moreover, in this process, the Jewish welfare offices were forced to provide Nazi authorities with updated information about the changing addresses and situations of the people entrusted to their care. They were, of course, like the Nazis themselves, unaware of the purposes for which this information would be used in the future stages of exclusion and deportation. But even if they had had some foreboding, they were right to believe that their cooperation was in the interest of the people in their care. After 1938, of course, they lost all freedom of decision in these matters.

This is only one example of the necessary, and often unavoidable, cooperation of Jewish organizations with the Nazi regime. Not every one of these examples posed a dilemma. The Reichsausschuss der jüdischen Jugendverbände (Reich Committee of Jewish Youth Associations) was recognized by the Nazi Reichsjugendführung (Reich Youth Leadership), and every leader of a Jewish youth group was equipped with a Swastika-stamped identification card. Thanks to this recognition, Jewish youth could continue to have reunions and, for some years, even use youth hostels and other facilities that were later denied them. On another level, officials of the legal and economic advisory offices of the Centralverein intervened to safeguard the legal rights of dismissed workers or civil servants in labor courts or in official silent negotiations. Often, they just continued to remain connected to their former contacts of well-meaning or at least law-abiding bureaucrats with whom they had dealt before and who now received them in a matter-of-fact way as negotiation partners, whether they came as officials of the Centralverein or of the Reichsvertretung.

The Dilemmas of the Zionists

Contact with the Nazi regime was also necessary for the officials of the Zionistische Vereinigung für Deutschland (Zionist Federation for Germany, or ZVfD) and for the Palästina-Amt (Palestine Office of the Jewish Agency for Palestine) in Berlin, especially in matters of vocational training (*hachschara*) and emigration to Palestine. The German Zionists were (and sometimes still are) criticized for cooperating with the Nazi government. The preferential treatment of the Zionists by many Nazi agencies, including the Gestapo, is an undeniable fact. It is evident from the many contemporary documents and later personal accounts referred to and quoted by our colleague Francis Nicosia in his pilot study of 1985 and in his later writings. To mention only two examples: a circular letter of the German Foreign Ministry from February 1934 stated that "Zionism comes closest to the goals of German Jewish policy. Official German authorities are cooperating fully with Jewish organizations, especially in the promotion of emigration to Palestine." And a prominent Zionist leader confirmed in 1957: "The Gestapo did everything in those days to promote emigration, particularly to Palestine. We often received their help when we required anything from other authorities."[11] In the nineteenth century and the first half of the twentieth century, there were numerous anti-Semites who supported Zionism. Only after the foundation of the Jewish state in 1948 have Jew-hatred and anti-Zionism become indistinguishably intertwined.

It is true that there are some similarities in the symbols and terminology of both German and Jewish nationalism, if one views them as purely philosophical constructions. But those similarities were not the reason for the preference granted by the Nazis to Zionist organizations and their work. Their motives were more practical in that the Nazis wanted to expel the Jews from Germany, and the Zionists wanted them to go to Palestine. Many contemporary sources, often quoted from both Jewish and official Nazi documents,[12] prove that it was a temporary common interest arising from completely opposite motives. It is also evident that the Zionists in Germany and in Palestine did not hesitate to take advantage of this preferential treatment. The question is whether they were, at the time or merely in retrospect, right to do so. I have chosen two examples to deal with this dilemma, namely, the vocational (mainly agricultural) training centers for young emigrants, and the capital transfer agreement, both known by their Hebrew names of *hachschara* (training) and *haavara* (transfer), respectively.

Since the early nineteenth century, the "abnormal" vocational structure of the Jews in Germany, mainly their concentration in the financial and commercial sectors and the professions, had troubled Jewish and non-Jewish "emancipationist" reformers who meant well; it also fueled the vicious anti-Semitism of the day. The former founded associations for the promotion of agriculture and the crafts among Jews, while the latter accused them of being a tribe of bloodsucking usurers who should best be eliminated, one way or the other. For the Zionists, the return to the soil and to manual labor was regarded as a precondition to a "normal" Jewish society in the "old-new" Jewish homeland. Vocational training or retraining in agriculture and the manual trades was a central aim in the program of the Zionist movement and its youth organizations and movements everywhere, and not just in Germany. Tens of thousands of young men and women awaited their turn for *aliyah* to Palestine in the *hachschara* farms of Eastern Europe.[13] In Germany, too, a few such farms existed before the Nazis attained power; after 1933, more occupational training and retraining programs and camps were established for the rapidly growing numbers of German Jews, mainly young people, who sought immigration certificates for Palestine.

In Nazi Germany, agriculture was ideologically romanticized. Farmers were cherished as the preservers of German *Blut und Boden* (blood and soil), and were tightly organized and economically protected. Their leaders were ardent Nazis who abhorred any contact of Jews with German soil, and even more so with the "honored maidens" of German blood. Therefore, the Ministry of Agriculture opposed the *hachschara* programs, even on separate collective farms and especially in the households of individual German farmers. However, the Zionist functionaries succeeded in overcoming this opposition with the help of other Nazi authorities, particularly within the SS. Francis Nicosia has rightly called the SS "the national executioner of Jewish policy between 1933 and 1945."[14] Although the Judenreferat (Jewish desk) of the SS-Sicherheitsdienst (SS-Security Service, or SD) was founded only in 1935 and became the launching pad for the ominous careers of Adolf Eichmann and his henchmen, the Gestapo had already intervened in 1933, and was in favor of what it termed the *jüdisches Umschulungswerk* (work of Jewish retraining), assuming control over its activities. Paradoxically, this included not only the 'good behavior' of the young people in the *hachschara* programs and their isolation from other Germans, but in some cases meant the expansion of Hebrew language courses as well.

Thanks to this "protection," the *hachschara* farms continued to exist even after November 1938, some of them even until 1943.

In a recently published and very informative article on the *hachschara* and the disagreements among German governmental and party agencies about Jewish occupational retraining, Nicosia demonstrates the manner in which the Gestapo and the SS gained the upper hand in the debates.[15] There is nothing I would add to this, but I wish to deal briefly first with the internal Jewish aspects, and second with the experience of the young people who lived and worked on the *hachschara* farms. I personally shared in this experience in 1936–1937. It is true that the Gestapo's "sponsorship" and ultimate control over the programs required detailed reports about all persons who lived and worked in those programs. In 1939, however, the *hachschara* farms were forced to give up most of their own production and to serve essentially as living quarters for their members, young Jews who performed forced labor in the surrounding farms and factories. If one insists on fitting the *hachschara* farms into a particular scheme, one may certainly classify them as part of what Hilberg has defined as the stage of "concentration." However, even according to Hilberg's matrix, the next step from there led not only to extermination but, at least until the end of 1941, to the alternative of emigration. The leaders of the Hechaluz (Hebrew for the Pioneer, the association of all Zionist youth movements) and of the Reichsvertretung, who struggled for the continuity and expansion of the *hachschara* farms in cooperation with the police and the Gestapo, could not, of course, foresee what was to come. Still, I wonder if they would have given up their struggle and closed down the *hachscharoth*, even if they knew or had some foreboding for the future.

It is unlikely that the Hechaluz would have done this because they would have foreseen at the same time that the *hachschara* programs helped many thousands of young Jews to escape with their lives. In the meantime, the programs also enabled the trainees to spend their remaining time in Germany, before emigration or deportation, in an oasis of creative work, learning, and the comradeship of young Jews. Reading Nicosia's article, I was glad to note that he no longer used the terms *Lager* or *Umschulungslager* (camps, or retraining camps), terms that appeared in his 1985 book, except when quoting Nazi documents. He also omitted describing the programs as "rigorous retraining programs."[16] Having spent over a year at the *hachschara* in Steckelsdorf, I do not remember anything "rigorous" about the experience and regard it as the happiest time of my life in Nazi Germany. There were no relations with the Germans around us, except for the periodic control visits of the rural policeman.

I left Steckelsdorf and Germany early in 1938, and did not suffer the fate of many of my comrades who remained there during and, for some of them, even after the pogrom of 9–10 November 1938. But we have a vivid description of the life there in the autobiography of a survivor who lived in Steckelsdorf from December 1939 until April 1942. Published in 1967, his book became an acclaimed German movie. This is what he wrote about Steckelsdorf in its last years, before his comrades shared the fate of the remnants of German Jewry: "In the midst of Germany, crowded with uniforms and weapons, there was a peaceful enclave in which neither policemen nor SA-storm troopers were to be seen. And there we were allowed to live." Furthermore, as all Jews had to turn in their radios at the beginning of the war:

> We were saved from listening to Goebbels' propaganda that was transmitted day after day over all stations . . . We rarely paid attention to what the papers had to report during the first winter of the war. But we were alert to every piece of news from the Palästina-Amt [the Palestine Office of the Jewish Agency for Palestine]. Little did we care about our ignorance, as our existence in Germany was in any case regarded as temporary. Internally we felt we belonged to the Holy Land, which we did not know, but which we painted with all the beautiful colors of our yearning.[17]

Toward the end, it was, of course, a very sad enclave of hungry, hardworking young people, always worrying about their parents and relatives. But compared with Jewish life elsewhere in Germany, it nevertheless was still an oasis.

Finally, it is necessary to consider the Haavara Transfer Agreement, perhaps the most prominent case in which the Zionists were, at the time and later, openly accused of collaboration with the Nazis. Some have said that the Haavara Agreement served the interests of German Jews and the Jewish *yishuv* (community) in Palestine at the expense of any chance of bringing down the Nazi regime early on through a worldwide economic boycott. The agreement's rationale was the assumption that the new Nazi government in Germany, with over 6 million unemployed and almost no reserves of foreign currency, could be brought down by blocking German exports. The Haavara Agreement evidently undercut this boycott since it was based on the continued export of German goods and equipment to Palestine and neighboring countries in the

Middle East. Undermining this boycott was indeed one of the central arguments of the German supporters of the Haavara. They claimed that German exports to Palestine would expand German foreign trade to additional countries, and promote German economic growth and employment. Therefore, the Foreign and Economic Ministries and the SS closely followed the Jewish debates outside of Germany with regard to the boycott. They even sent observers to the Zionist world congresses of 1933 in Prague and 1935 in Lucerne where the Haavara agreement was discussed and debated. Aware of this dilemma, the World Zionist Organization and its Jewish Agency avoided openly admitting its leading role, and the Haavara Transfer Agreement operated until 1935 under the cover of private firms (Hanotiah Ltd. and the Anglo-Palestine Bank). Only in 1935 was the Haavara Transfer Agreement officially confirmed at the World Zionist Congress in Lucerne as being controlled by the World Zionist Organization and the Jewish Agency for Palestine.[18]

In the space allowed for this essay, it is not possible to go into the details of the agreement and its results; nor is there any need to do so here. The subject has been dealt with extensively and in great detail elsewhere. However, I will make a few remarks based on the present state of research on the topic. First, I believe that both the boycott movement and the alarmed reaction of the Germans in response to it were based on presumptions that turned out to be incorrect. The surprisingly fast recovery of the German economy was not caused by the growth of its foreign trade, but rather by the expansion of aggregate demand on the home-market. It resulted mainly from increased "deficit spending" by the public sector, which as early as 1934 was based mainly on rearmament.[19] Between 1933 and 1939, Germany's exports never exceeded 10 percent of GNP. True, thanks to the Haavara agreement, which served all sectors of the Palestinian economy, including the Arabs and the approximately 2,500 German-Christian settlers, Germany ranked first among the countries exporting to Palestine. But all of these transactions accounted for no more than a mere half percent of all German exports. These facts demonstrate that the boycott of German goods never had any chance of bringing down the new regime in Berlin, and that the Haavara Agreement played absolutely no role in, and therefore was not responsible for, its survival.

In hindsight, it may be that Jewish expectations and German apprehensions were real at that time; but it did not take long before German economists and politicians became aware of the weakness of the anti-German economic boycott movement. If they had become aware of this weakness and the needlessness of the agreement for political capital, why did the Nazis allow the Haavara Agreement to continue even after their economy had reached the peak of full employment by the end of 1935? There is, indeed, ample evidence of growing opposition to the Haavara Agreement within the Nazi government. In November 1935, and again in November 1936 and October 1937, interministerial conferences discussed the continuation of the Haavara Agreement. Spokesmen for the Reichsbank, the Auslandsorganisation (Overseas Organization) of the Nazi party, German settlers in Palestine, and the Foreign Ministry argued that the Haavara system endangered German political interests in the Middle East by alienating the Arab nationalist movement in Palestine and in neighboring countries. At this time, even the most ardent supporters of the Haavara, for instance, officials in the Ministry of Economics who had signed the agreement in 1933, were convinced that the Jews could be pressured to emigrate without their property or with only a negligible part of it. Nevertheless, the Haavara transfer system continued to function until the outbreak of the war, and its volume increased from year to year until 1939, when the agreement was terminated. After a total of 27.3 million Reichsmarks was transferred in the years 1933 and 1934, 78.5 million were transferred from 1935 to 1939, almost half of which (31.5 million Reichsmarks) were transferred in the peak year of 1937 alone.[20] The ever-declining part of their capital that was paid out in Palestine and not in Germany—in the last stage, scarcely one-third of the amount was paid to the Haavara offices in Berlin—did not deter other Jewish refugees from leaving, even though emigrants to other countries could transfer only a miniscule part of their frozen accounts of so-called *Sperrmarks*.

In the years following the war, Jewish officials who had been involved in the Haavara transfer system came to the conclusion that it was solely based on Hitler's personal decision to prevent the termination of Haavara transfers after 1935, to the displeasure of some of the involved government and party agencies.[21] The political and economic arguments of those agencies opposed to the Haavara transfer system were well founded and reflected real German interests. However, Hitler decided against them in the interest of promoting Jewish emigration. Still, it remains an enigma as to why similar incentives were not granted to emigrants to other countries. Many informed guesses and speculations have tried to explain this, but have not come up with a convincing answer. What is certain is the significance of the subject in the broader context of the road to the *Shoah*. Protagonists of the so-called "intentionalist" and "functionalist" schools of interpretation are faced with two undisputed facts: the first is that up until the war and even later, until 1941, the expulsion of the Jews from Germany by emigration was the centerpiece of Nazi *Judenpolitik*; secondly, there was the relatively marginal question of whether to expel the hated Jews penniless or to let them take with them some small part of their possessions, preferably to Palestine. This was a question that had to be decided by Hitler himself.

For Germany's Jews, cooperation with the Nazis in the case of the Haavara Transfer Agreement did not pose a dilemma. In retrospect, I believe that it was also fully justified. Close to 40 percent of the 53,000 German Jews who were able to escape to Palestine between 1933 and 1941 arrived as "capitalists" thanks to the Haavara Agreement. It is true that the 140 million Reichsmarks they were able to rescue through Haavara represented only a very small part of the assets owned by German Jews in 1933. But for the people who brought those assets to Palestine, as well as for the economy of the Jewish *yishuv*, they were of great importance.

Conclusion and Postscript

Many questions still remain with regard to the dilemmas of cooperation. In a very few, very specific instances, it indeed turned into condemnable collaboration. Those scholars who dare to tread this path should beware of the pitfalls of historical hindsight. They should also try to mobilize all of the human empathy they can before they pass judgment on the unfortunate women and men who were burdened with the responsibility of making decisions under extremely inhuman and desperate conditions.

I am now in my eighty-eighth year. After having spent four decades researching the topics discussed at the Miller Symposium, the readers will (I hope) not regard it as improper if I conclude my essay on a personal note from my 1989 book, *From Boycott to Annihilation: The Economic Struggle of German Jews, 1933–1943*:[22]

> As long as Jews were still living in Germany, Jewish representatives considered it their duty to provide services for them. Since 1939, that had encompassed almost all spheres of life . . . all the way to providing for the basic necessities of everyday life . . . Even if, in

connection with deportations, they were forced to act as accomplices for the Gestapo, most of these leading officials were motivated by the best of intentions. They sincerely believed, rightly or wrongly, that they could ameliorate the sufferings of Jews and prevent worse things from happening. In this they may have been mistaken, but who today has the right to stand in judgment and condemn them for that error? Even after the beginning of the deportations in October 1941, there were still 150,000 Jews living in the *Altreich*. These individuals had to be provided for and given the most basic essentials for daily survival.

This paragraph was written long before 1985, the year I submitted the text of the German translation to the publishers. Both editions were given the cold shoulder by most scholars in the field, and rightly so given a number of technical errors that included some wrong dates and generally poor editing. For these, I have only myself to blame. But more importantly, there was also an almost general rejection of what was erroneously believed to be my main thesis. At the height of the heated debates between so-called "functionalists" and "intentionalists," the book was dismissed as an argument for an alleged deterministic linear development from the Nazis' party program of 1920 to the gas chambers of Auschwitz-Birkenau. But nowhere in this book or in my later publications is such an argument to be found. In fact, I was never an "intentionalist" or a "functionalist." To prove this, I need to quote myself again. The distinction was introduced by Tim Mason at a conference in London in June 1979, and appeared in print in Gerhard Hirschfeld and Lothar Kettenacker, *The "Führer-State": Myth and Reality*. In my review of this volume, I wrote:

> [after one has read Mason, Hans Mommsen and Klaus Hildebrand] who respectively represent the 'functionalist' versus the 'intentionalist' interpretation, it remains unclear, whether the multitude of competing authorities . . . or the dictatorship of the *Führer* was the decisive factor. One is rather forced to face the fundamental question about the methodological relevance of this highly theoretical debate. After all presented arguments, one remains in the dark why both elements could not have been involved, side by side and complementing each other, in the process [of 'cumulative radicalization' (Hans Mommsen)] . . . It is, on the contrary, my opinion, that the combination of ideologically fixed targets . . . and pragmatic-tactical improvisation was characteristic for the Nazi regime.[23]

Despite some technical shortcomings, my book has opened new vistas of research, and some of its theses that at the time were still partly hypothetical have been confirmed by many local and regional studies. I am aware that the impression of my claiming the gradual unfolding of a pre-conceived "master-plan" for the *Shoah* may easily have arisen in the minds of readers, and even (not so unusual) of reviewers, who are content with reading the introduction of a book, some random pages, and its conclusions. Today, being twenty-five years older and familiar with the current stage of historical knowledge, I certainly would have formulated many of my statements differently. Still, I see no reason to change my general approach and most of my theses, including my evaluation of the intentions and functions of most leading persons of the Jewish leadership as outlined above.

Notes

1. X. Verordnung zum Reichsbürgergesetz vom 4.7.1939 (Tenth Regulation to the Reich Citizenship Law, 4 July 1939), *Reichsgesetzblatt* I, 1097ff.
2. Raul Hilberg, *The Destruction of the European Jews* (Student Edition) (New York: Holmes and Meier, 1985), 62ff. The text is translated unchanged in the German edition, *Die Vernichtung der europäischen Juden* (Frankfurt am Main: Fischer Taschenbuch Verlag, 1990), 196ff. Here, "Jewish Council" is rightly translated as *Judenrat*.
3. Hannah Arendt, *Eichmann in Jerusalem. A Report on the Banality of Evil* (New York: Viking Press, 1963), 111.
4. Isaiah Trunk, *Judenrat: The Jewish Councils in Eastern Europe under Nazi Occupation* (New York: Macmillan, 1972).
5. See Avraham Barkai, *From Boycott to Annihilation: The Economic Struggle of German Jews, 1933–1943* (Hanover: University Press of New England, 1989), and Avraham Barkai and Paul Mendes-Flohr, *German-Jewish History in Modern Times*, Vol. IV, *Renewal and Destruction*, ed. Michael A. Meyer (New York: Columbia University Press, 1998).
6. See Shalom Adler-Rudel, *Ostjuden in Deutschland, 1880–1940. Zugleich eine Geschichte der Organisationen, die sie betreuten* (Tübingen: Mohr/Siebeck, 1959), and *Jüdische Selbsthilfe unter dem Naziregime 1933–1939* (Tübingen: Mohr/Siebeck, 1974). Of the more than half a million Jews in Germany at the end of World War I, some twenty percent were generally un-assimilated and were less affluent Jews from Eastern Europe.
7. Avraham Barkai, *"Wehr Dich!" Der Centralverein deutscher Staatsbürger jüdischen Glaubens 1893–1938* (Munich: C.H. Beck, 2002).
8. Isaac Deutscher, *The Non-Jewish Jew and Other Essays*, ed. Tamara Deutscher (London: Oxford University Press, 1968).

9. Eugen Fuchs, "Aus der Jugend des Centralvereins," in *CV-Zeitung*, 4 May 1922.
10. See Avraham Barkai, "Zionist and Non-Zionist Reactions to the Rise of the Nazi Party in Germany's September 1930 Elections," *Moreshet. Journal for the Study of the Holocaust and Antisemitism* 6 (Spring 2009): 119–136.
11. Francis R. Nicosia, *The Third Reich and the Palestine Question* (London: I.B. Tauris, 1985), 52ff.
12. See Michael Wildt, ed., *Die Judenpolitik des SD 1935 bis 1938* (Munich: Oldenbourg Verlag, 1995), 139ff.
13. Leaning on the centuries-old tradition of pilgrimage to Jerusalem, immigration to Israel is termed *aliyah* (Hebrew for "ascent" or "improvement") in Zionist terminology. *Hachschara* is the Hebrew term used for the "occupational retraining" that many young Jews in Europe underwent before their *aliyah* to what was then the British Mandate of Palestine.
14. Nicosia, *Third Reich*, 54.
15. See Francis R. Nicosia, "Jewish Farmers in Hitler's Germany: Zionist Occupational Retraining and Nazi 'Jewish Policy,'" *Holocaust and Genocide Studies* 19 (2005): 365–389.
16. Nicosia, *Third Reich*, 58.
17. Joel König (Ezra Ben-Gershom), *David: Aufzeichnungen eines Überlebenden* (Frankfurt am Main: Fischer Taschenbuch Verlag, 1980), 115ff.
18. The most comprehensive study of internal Jewish discussions about the Haavara Agreement and its influence on the anti-German boycott is Yoav Gelber's MA thesis, "Zionist Policy and the Haavara Agreement," published only in Hebrew in Nos. XVII and XVIII (January/November 1974) of *Yalkut Moreshet*, Tel Aviv. For a condensed version, see his "Reactions of the Zionist Movement and the Yishuv to the Nazis' Rise to Power," *Yad Vashem Studies* 18 (1987): 41–69. See also Nicosia, *Third Reich*, ch. 3, and Edwin Black, *The Transfer Agreement: The Dramatic Story of the Pact between the Third Reich and Jewish Palestine* (New York: Brookline Books, 1999). Black's volume is a new edition of the book that was originally published by Macmillan in 1984 with the different and entirely misleading subtitle "The Untold Story of the Secret Pact Between the Third Reich and Jewish Palestine." The reader can find much interesting and detailed information in both editions, although Black incorrectly believes that the boycott could have toppled the Third Reich at its very start.
19. See Avraham Barkai, *Nazi Economics: Ideology, Theory, and Policy* (New Haven: Yale University Press, 1990).
20. Werner Feilchenfeld, Dolf Michaelis, and Ludwig Pinner, *Haavara-Transfer nach Palästina und Einwanderung deutscher Juden 1933–1939* (Tübingen: Mohr/Siebeck, 1972), 75.
21. See Avraham Barkai, "German Interests in the Haavara-Transfer Agreement," *Leo Baeck Institute Yearbook* XXXV (1990): 245–266.
22. Barkai, *From Boycott*, 183–184.
23. Review in *Tel Aviver Jahrbuch für Deutsche Geschichte* XIV (1985): 376ff.

Chapter Four

GERMAN ZIONISM AND JEWISH LIFE IN NAZI BERLIN

Francis R. Nicosia

Introduction

THERE IS GENERAL AGREEMENT ABOUT the decisive role that the Jews of Berlin played in the economic and cultural life of the city during the age of Jewish emancipation. Indeed, without them it seems unlikely that Berlin would have become a major world city in such a short period of time. As Peter Gay has observed in his memoir, "Berlin's Jews . . . helped to shape its [Berlin's] culture, far out of proportion to their numbers, as scientists, historians, poets, musicians, editors, critics, lawyers, physicians, art dealers, munificent collectors, and donors to museums."[1] And, in his recently published autobiography, the late Rabbi Joachim Prinz comments on the pivotal role of Berlin's Jews, during the century or so prior to 1933, in the development of music, theater, art and architecture, literature, and the media in the Reich capital and throughout Germany.[2] As a consequence, much of Jewish institutional and cultural life in Germany was centered in and dominated by Berlin, a reality that would become even more apparent under the harsh totalitarian rule of the Nazis after 1933. The demographics of German Jewry from German unification and the establishment of the *Kaiserreich* in 1871 to the Holocaust provide an essential analytical framework for any study of modern German-Jewish history that must at least begin with Berlin.

Jews in Germany flocked to Berlin in the nineteenth century, as Ruth Gay has written, because its size, rapidly expanding importance, and its proximity to the Prussian court offered them opportunities unavailable in other German cities.[3] From a mere 6,000 in 1837, the Jewish population of Berlin increased six fold to 36,000 by 1871; by 1925, there were almost 170,000 Jews living in Berlin, constituting about one-third of the Jewish population in Germany, and about 4 percent of the total population of the city.[4] By 1933, the Jewish population of Berlin had declined to 160,564. The city's largely assimilated Jewish community was by far the largest in Germany, followed by Frankfurt, Breslau, Hamburg, Cologne, and Leipzig, in that order. The majority of Berlin's Jews were middle class and politically liberal, with some 80 percent living in Tiergarten, Mitte, Charlottenburg, Wilmersdorf, Schöneberg, and Prenzlauer Berg.[5] Moreover, since the late nineteenth century, Berlin's geographical location and economic importance made it a major gateway for millions of Eastern European Jews on their way west, with thousands staying on in the Reich capital. Of the approximately 560,000 Jews in Germany in 1925, about 100,000, or almost 20 percent, were foreign Jews, mostly from Eastern Europe.[6] Almost one-quarter of the Jews in Berlin, some 45,000, made up not quite half of all of the *Ostjuden* in Germany.[7] They were more inclined to retain their Jewish cultural and religious identity and traditions, which prompted a natural growth in Hebrew and Yiddish periodicals, publishing houses, and literature in general during the pre-Nazi years. This, along with the growing intensity and public acceptance of anti-Semitism throughout Germany, contributed to a renewed interest and renaissance in Jewish culture in Germany.[8] They strengthened somewhat the conservative and religiously orthodox minority within German Jewry, and certainly accounted for some of the membership growth in the Zionist movement in Berlin and other cities following World War I.[9]

At the turn of the twentieth century, relatively few Jews in Germany embraced Zionism. This was particularly so in Berlin, where fears of anti-Semitism seemed to be off-set for many by the Jewish community's many successes and considerable prominence in the life of the city, as well as by a parallel trust in a German legal system that most believed would protect the Jews. They vehemently rejected Zionist arguments that Jewish emancipation could never be a solution to the Jewish question; that the assimilation of Jews as Jews into German life was futile; that the Jews were Jewish by nationality, and not German; and, that they must leave Germany and rebuild their national, cultural, and spiritual life in Palestine.

Most saw Zionism as an apparent confirmation of the anti-Semitism around them, and thus part of the problem.[10] But Zionism did become a viable alternative and minority movement among German Jews during the Weimar years, particularly in Berlin. Despite fluctuations, membership in Zionist organizations increased significantly, due in large measure to the slow but steady development of the Jewish National Home in Palestine, the effectiveness of a multitude of Zionist institutions inside and outside of Palestine, among them the Jewish Agency for Palestine and the World Zionist Organization, the influx of more *Ostjuden* into Germany during the 1920s, and the growing public tolerance of anti-Semitism and acceptance of National Socialism in Germany after 1930.

Despite its relative unpopularity among Berlin Jews, and German Jews in general, Zionism was able to establish itself in Germany before 1914. The headquarters of the World Zionist Organization opened in Berlin in 1911, and the leadership of the Zionistische Vereinigung für Deutschland (Zionist Federation for Germany, or ZVfD), established in 1897, required all of its members at a minimum to embrace the principle of eventual emigration to and settlement in a future Jewish state in Palestine. Still, the great majority of German Jews, particularly in Berlin, subscribed to the arguments of the much larger, liberal Berlin-based Centralverein deutscher Staatsbürger jüdischen Glaubens (Central Association of German Citizens of the Jewish Faith, or CV), established in 1893. The CV pursued the ideal of a symbiosis between *Deutschtum* and *Judentum*, and a vigorous program of *Abwehr* (self-defense) of German Jews against anti-Semitism. The CV proclaimed in 1913: "We cannot, however, claim unity with the Zionist, who denies his German national feeling, who considers himself to be a guest among a foreign host people, and whose national sentiment is exclusively Jewish."[11]

During the Weimar and Nazi years, institutional Jewish life became even more centralized in Berlin. Kantstrasse 158 housed the headquarters of such important Jewish organizations as the Preussische Landesverband jüdischer Gemeinden (Prussian State Association of Jewish Communities), the Reichsvertretung der deutschen Juden (Reich Representation of German Jews), the Zentralausschuss der deutschen Juden für Hilfe und Aufbau (Central Committee of German Jews for Assistance and Construction), the Kinder und Jugendalijah (Children and Youth Aliyah), the Zentralwohlfahrtsstelle der deutschen Juden (Central Welfare Agency of German Jews), the

Jüdische Frauenbund (Jewish League of Women), and others. The Zionist movement, led by the ZVfD, established its headquarters in the Charlottenburg district of Berlin at Meineckestrasse 10. The offices of the ZVfD, the Palestine Office (Palästinaamt) of the Jewish Agency for Palestine, the Jüdische Sportvereine (Jewish Sports Associations), the international Zionist youth movement Hechaluz, the Zionist newspaper *Jüdische Rundschau*, and other Zionist agencies were located in the same building at Meinecke Strasse 10. The Misrachi, the Zionist organization adhering to orthodox Judaism, was also headquartered in Berlin, with its own youth movement Brith Chaluzim Datiim (Bachad) and its own monthly journal, *Zion*. There were some forty Jewish publishing houses and major bookstores in Berlin, most notably the Jüdischer Verlag, established by German Zionists in 1909 under the literary direction of Martin Buber. Among the fifty or so Jewish newspapers and magazines published in Berlin in 1930 were such influential Zionist or Zionist-oriented newspapers and magazines as the *Jüdische Rundschau*, *Hed Bethar*, *Der Junge Jude*, *Der Makkabi*, *Der Jüdische Student*, *Unser Werk*, the *Berliner Jüdische Zeitung*, and *Zion*.

One of the most influential political organizations in Berlin was the Jüdische Volkspartei (Jewish Peoples Party, or JVP), founded in 1920 in Berlin to represent Zionist interests at communal bodies in the city. Its goal was to win over Berlin's Jews to Zionism, and its strong Zionist activism often proved effective in political battles within the Berlin Jewish community and, by example, in Jewish communities in other cities in Germany before 1933. The party drew much of its support from the relatively large community of Eastern European Jews in Berlin as it promoted community programs that were intended to help the *Ostjuden*. The leadership of the ZVfD, situated as it was in Berlin, played an active role in the JVP, which provided the Zionist movement with a platform from which to promote the Zionist idea and Zionist programs in the Reich capital and beyond.[12]

Hitler's anti-Jewish measures during the 1930s were especially harsh on the Berlin Jewish community because of its comparative size and location in the German capital, and its relatively large number of Eastern European Jewish immigrants. Berlin Jews were also subject to the administration of the city's Gauleiter, Joseph Goebbels, who never tired of making their lives perilous, particularly through intimidation and violence, in an effort to get them to leave.[13] Moreover, after 1933, Jews from the countryside and smaller cities moved in significant numbers to

Figure 4.1.: The *Hauswegweiser* (Office Directory) at the headquarters of the Zionistische Vereinigung für Deutschland and the Jewish Agency for Palestine at Meineckestrasse 10, Berlin. *Courtesy*: Central Zionist Archives, Jerusalem.

the larger urban centers, especially to Berlin.[14] As they felt increasingly exposed and vulnerable in the smaller cities, towns, and rural areas of Germany, tens of thousands sought refuge in large cities such as Berlin with their larger Jewish communities and established Jewish institutions and support networks. The 1 April 1933 anti-Jewish boycott seemed focused on Berlin in part because of the large number of major Jewish retail businesses, while the laws in 1933 regarding the legal and medical professions, the media and culture, and the schools were especially hard on Berlin Jews due to the relatively high percentage of Jewish lawyers, physicians, writers, artists of all sorts, and university students in the city.[15] The Nazi assault on Jews in the media and the arts had some of its most devastating consequences for the Jews of Berlin. The Reich capital was the location of such media giants as the *Berliner Tageblatt,* published by the Mosse Verlag, and the *Vossische Zeitung* and the *Berliner Illustrierte,* published by Ullstein Verlag. The exodus of Jewish writers and artists from Berlin, even before 1933, was huge. Jewish-owned independent theaters, operated by the newly formed Kulturbund der deutschen Juden (Cultural League of German Jews) opened in Berlin and elsewhere in June 1933. Jews in the German film industry in Babelsberg, just outside of Berlin, were also forced to leave their jobs and many emigrated.[16]

The National Socialist *Machtübernahme* (assumption of power) in January 1933 confronted German Zionist leaders in Berlin with both obvious dangers as well as opportunities for growth in Germany. After almost four decades of modest success among German Jews, the advent of National Socialism in Germany seemed to confirm the Zionist message and to lend an air of prophecy to its theoretical and political arguments. In other words, the radically new circumstances created conditions that seemed likely to ensure the ultimate success of Zionist efforts to win over more German Jews to Zionism and emigration to Palestine. Berlin's central role in Jewish affairs and its increasing influence over Jewish communities throughout Germany, coupled with Nazi efforts after 1933 to further centralize authority in Jewish institutional life in the capital, meant that the critical efforts of the Zionist leadership would naturally originate in Berlin. But the anticipation among Zionists that their efforts in Germany would finally achieve success would soon be frustrated, as the realities of Nazi anti-Semitism and Jewish policy after 1933 created conditions that made effective Zionist work problematic and Zionist hopes and goals in the end unachievable.

Zionist Hopes

Germany's defeat in World War I, coupled with London's replacement of Berlin as headquarters of the World Zionist Organization and Britain's sponsorship of the Balfour Declaration and the Jewish National Home in Palestine, diminished German Zionism's prewar influence in the international Zionist movement. On the other hand, the influence of the ZVfD within the larger German-Jewish community, particularly among young Jews, increased considerably during the Weimar years. The establishment of the Jewish National Home in Palestine bolstered the Jewish national idea which, coupled with the sharp rise in both the virulence and public tolerance of anti-Semitism in Germany during the Weimar period, produced an overall increase in the ZVfD's membership, in the number of Zionist youth, sports, and other organizations,[17] and in the circulation of Zionist publications, especially the newspaper *Jüdische Rundschau*. This was particularly evident among Jewish youths in Berlin and in other large cities; as their hopes for a secure future in their native Germany seemed threatened in the new postwar environment, they were increasingly inclined to reject the liberal and "assimilationist"[18] inclinations of their parents. The growing appeal of Zionism among the young also heightened the traditional rivalries within the Jewish community between the Zionist movement and the major non-Zionist Jewish organizations. Their differences became sharper as the deteriorating political environment for Jews seemed to confirm the Zionist prognosis and to raise more doubts about the arguments of the Centralverein.[19] Still, of the approximately 40,000 Jews who emigrated from Germany between 1920 and the end of 1932, only some 3,000 went to Palestine. Moreover, the membership level of the ZVfD, despite respectable growth, never reached even half of that of the CV during the Weimar years.[20]

On 12 August 1932, the Zionist newspaper *Jüdische Rundschau* printed an editorial entitled "Challenges and Tasks in the event of a National Socialist Victory."[21] It predicted the final collapse of the idea of assimilation among Jews in Germany and called on all Jews "to adapt themselves to a new reality." In a letter to Chaim Weizmann of the World Zionist Organization dated 15 June 1932, Kurt Blumenfeld, president of the ZVfD, wrote: "The German Jews are slipping into a new situation without taking completely into account the fundamental changes." He further asserted that the deepening economic crisis might be the primary motivation for future converts to Zionism from among the Jews of Germany.[22] And in his speech to the delegates to the twenty-fourth *Delegiertentag* (congress) of the ZVfD in Frankfurt am Main on 11 September 1932, Blumenfeld outlined the grim prospects for Jews in Germany, as well as the essential nature and the undeniable correctness of the Zionist alternative for all German Jews.[23]

In these and other references to the ever-deepening political and economic crisis in Germany and its likely impact on the Jewish community just before January 1933, German Zionists generally did not join with non-Zionist Jewish organizations such as the CV in political activity that might work against a Nazi political victory. This is not surprising in view of the traditional Zionist emphasis on emigration and Palestine, and ambivalence toward *Abwehr* (self-defense) against anti-Semitism.[24] Instead, Zionists focused their efforts on the correctness of the traditional Zionist message, the failure of most German Jews to heed that message in the past, and the singular importance of that message in the coming upheaval. The *Jüdische Rundschau* also followed this editorial approach during the early weeks of the Nazi regime.[25] However, it is also clear that the Zionist leadership in Berlin saw the events of 1932–1933 as an opportunity for Zionism to finally assume a dominant role in German-Jewish life. As Kurt Blumenfeld, president of the ZVfD, remarked in a letter to all Zionist local branches (*Ortsgruppen*) in Germany on 20 April 1933: "Nevertheless there exists for us today a unique opportunity to win over German Jews to the Zionist idea. In these days we have the obligation to actively enlighten and recruit."[26] And this prescribed transformation in Jewish life in Germany would have to play itself out first and foremost within Jewish communal and institutional life in Berlin after January 1933.

By the end of March 1936, there were 23,355 active members of the ZVfD, which consisted of 205 *Ortsgruppen* (local branches) throughout Germany.[27] With almost 6,300 members as of 1936, the Berlin Zionist organization was by far the largest branch in the ZVfD, containing one-quarter of all members of the ZVfD, and was almost six times as large as the *Ortsgruppe* in Leipzig, the second largest branch in Germany. There were also about one thousand members of the revisionist Staatszionistische Organisation (State Zionist Organization) throughout Germany, with the majority of its members in Berlin.[28] Of course, by the spring of 1934, all Jewish organizations in Germany were under the strict supervision of police authorities. This required an even more centralized Jewish authority in Berlin for all Jewish organizations, a reality that was intensified in September 1933 with the official opening of the Reichsvertretung der deutschen Juden in Berlin.

In a 26 June 1934 directive to state police agencies throughout Germany, Reinhard Heydrich ordered all Jewish organizations to register all events with the local police authorities, regardless of the nature of those events.[29] Throughout the Reich, meetings and events of all kinds, whether political, youth, women, sports, educational, or otherwise were usually attended by police observers who filed detailed reports with Berlin on the nature of the events, the number of people in attendance, the purposes and program, and whether the events proceeded without incident. The police authorities strictly prohibited all activities that in any way encouraged Jews to ride out the storm and remain in Germany, stipulating that any organization that did not follow this directive was to be dissolved immediately.[30] Since most events were attended by police observers, these directives had a debilitating impact on the non-Zionist organizations such as the CV, the Reichsbund jüdischer Frontsoldaten (Reich League of Jewish War Veterans, or RjF), and the Verband nationaldeutscher Juden (Association of National German Jews, or VnJ), greatly reducing the number of, and attendance at, their various events. Zionist and Zionist-affiliated groups, on the other hand, were constantly visited and encouraged to continue by police observers, who reported large crowds and a consistent emphasis on Jewish emigration from Germany and settlement in Palestine.

In short, between 1933 and 1935, the Zionist movement rapidly became the only political option for Jews in Germany as its growth soon outstripped that of the non-Zionist organizations and it came to dominate the political discourse among the German-Jewish leadership in Berlin.[31] In November 1935, the Verband nationaldeutscher Juden (VnJ) was dissolved, and the CV was forced to change its name to the Centralverein der Juden in Deutschland (Central Association of Jews in Germany) and to eliminate any and all "assimilationist" tendencies. The Jewish war veterans' organization was slowly eliminated over the next three years. With the CV and the RjF rendered increasingly irrelevant, the two Zionist organizations were the only Jewish organizations of a political nature that continued to function and grow, albeit under increasingly difficult conditions.

The dramatic increase in the public activities of the various organizations affiliated with the Zionist movement in Germany is indicative of its increasingly dominant role in Jewish life in Germany during the 1930s. Zionist youth and sports movements such as the Jüdische Turn- und Sportverein Bar Kochba, the Hechaluz, Habonim noar Chaluzi, Hashomer Hazair, and the Jüdische Pfadfinderbund Makkabi Hazair, as well as women's organizations such as the Verband jüdischer Frauen für Palästina-Arbeit (Association of Jewish Women for Palestine Work), held many public events at which speakers, films, and panel discussions about Zionism and settlement work in Palestine were featured.[32] All of these organizations were headquartered in Berlin, mostly at Meineckestrasse 10. At events that were almost daily occurrences in Berlin and other major cities in Germany, topics under discussion included the futility of emancipation and assimilation as solutions to the Jewish Question, the correctness of Zionism, and the issues and problems involved in settlement work in Palestine, such as Jewish land purchases, relations with the Arabs and the British Mandate authorities and the integration of German Jews into the *yishuv* (Palestine Jewish community).[33] Hebrew courses were increasingly in demand as more and more youths considered emigrating from Germany to Palestine. Prominent Berlin Zionists such as Rabbi Joachim Prinz, Kurt Blumenfeld, Georg Landauer, Siegfried Moses, and others spoke often in Berlin and traveled constantly to other German cities to be featured speakers. Some, like Blumenfeld, Landauer, and others, were permitted to return to Germany from time to time after their emigration to Palestine in 1933 to speak at Zionist events. All events were registered with the authorities, and police observers were always in attendance.[34] According to police reports, attendance, especially in Berlin, was almost always very high, ranging from one hundred to one thousand or more, and the police reports always expressed satisfaction with the course of the events, particularly with the programs' emphasis on doing everything to promote emigration to Palestine.

Figure 4.2.: An all-day seminar sponsored by the Zionistische Vereinigung für Deutschland, Berlin, 1935. *Courtesy*: Central Zionist Archives, Jerusalem.

Zionist institutions rapidly grew in size as well as in influence. Zionist meetings that before 1933 rarely drew more than 100 people soon filled the meeting room at Meineckestrasse 10 beyond its capacity of 800. By 1936, Zionists occupied half of the seats on the committees of the Berlin Jewish community, and shared power equally with the CV in the Reichsvertretung in Berlin as it focused most of its efforts on preparing German Jews for emigration, especially to Palestine. Moreover, in Berlin in December 1938, the Palestine Office of the Jewish Agency for Palestine was incorporated into the Reichsvertretung (and its successor in 1939, the Reichsvereinigung der Juden in Deutschland [Reich Association of Jews in Germany]) after the two German Zionist organizations, along with all other autonomous Jewish organizations, were dissolved. By October 1935, the 38,000 circulation of the twice-weekly *Jüdische Rundschau* almost matched that of the older and hitherto dominant 40,000 circulation *CV-Zeitung*, the newspaper of the Centralverein. Jewish schools, with an academic emphasis on Jewish culture and history, and on the teaching of Hebrew and the geography of Palestine, naturally experienced an unprecedented boom throughout Germany, especially in Berlin, where the number of Jewish students in public high schools dropped precipitously after 1933.[35] Membership in the two Zionist sports organizations in Berlin, Makkabi and Bar Kochba, soon exceeded that of the comparable non-Zionist organizations, with 22,000 and 2,800 members, respectively, by 1938.

The rapid expansion of Zionist occupational retraining efforts throughout Germany was particularly evident in and around Berlin.[36] The occupational retraining of prospective young immigrants to Palestine was certainly one of the most important and practical tasks of the Zionist movement during the 1930s. The social, economic, and occupational background of most German Jews meant that they were ill-prepared for a new life in Palestine, with an economy in need of agricultural workers and other skilled artisans and craftsmen. Immigration restrictions and quotas imposed by potential destination countries were based in part on the kinds of skills and occupations their economies could or could not absorb. Zionists pursued occupational retraining for ideological reasons as well, with a view of agriculture and the manual trades as necessary components of the "normalization" of the Jews as a people, and the rejection of anti-Semitic assertions that Jews did not engage in wholesome and honest work. Thus, the occupational retraining of German Jews was quickly recognized by Jewish as well as Nazi authorities as critically important in their mutual efforts to facilitate Jewish emigration.

FIGURE 4.3.: Jewish Gymnasium graduates train as carpenters under the auspices of the Jewish community in Berlin. Photograph by Abraham Pisarek. *Courtesy*: Bildarchiv Preussischer Kulturbesitz, Berlin, and Art Resource, New York.

According to the ZJHA, there were already 6,069 Jews in mostly Zionist occupational retraining programs in Germany in March 1934, and that number was expected to increase dramatically in the months to follow.[37] The Zionists had provided occupational retraining in Germany before 1933, and a systematic network of occupational retraining centers (*hachschara* camps in Hebrew, *Umschulungslager* in German) run by the Hechaluz and other largely Zionist-oriented organizations, and sponsored by various Zionist organizations and relief agencies in Berlin, was operating within a year of Hitler's appointment as chancellor.[38] Indeed, membership in the Hechaluz in Germany rose from about 500 in 1933 to 14,000 in 1935.[39] Other Jewish organizations, including the Jewish communities in smaller towns and cities, the ZJHA, the Kulturbund der deutschen Juden, the Talmud-Torah School in Hamburg, the Advisory Office for Jewish Economic Assistance, Jewish Agriculture, and small individual groups, such as the orthodox Beth Chaluz of Magdeburg and the Keren Tora Wa'awoda of Hamburg, established centers throughout Germany for the occupational retraining of German Jews in preparation for emigration. Even non-Zionist organizations eventually established occupational retraining camps. The CV and the RjF opened one at Gross-Breesen near Breslau in 1936 to facilitate the emigration of young Jews to destinations other than Palestine.[40] And in 1937, the Gesellschaft für handwerkliche Arbeit (Society for Manual Labor), the German branch of the international organization ORT, opened an *Auswanderungsschule* (emigration school) in Berlin with programs designed to teach young Jews the manual trades and to prepare them for emigration to Palestine and elsewhere.[41]

Jewish occupational retraining was naturally focused on agriculture, and therefore likely to be found primarily in the rural areas of the Reich rather than in the urban environs of a city such as Berlin. Of course, all retraining programs were generally administered from Berlin, requiring as they did the approval of and strict supervision by both Jewish officials in the Reichsvertretung and Nazi police authorities. These officials also had to negotiate with the regime for the necessary permits. For example, in 1936, the Reichsvertretung concluded an agreement with the Reichsnährstand (Reich Farmers' Bureau) that formally regulated the establishment, enrollments, programs, and outcomes of agricultural retraining programs throughout the Reich.[42] Notwithstanding the fact that much of the retraining effort was in agriculture, and therefore centered in the countryside, there were significant retraining programs during the 1930s, particularly in the manual trades, that were very much in evidence in the life of Berlin Jewry. Of the fifty-four retraining centers operated by the Hechaluz throughout Germany, twelve were within the city limits of Berlin, and another five were within commuting distance from the city. Altogether, some twenty-four programs were operating in and around Berlin by December 1937, engaged in teaching young Jews such trades as metallurgy and metal processing, carpentry and furniture making, construction work, electronics, plumbing, locksmithing, gardening, horticulture, childcare, and home economics. Some agriculture students from Berlin were able to commute by train to programs on farms not far from the city.

Individual Jews also established small retraining sites on their property, such as the agricultural retraining center at Altkarbe-Obermüle in Brandenburg run by a Jewish farmer, Siegmund Levy, and the small retraining programs in Jewish homes in Berlin that taught young Jews many of the skills needed in Palestine.[43] By the summer of 1936, the practice of allowing Jewish agricultural trainees to learn their new trades in non-Jewish settings (farms and other agricultural enterprises) and with "Aryan" instructors had, with some reluctance, become acceptable to Nazi authorities. The police had come to recognize that the number of qualified Jewish teachers in agriculture, gardening, etc., was small, and that the employment of "Aryan" teachers was unavoidable.[44] Moreover, Nazi authorities permitted German Jews to enroll in occupational retraining programs outside of Germany, in Holland, France, Denmark, and Czechoslovakia. By 1938, for example, 226 German Jews were enrolled in "practical training" (*praktische Ausbildung*) programs abroad to become technicians, farmers, and craftsmen.[45] All of these programs were designed to teach young Jews the kinds of occupational skills that were in demand in Palestine and elsewhere, skills that they would not otherwise have had the opportunity to acquire in Germany. Most, but not all, of the graduates of Zionist retraining programs ended up in Palestine.[46]

Finally, Jewish sports clubs also grew rapidly in Germany during the 1930s. Of the 126 sports clubs of all kinds throughout Germany, nine were located in Berlin.[47] But the Berlin clubs maintained a membership that comprised about one-third of all German Jews enrolled in such organizations. Moreover, almost three-quarters of those in the Berlin clubs were members of Zionist sports organizations such as the Bar Kochba and Makkabi clubs.

Nazi Reality

In spite of considerable growth and progress in its efforts to change German-Jewish life in preparation for emigration after 1933, the German Zionist movement would have to face unanticipated obstacles presented by Nazi Jewish policy. For example, the National Socialist assumption of power tended to aggravate rather than neutralize some of the long-standing conflicts between the Zionists and the assimilationist Jewish organizations in Germany. The conflict was exacerbated no doubt by the ZVfD's interpretation of the new realities facing Jews in Germany after 30 January 1933 as affording it an opportunity to assume a dominant role in German-Jewish life. Traditional differences and rivalries were placed in a different and more dangerous context when the state declared all Jews to be the enemy of Germany, which necessitated that the various Jewish organizations create a single Jewish response.[48] These tensions were particularly evident in Berlin, where all of the major Jewish institutions, organizations, and media outlets were headquartered.

The tenuous and often difficult relationship between the ZVfD and the CV, which existed prior to 1933, continued for the next five years, until all autonomous Jewish organizations were dissolved in 1938. Of course, the CV resented and initially resisted the ZVfD's public drive for political pre-eminence in Jewish life in Berlin and throughout Germany. Notwithstanding the obvious dependence of the Reichsvertretung on the cooperation of the CV and the ZVfD, the mounting pressures on the non-Zionist CV to support Jewish emigration, if not the Zionist preoccupation with Palestine, did not at all reflect any inclination to accept Zionist ideology as the salvation of German Jews, let alone Zionist leadership in Jewish affairs. Even when it reluctantly accepted the inevitability of Jewish emigration by 1936, the CV criticized what it believed were the efforts of the ZVfD to direct Jewish emigration to Palestine at the expense of other suitable destinations.[49] Moreover, the fundamental aim of Nazi Jewish policy to promote the emigration of Jews from Germany naturally resulted in a much larger role and higher profile for the ZVfD in the Jewish community, particularly in the Reichsvertretung. This also entailed the steady decline of the CV, as Jewish emigration became the only permissible option.[50]

The relationship between the ZVfD and the RjF was also characterized by friction. At times, the new realities in Jewish life in Germany threw the two into open conflict, reflecting the tensions inherent in the traditional Zionist-assimilationist rivalry among Jews in Germany.[51] While some in the RjF and the CV had long accepted the idea of Zionist work in Palestine for the benefit of persecuted Jews from Eastern Europe, they always rejected Zionism as anything remotely relevant to the situation of Jews in Germany. The RjF, although neutral in internal Jewish politics before Hitler's appointment as chancellor on 30 January 1933 and generally content to defend the interests of Jewish veterans of World War I, was forced to adopt a more politically active role in Jewish affairs in Germany after 1933. While it supported Zionist efforts to create a refuge for a small number of Jews as well as for Jewish religious traditions in Palestine, the RjF initially would not countenance any rationale for nation-building abroad by any German-Jewish organization.[52] In July 1934, Captain Leo Löwenstein, Chairman of the RjF, prepared a lengthy report outlining the continuing conflict between the RjF and the ZVfD.[53] The report emphasized the RjF's rejection of a Zionist "building of a political national Jewish community" and reaffirmed its "ties of more than a thousand years to the German homeland." Although Löwenstein described the willingness of his organization to cooperate with the ZVfD and the CV in the creation of the Reichsvertretung in 1933 as a unified Jewish response to the altered conditions of Jewish life in Germany, the RjF and the ZVfD would remain in fundamental conflict over the nature and form of that response at least until 1937.

Certainly the ZVfD's most bitterly contentious relationship, one played out mainly within the institutional framework of the Zionist movement in Berlin until the dissolution of all Jewish organizations in 1938, was with the small right-wing Revisionist Zionist movement in Germany. The remnants from the internal divisions within Revisionist ranks in Germany in 1931 were forced by the Nazi assumption of power to come together in April 1934 in the new Staatszionistische Organisation (State Zionist Organization) under Georg Kareski.[54] The reconstituted organization worked independently of and usually in opposition to the ZVfD in an effort to establish its own separate relationship with the authorities, control over the Zionist movement in Germany, and, by extension, over the affairs of the Jewish community as a whole. Like all other Jewish organizations inside Germany, the State Zionists also sought to accommodate themselves, albeit in a more public manner, to the policies of the Nazi regime. The ZVfD was already sufficiently alarmed by July of 1934 over the activities of the Staatszionisten when, in a circular letter to all of its local branches, it noted that Revisionist activities "deserve the attention of all members of the ZVfD and forces us to take decisive counter-action."[55]

Beginning in 1934, the main points of the Revisionist attack against the ZVfD included many of the old contentions from its struggles with the ZVfD leadership during the 1920s. These included arguments that the ZVfD promoted Jewish assimilation in Germany, that it was a thoroughly Marxist organization, and that it opposed the creation of an independent Jewish state in Palestine. While these themes were not entirely new, they were significantly different in emphasis and intensity, and possessed far more dangerous implications for the ZVfD in an environment of Nazi hatred and persecution. In particular, public charges against any Jewish organization that it encouraged Jews to remain in Germany, or that it was Marxist, were dangerous in light of the ideological foundations of Nazism and Hitler's regime.

From the very beginning of Nazi rule, however, the Zionist movement in Germany was faced with specific problems and dilemmas rendering problematic its quest to transform German Jewry and secure its orderly and economically viable departure from Germany. While

Nazi authorities were soon satisfied that emigration in general, and Zionism in particular, were being embraced by more and more Jews in Germany,[56] the growing position of Zionism among Jews in Germany only generated complications that, in the end, impeded effective Zionist work. The ZVfD, while noting its significant membership growth and its prominent role in the functioning of the Reichsvertretung, nevertheless fretted over the difficulties caused by the combination of rapid growth and the anti-Jewish measures of the regime.[57]

One such problem was the loss of prominent Zionist leaders in Berlin who began emigrating to Palestine in greater numbers after 1933. This leadership exodus occurred at a time when competent and experienced Zionist leaders were needed even more to cope with the sudden growth of the German Zionist movement. In 1933 alone, officials such as Kurt Blumenfeld and Georg Landauer emigrated to Palestine, and Martin Rosenblüth temporarily moved to England. The ZVfD in Berlin described this problem in greater detail in a circular letter to its local branches in February 1934: "The danger of this sudden progress in many areas should not be missed. As a result of emigration, the core of German Zionism has dwindled considerably. The organization, as large as it has become, nevertheless finds itself today in an amorphous condition."[58] This problem intensified as the decade wore on and as more and more Zionist officials departed from Berlin. In December 1935, Robert Weltsch, editor of the *Jüdische Rundschau*, wrote with regret from Berlin to Kurt Blumenfeld in Jerusalem that: "The departure of leading Zionist personalities is having a negative impact. The question whether the new generation and the new Zionists are capable of doing the job is not entirely clear. I doubt they can."[59]

In May 1938, shortly after the 26 April decree making it compulsory for Jews to register their property in Germany and abroad, the ZVfD in Berlin reported unusually large numbers of Jews at the Jewish Agency's Palestine Office, housed in the ZVfD headquarters at Meineckestrasse 10 in Berlin.[60] The report mentioned the impossibility of effectively serving the growing number of people interested in emigration to Palestine, given the shortages of personnel and resources. The personnel problem was only compounded by the limits that Nazi authorities had imposed on foreign Jews entering Germany to assist in preparing Jews for emigration. This problem became particularly acute after the *Kristallnacht* pogrom of November 1938 as Benno Cohn, president of the ZVfD, reported in a letter from Berlin to Georg Landauer in Jerusalem: "Once again the problem of personnel and the leading people is very difficult. At this time, all want to leave and there is hardly anyone to take over."[61] Moreover, periodic arrests of Jewish leaders by the authorities, a common occurrence in Germany during the 1930s, often included prominent members of the ZVfD. In reporting the release from police custody of Zionist leaders Franz Meyer and Benno Cohn in Berlin in early October 1936, Martin Rosenblüth of the London Office of the Central Bureau for the Settlement of German Jews in Palestine expressed his frustration over never being quite sure of the reasons that prompted such arrests, notwithstanding Zionist cooperation in overall Nazi emigration policy.[62] Moreover, during the November pogrom, Zionist officials and others connected with the Jewish Agency's Palestine Office in Berlin were arrested along with thousands of other Jews. They were soon released by the police and were permitted to re-open the office in order to continue the work of Jewish emigration from Germany to Palestine.[63]

Contact between the ZVfD in Berlin and the Jewish Agency in London and Jerusalem became more infrequent and difficult to maintain. Of course, the ZVfD, like all Jewish organizations in Germany, was under constant police surveillance and thus exposed to considerable potential danger from any exchange of correspondence between Germany and the outside world. In October 1936, the ZVfD complained to the Executive of the Jewish Agency for Palestine in Jerusalem that German Zionism was virtually cut off from information concerning the situation in Palestine and in the larger Zionist movement worldwide, which impeded the effectiveness of Zionist work.[64] In July 1938, Franz Meyer of the ZVfD wrote to the Executive of the Jewish Agency in London: "With regret I must once again state how deficient the contact is between you and Zionists working in Germany."[65] Later that month, in another letter to the Jewish Agency in London, Meyer reiterated the concern of the ZVfD over its isolation. After expressing his understanding for the communication difficulties between Germany and the outside world, he insisted nevertheless: "I beg you to make every effort in the future, in spite of the existing impediments, not to desist from sending us all necessary materials."[66]

Finally, and perhaps most important, the spate of anti-Jewish legislation between 1933 and 1938, designed to achieve the political, social, and cultural dissimilation of the Jewish community, had severe economic repercussions for all Jews and their institutions. The negative economic consequences of the anti-Jewish legislation and the "Aryanization" of Jewish businesses during the 1930s included unemployment and loss of livelihood for tens of thousands of Jews, which meant, of course, a growing dependence on Jewish welfare agencies both inside and outside of Germany.[67] While exceptions were made for Jewish war veterans at least until the Nuremberg Race Laws of September 1935, none were made for the Zionists, despite their central role in the emigration policy of the regime. That the activities of Zionist and other Jewish organizations in Germany had always depended on the financial support of their members goes without saying; but the steady pauperization of the entire Jewish community after 1933, coupled with the dramatic growth in membership, activity, and responsibility, created enormous and unprecedented new strains on the German Zionist movement.

The erosion of the economic position of Jews in Germany was in many ways the most difficult burden with which the ZVfD and other Jewish organizations had to cope, even with the extraordinary self-help efforts of the entire Jewish community. As early as October 1933, in a letter to Martin Rosenblüth in London, Michael Traub, the Director of the Keren Hayesod (Palestine Foundation Fund) in Berlin and a member of the Reichsvertretung, observed: "Regarding the situation in Germany, it can only be said in a letter that the process of economic deprivation which is inexorably and systematically being pursued is worse than all acts of violence (which have recently subsided) . . . And since this process encompasses not only large concerns . . . but also medium-sized ones, we must face a very strong decline in Jewish wealth in the next few months."[68]

The economic disintegration of the Jewish community during the 1930s constituted a significant brake on effective Zionist work in Germany. Of course, all of the anti-Jewish measures of the Nazi state between 1933 and 1939, particularly the expulsion from the economy, were designed to encourage Jews to leave Germany, albeit under conditions that made effective Zionist work in Germany extraordinarily difficult. By the end of 1935, Salomon Adler-Rudel of the ZVfD and the Reichsvertretung reported on the negative impact of the growing economic crisis of the Jewish community on Zionist activity in Germany.[69] He observed that the rapidly growing economic deprivation of the Jewish community was contributing to the emigration of those with means and to the flood of prospective emigrants at the Jewish Agency's Palestine Office in Berlin. These realities placed enormous burdens on declining Jewish communities throughout Germany, on the Zionist movement, and, in general, on the relief efforts of various Jewish agencies in Berlin:

These factors which have been outlined briefly have resulted in an enormous increase in the emigration requirements of the Jews, and it is now not only the younger and poorer people who have decided to emigrate, but also the well-off and prosperous families see themselves as forced to leave . . . the Palestine Offices are so flooded with people willing to emigrate that they can hardly manage the numbers streaming to them . . . The economic collapse, the increase in the number of the needy, demand from the Jewish communities the greatest effort and sacrifice in order to be able to satisfy the enormous need for relief.

The rapid departure of the Zionist leadership, a problem referred to above, was in part a natural consequence of ever-worsening economic conditions for all Jews. In a letter to Georg Landauer in Jerusalem in August 1938, Benno Cohn of the ZVfD warned: "This very anarchistic emigration will have grave consequences."[70] Cohn was referring to the economic crisis of German Jewry as a natural cause of this problem and warned of the far greater difficulties that would soon result from the coming Nazi onslaught on the remaining Jewish stake in the economy: "In view of the new economic measures, we face massive unemployment in the winter, which is estimated to be 30,000 wage earners, thus affecting about 100,000 family members. Therefore we will not be able to get by with previous methods of social work."

Georg Landauer, General Secretary of the ZVfD in Berlin before his emigration to Palestine in 1933, visited Berlin in February 1939 to assess Zionist efforts and the emigration process. This letter is briefly referred to above, in the Introduction to this book. Writing from Berlin to his colleague Arthur Ruppin in Jerusalem on 17 February 1939, Landauer described the situation for Jews in Berlin as grim, and for Zionist efforts there as very difficult.[71] The disastrous economic situation had resulted in the impoverishment of the remaining Jewish community, and he related that to the organizational problems afflicting the Zionist movement, especially the Jewish Agency's Palestine Office in Berlin, in the following way:

> All competent Zionist functionaries have emigrated or will emigrate this week. The re-staffing of the offices is virtually impossible. Representing Zionist interests in the Reichsvertretung has been difficult lately . . . our friends in the Meineckestrasse believe that even their second-level people have all left as well, and that they fear they will have to turn things over to incompetent bureaucrats who themselves

would prefer to emigrate today rather than tomorrow ... Who knows what will happen.

Landauer was clearly pessimistic about the retraining and reeducation programs and about moving substantially more Jews safely out of Germany.

Conclusions

From the beginning of Hitler's regime in 1933, the ZVfD attempted to convince Nazi authorities of the need to maintain suitable conditions for Jewish life in Germany, at least until the emigration process ran its course. For instance, Martin Rosenblüth's general memorandum of 13 September 1933 to the membership of the ZVfD addressed this question in some detail.[72] He reasoned that German Zionism had little choice but to seek conditions that would best ensure orderly Jewish emigration, and that those conditions were possible only with the cooperation and support of the Nazi state. In other words, there was no alternative to working with Nazi authorities to facilitate Jewish emigration safely and effectively from Germany. He elaborated on the conditions that he hoped would prevail for the Jews in the new Germany during the emigration process. These included preservation of the civil equality of Jews and the avoidance of restrictions on their economic livelihood. He also appealed for state support for the occupational retraining of German Jews in order to ensure a livelihood while still in Germany and to prepare them for a new life in Palestine once they emigrated. Protection for autonomous Jewish religious institutions, schools, sports organizations, welfare agencies, and emigration offices was also proposed, and Rosenblüth called for the free emigration of at least half of German Jewry with its assets. Three months earlier, the ZVfD had addressed a direct appeal to Hitler to allow the continued economic and political freedom of Jews in Germany until the emigration process was completed.[73] Hitler never responded, and the regime's ideology would preclude Zionist requirements almost entirely. Instead, Nazi policy imposed onerous conditions on all Jews, making the desired reeducation and economically viable departure, mostly to Palestine, problematic.

In Berlin, perhaps more than any other city in Germany or, for that matter, the rest of Europe, the culture of emancipation and assimilation had enabled Jews to have the most profound and positive effect on the larger society in which they lived. David Clay Large observes that the Zionists were critical of Berlin's Jews for trying to hold onto something that was in reality "alien" to them, but also noting in agreement with Peter Gay that the Nazis, not the Jews, were the real aliens in Berlin. He seems to put his finger on the central dilemma under which the Zionists labored in their efforts to transform the culture of Jews in Berlin.[74] For in the end, the German Zionist movement, notwithstanding its new-found political pre-eminence during the 1930s in Jewish life in Berlin, was never able to transform that culture as a necessary or even desirable preliminary step to a new life in a Jewish state in Palestine, even under the harsh conditions of Nazi rule. One German Zionist observed in a letter to Palestine in November 1933, written while on a trip to Yugoslavia, that the brief respite in Nazi pressure on Jews in the fall of 1933, and the consequent slowdown in Zionist activity at that time, demonstrated that "the Jews cling to every hope and are always ready to adapt to the status-quo. This is nothing to be proud of, and this tendency is not one of the positive characteristics of German Jewry."[75]

The desired transformation would require time and, of necessity, an environment that preserved some of the basic elements of Jewish emancipation. This is particularly apparent because Zionist work was naturally so clearly focused on the young. Zionist strategy had always sought to re-educate mainly younger Jews before their departure for Palestine; their established and largely assimilated parents and grandparents would live out their days as Jews in Germany. This necessary re-education and training of the young would require a relatively benign environment to effectively accomplish those ends. But the Nazis rapidly dismantled the foundations of Jewish emancipation after 1933 so that the necessary environment for a long-term transformation could not materialize. Instead, Zionist efforts had to be undertaken under the most adverse of conditions. It is true that the Nazis, in their determination to remove Jews from Germany, encouraged Zionist work in Germany and the promotion of Jewish emigration. However, what appeared on the surface to be a community of interests between the Zionists and the Nazis was in fact a relationship in which the all-powerful Nazi state used the Zionist movement to implement its policy of disenfranchising and expelling the Jews from Germany. Zionists in Germany were generally not exempt from the brutality of political, economic, and social disenfranchisement meted out to all Jews. Thus, Zionist work in the Third Reich, unlike in the Weimar years, was rendered extraordinarily difficult and dangerous.

Approximately 53,000 German Jews, or about 10 percent of the 1933 Jewish population in the *Altreich*, made it to Palestine between 1933 and 1941, with an additional almost 12,000 from Austria, Bohemia, and Moravia beginning in 1938. Most were young, with about 58 percent under the age of thirty.[76] Some ended up leaving Palestine for other destinations after the war. Most of those who made it to Palestine were probably committed Zionists, and some no doubt considered emigration to Palestine as the only way out of an impossible situation with very few options.

The German Zionist movement did become a major force in the political and cultural life of Berlin Jews between 1933 and 1941. This was particularly evident among Jewish youths in Berlin, as noted by ZVfD president Benno Cohn in a February 1938 memo that described the considerable impact of Zionist *hachschara* programs on the attitudes and lives of non-Zionist youths in Berlin and elsewhere.[77] But the Zionist movement was permitted neither the time nor the conditions conducive to gradually transforming the culture of Berlin's Jewish community; in the end, it had to scramble to secure the departure of as many Jews as possible from Berlin and the rest of Germany, as quickly as possible, regardless of their commitment to Zionism and Palestine. Certainly by the outbreak of war in 1939, rescue had replaced re-education as the imperative in the efforts of the Zionist leadership in Berlin; and with that, some of Zionism's youthful idealism was forced to give way to harsh reality.

Notes

1. See Peter Gay, *My German Question: Growing Up in Nazi Berlin* (New Haven: Yale University Press, 1998), 15.
2. See Michael Meyer, ed., *Joachim Prinz, Rebellious Rabbi: An Autobiography—the German and Early American Years* (Bloomington: Indiana University Press, 2008), 87–88, 90–92.
3. Ruth Gay, *The Jews of Germany: A Historical Portrait* (New Haven: Yale University Press, 1992), 126, 145–146.
4. See Joseph Walk, *Jüdische Schule und Erziehung im Dritten Reich* (Frankfurt a.M.: Verlag Anton Hain Meisenheim, 1991), 14ff.
5. See Hermann Meier-Cronemeyer, ed., *Juden in Berlin 1671–1945: Ein Lesebuch* (Berlin: Nicolai, 1988), 183. See also Andreas Nachama, Julius Schoeps, and Hermann Simon, eds., *Jews in Berlin* (Berlin: Henschel Verlag, 2002), 141ff. In 1871, only 7 percent of German Jews lived in Berlin. By 1910, some 23 percent lived there.

6. See S. Adler-Rudel, *Jüdische Selbsthilfe unter dem Naziregime 1933–1939. Im Spiegel der Berichte der Reichsvertretung der Juden in Deutschland* (Tübingen: Mohr/Siebeck, 1974), 8.
7. Meier-Cronemeyer, *Juden in Berlin*, 191.
8. On the general subject, see Michael Brenner, *The Renaissance of Jewish Culture in Weimar Germany* (New Haven: Yale University Press, 1996).
9. See Francis R. Nicosia, "Der Zionismus in Leipzig im Dritten Reich," in *Judaica Lipsiensa: Zur Geschichte der Juden in Leipzig*, ed. Ephraim Carlebach Stiftung (Leipzig: Edition Leipzig, 1994), 167–178.
10. See most recently Francis R. Nicosia, *Zionism and Anti-Semitism in Nazi Germany* (New York: Cambridge University Press, 2008), chs. 1–3.
11. Nachama et al., *Jews in Berlin*, 128.
12. See Kurt Jacob Ball-Kaduri, *Das Leben der Juden in Deutschland im Jahre 1933* (Frankfurt am Main: Europäische Verlags-Anstalt, 1963), 33, 39, 42, 122; and Donald Niewyk, *The Jews in Weimar Germany* (New Brunswick, NJ: Transaction Publishers, 2001), 148–152.
13. See for example his diary entry for 11 June 1938 and his assertion that "the Jews must get out of Berlin. The police will help me accomplish this." Ralf Georg Reuth, ed., *Joseph Goebbels: Tagebücher, 1935–1939*, Bd. 3 (München: Piper-Verlag, 2003), 1223.
14. In spite of the pace of Jewish emigration from Germany after 1933, especially from Berlin, there were still some 140,000 Jews in Berlin in 1938. Whereas about one-third of all German Jews had lived in Berlin in 1933, in 1938, the percentage had actually risen to about 40 percent. This can be explained only by the internal migration of Jews from smaller towns and the countryside to cities such as Berlin, a phenomenon that was usually encouraged by the police authorities. See Walk, *Jüdische Schule*, 102.
15. See David Clay Large, *Berlin* (New York: Basic Books, 2000), 289ff.
16. Ibid., 272ff.
17. See for example Jacob Borut, "'Verjudung des Judentums': Was There a Zionist Subculture in Weimar Germany?" in *In Search of Jewish Community: Jewish Identities in Germany and Austria, 1918–1933*, ed. Michael Brenner and Derek J. Penslar (Bloomington: Indiana University Press, 1998), 92–114.
18. I use the term "assimilationist" to refer to those secular, non-Zionist or anti-Zionist German Jews who viewed themselves as Jewish by some confessional or cultural identity or practice, but German by nationality and culture, and who were very much integrated into the political, economic, social, and cultural life of their German homeland. It is important to remember that both the Zionists and the Nazis referred to them and their various organizations as "assimilationist." However, the great majority of these so-called assimilationist German Jews neither sought to deny their Jewish identity nor stopped believing that one could be both Jewish and German at the same time. See Ruth Gay, *The Jews of Germany*, 202; and Saul Friedländer, *The Years of Extermination: Nazi Germany and the Jews, 1939–1945* (New York: HarperCollins, 2007), 5.
19. Avraham Barkai, "*Wehr Dich!" Der Centralverein deutscher Staatsbürger jüdischen Glaubens 1893–1938* (Munich: C.H. Beck, 2002), 257. See also Avraham Barkai, "Between Deutschtum and Judentum: Ideological Controversies within the Centralverein," in Brenner and Penslar, *In Search of Jewish Community: Jewish Identities in Germany and Austria, 1918–1933*, 74–75, 84–86.

20. Moshe Zimmermann, *Die Deutschen Juden 1914–1945* (Munich: R. Oldenbourg, 1997), 32–35. See also Richard Lichtheim, *Geschichte des deutschen Zionismus* (Jerusalem: R. Maas, 1954), 234–235.
21. *Jüdische Rundschau,* 12 August 1932, reprinted in Jehuda Reinharz, ed., *Dokumente zur Geschichte des deutschen Zionismus 1882–1933* (Tübingen: Mohr/ Siebeck, 1981), No. 210: 528–530.
22. Kurt Blumenfeld, *Im Kampf um den Zionismus. Briefe aus fünf Jahrzehnten* (Stuttgart: Deutsche Verlagsanstalt, 1976), 122.
23. *Jüdische Rundschau,* 16 September 1932, as reprinted in Reinharz, ed., *Dokumente,* No. 211: 530–542.
24. For the ambiguous relationship between the ZVfD and the idea of defense against anti-Semitism in Weimar Germany, see Arnold Paucker, *Der jüdische Abwehrkampf gegen Antisemitismus und Nationalsozialismus in den letzten Jahren der Weimarer Republik* (Hamburg: Leibnitz, 1969), 391f.; and Jehuda Reinharz, "The Zionist Response to Antisemitism in Germany," *Leo Baeck Institute Yearbook* 30 (1985): 105–140.
25. See for example *Jüdische Rundschau,* 31 January and 29 March 1933.
26. Central Zionist Archives, Jerusalem (hereafter CZA): Z4–3567 VIII, Rundschreiben der Zionistischen Vereinigung für Deutschland, 20 April 1933.
27. See Bundesarchiv, Berlin (hereafter BArch): Z/B1–96, "Stärke der Zionistischen Vereinigung für Deutschland," (no date).
28. Francis R. Nicosia, "Revisionist Zionism in Germany (II). Georg Kareski and the Staatszionistische Organisation, 1933–1938," *Leo Baeck Institute Year Book* 32 (1987): 265.
29. Brandenburgisches Landeshauptarchiv (hereafter BLHA), Potsdam: Pr.Br. Rep. 2A I pol., 1167. Geheimes Staatspolizeiamt/Berlin to alle Staatspolizeistellen, II 1 B.2 24650, 26 June 1934.
30. BArch: R/58–276, Geheimes Staatspolizeiamt to alle Staatspolizeistellen, III B2–60934/J.191/35, 10 February 1935.
31. Stephen Poppel, *Zionism in Germany, 1897–1933: The Shaping of a Jewish Identity* (Philadelphia: Jewish Publication Society of America, 1977), 176–177.
32. For instance, during the 1930s, there were 4,239 members of the *Verband jüdischer Frauen für Palästina-Arbeit,* with more than 600 in Berlin alone. See: BArch: Z/B1–96, "Ortsgruppen des Verbandes jüdischer Frauen für Palästina-Arbeit," (no date).
33. Nicosia, "Der Zionismus in Leipzig," 171–173.
34. See for example BArch: Z/B1–582, Zionistische Vereinigung für Deutschland to die Geheime Staatspolizei Berlin, Betr. Landesvorstandssitzung der ZVfD, 16 July 1937.
35. Walk, *Jüdische Schule,* 74ff.
36. See Nicosia, *Zionism and Anti-Semitism,* ch. 7.
37. United States Holocaust Memorial Museum, Washington, DC (hereafter USHMM): 11.001M.01, 2–173, Abschrift aus der Jüdischen Telegraphen-Agentur (J.T.A.), Nr. 70, Jahrgang XIII, vom 24 March 1934.
38. See Avraham Barkai, *From Boycott to Annihilation: The Economic Struggle of German Jews, 1933–1943* (Hanover: University Press of New England, 1989), 85ff.
39. Otto Dov Kulka, ed., *Deutsches Judentum unter dem Nationalsozialismus: Dokumente zur Geschichte der Reichsvertretung der deutschen Juden 1933–1939* (Tübingen: Mohr/Siebeck, 1997), 483.

40. See Werner Angress, *Between Fear and Hope: Jewish Youth in the Third Reich* (New York: Columbia University Press, 1988).
41. See Leon Shapiro, *The History of ORT: A Jewish Movement for Social Change* (New York: Schocken Books, 1980).
42. USHMM: 11.001M.01, 3, "Entwurf einer Vereinbarung zwischen Reichsnährstand und Reichsvertretung der Juden in Deutschland betr. die landwirtschaftliche und gärtnerische Ausbildung von Juden zur Vorbereitung der künftigen Auswanderung," (no date).
43. USHMM: 11.001M.01, 2–137, "Jüdisches Umschulungslager Altkarbe", 23 July 1935; and 4–305, "Umschulungslehrgänge für Juden," from the magazine *Der jüdische Handwerker*, XXVII, Nr.9, 9 September 1935.
44. USHMM: 11.001M.01, 2–173, Staatspolizeistelle für den Landespolizeibezirk Berlin to die Preussische Geheime Staatspolizei, Berlin, Stapo. 8 A 1777/36, 15 May 1936.
45. USHMM: 11.001M.01, 4–305, Reichsvertretung der Juden in Deutschland to die Geheime Staatspolizei, "Berufsausbildung von Juden im Ausland, Erziehungsclearing," 7 March 1938. For details on agricultural retraining for German Jews in Holland, see USHMM: 11.001M.01, 4–237, Abschrift aus der Jüdischen Telegraphen-Agentur, XIII, Nr. 65, 19 March 1934.
46. USHMM: 11.001M.01, 7–514, Reichsvertretung der Juden in Deutschland, "Übersicht über die nach Durchführung einer Berufsausbildung ausgewanderten Personen," 17 January 1938. Although most of the trainees from the various Zionist retraining centers emigrated from Germany to Palestine, a considerable number went elsewhere. For example, the agricultural retraining site in Neuendorf sent 689 of its 1182 graduates to Palestine between July 1932 and January 1938, with 263 going to Argentina, and the remainder going to Denmark, Brazil, France, Holland, the United States, Luxemburg, Sweden, Czechoslovakia, Poland, Austria, New Zealand, Ecuador, and elsewhere. See USHMM: 11.001M.01, 4–305, "Landwirtschaftliches Lehrgut Landwerk Neuendorf," (no date).
47. BArch: Z/B1–96, entire file.
48. For a concise account of the internal politics among German-Jewish organizations during the 1930s, particularly the ongoing rivalries among the Zionists, non-Zionists, and anti-Zionists in the Reichsvertretung, see Jacob Boas, "German-Jewish Internal Politics under Hitler 1933–1938," *Leo Baeck Institute Year Book* 29 (1984): 3–25.
49. See for example *CV-Zeitung*, 13 October 1935.
50. Boas, "German-Jewish Internal," 23–25.
51. For the history of the RjF see Ulrich Dunker, *Der Reichsbund jüdischer Frontsoldaten 1919–1938. Geschichte eines jüdischen Abwehrvereins* (Düsseldorf: Droste Verlag, 1977).
52. See for example *Der Schild*, 1 June 1934.
53. CZA: AI42/47/7, "Zionisten und RjF, insbesondere ihre Mitarbeit in der Reichsvertretung der deutschen Juden," von Leo Löwenstein, 23 July 1934.
54. See Yehoyakim Cochavi, "Georg Kareski's Nomination as Head of the Kulturbund. The Gestapo's First Attempt—and Last Failure—to Impose a Jewish Leadership," *Leo Baeck Institute Year Book* XXXIV(1989): 227–246; Herbert S. Levine, "A Jewish Collaborator in Nazi Germany. The Strange Career of Georg Kareski, 1933–1937," *Central European History* 8 (1975), 251–281; and Nicosia, "Revisionist Zionism II," 231–267.

55. CZA: AI42/47/7, ZVfD Berlin (Meyer) to die Zionistischen Ortsgruppen und Vertrauensleute, 26 July 1934.
56. See for example CZA: F4/1O0, Württembergisches Innenministerium und Württembergische Politische Polizei to das Reichsministerium des Innern, Nr. 3/1376/33a, 4 September 1933.
57. See for example CZA: S7/93, Zionistische Vereinigung für Deutschland to die Zionistischen Ortsgruppen und Vertrauensleute, 24 October 1933.
58. CZA: Ll3/138, Zionistische Vereinigung für Deutschland to die Zionistischen Ortsgruppen und Vertrauensleute, 8 February 1934.
59. CZA: A222/98, Robert Weltsch, Berlin Kurt Blumenfeld, Jerusalem, 6 December 1935.
60. CZA: S7/689, Martin Rosenblüth, Berlin to Werner Senator, London, 6 May 1938.
61. CZA: S7/902, Benno Cohn, Berlin to Georg Landauer, Jerusalem, 22 November 1938.
62. CZA: S7/493, Martin Rosenblüth, London to Nahum Goldmann, Paris, 6 October 1936.
63. See Institut für Zeitgeschichte, Munich (IfZ): Beweisdokumente, Eichmannprozess, No. 742, interview with Dr. Kurt Jacob Ball-Kaduri by Hans Friedenthal, March 1957.
64. CZA: S5/2194, ZVfD to die Executive der Jewish Agency for Palestine, Jerusalem, 13 October 1936.
65. CZA: S5/432, Franz Meyer, Berlin to das Büro der Exekutive der Jewish Agency for Palestine, London, 13 July 1938.
66. CZA: S5/432, Franz Meyer, Berlin to die Jewish Agency for Palestine, London, 29 July 1938.
67. See Salomon Adler-Rudel, *Jüdische Selbsthilfe unter dem Nazi-Regime 1933–1939. 1m Spiegel der Berichte der Reichsvertretung der Juden in Deutschland* (Tübingen: Mohr/Siebeck, 1974), 177ff. See in particular the memorandum from the Reichsvertretung to Hans Heinrich Lammers, the State Secretary in the Reich Chancellory, of January 1934 in which the disastrous economic consequences of unemployment and loss of livelihood among Jews is described. The memorandum is reprinted Adler-Rudel, *Jüdische Selbsthilfe*, 188–191.
68. CZA: S7/93, Michael Traub, z. Zt. Paris to Martin Rosenblüth, London, 21 October 1933.
69. CZA: S7/357, Aufzeichnung von S. Adler-Rudel, z.Zt. in Genf über die Lage der Juden in Deutschland, 29 November 1935.
70. CZA: S 7 /689, Benno Cohn, Berlin to Georg Landauer, Jerusalem, 3 August 1938.
71. CZA: S7–902, Georg Landauer, Berlin to Arthur Ruppin, Jerusalem, 17 February 1939.
72. Politisches Archiv des Auswärtigen Amts, Berlin (hereafter PA): Ref. D., P05 NE adh 6, Nr. 4, Bd. 2, "Zusätzliche Bemerkungen zur deutschen Judenfrage," 13 September 1933.
73. PA: Inland II A/B, 83–21, Bd.1, "Äusserung der Zionistischen Vereinigung für Deutschland zur Stellung der Juden im neuen deutschen Staat," Berlin, 21 June 1933.
74. Large, *Berlin*, 289–290.

75. CZA: S7–93, Eliezer Liebenstein to Georg Landauer, 7 November 1933.
76. See BArch: R8150, 31, Reichsvereinigung der Juden in Deutschland, Organisation Auswanderung 1933 bis 1941, 8.
77. Osobyi Special Archive, Moscow (Osb): 713-1-32. ZVfD/Berlin to die Zionistischen Vereinigungen und Arbeitsgemeinschaften und to die Mitglieder des Landesvorstandes der ZVfD, 21 February 1938.

Chapter Five

WITHOUT NEIGHBORS

Daily Living in *Judenhäuser*[1]

Konrad Kwiet

NEIGHBORS IN THE POLISH VILLAGE of Jedwabne slaughtered hundreds of Jews in July 1941 before Nazi killers arrived to wipe out the Jewish community.[2] Such neighbors did not exist in Germany, not even in November 1938, when the inflamed "wrath of the people" vented itself in a bloody pogrom commonly known as *Reichskristallnacht* (Reich Crystal Night, or Night of Broken Glass). While some neighbors criticized the destruction of property or complained about "illegal" excesses, only a few had the courage or inclination to support or help the persecuted.

In 1933, the new Nazi racial state had entrusted officials with the task of carrying out its *Judenpolitik*, the anti-Jewish policy designed to remove the Jews from Germany once and for all. As early as 1919, Adolf Hitler, entering the world of politics in Munich, had prophesied that the final aim of his anti-Jewish policy would first lead to the revocation of Jewish emancipation and then to an "uncompromising removal" (*Entfernung*) of all Jews from Germany.[3] Within the vocabulary of the Nazis, *Entfernung* and *Entjudung* (de-Jewification) were identical, with several meanings, each of which later defined the stages of a gradual process of persecution. "Ordinary" Germans were invited to participate in and profit from the exclusion, expropriation, and expulsion of the unwanted Jews, especially from the "Aryanization" or robbery of Jewish property. As Frank Bajohr points out, it was an enterprise that "developed into the single greatest exchange of property in modern German history."[4]

This essay explores the termination of the cohabitation of Germans and Jews, and sheds light on Jewish daily life in segregated living quarters. The physical segregation of Germans and Jews, a crucial element in the program of the "final solution," did not require the establishment of ghettos. I will argue that as the German Jews were to be expelled as quickly as possible, there was no need to relocate them into ghettos that had been set up and guarded in districts of German cities and towns, or on their outskirts. Moreover, as they were already living without neighbors, there was no need to confine them behind walls. A *de facto* ghettoization, in fact, did take place, forcing the Jews to live, using the term coined by Avraham Barkai, in a *mauerlosen Ghetto*,[5] a ghetto without walls, until they were called up for deportation. In his classic study *Nazi Germany and the Jews,* Saul Friedländer also refers to "the New Ghetto" when shedding light on the early years of persecution.[6] The creation of *Judenhäuser* (Jews' Houses) and *Judensiedlungen* (Jews' Settlements) served as preparatory or transitional measures toward expulsion, deportation, and murder. Together with two other historical models—*Judenbann* (ostracism of Jews) and *Judenstern* (Jews' star)—once imposed upon pre-Emancipation Jewry, and the introduction of forced labor, the *Judenhäuser* radicalized the anti-Jewish policy by accelerating and achieving complete isolation and de-personalization, concentration, and control of the Jews. Some German Jews had experienced the feeling of living without neighbors at an early stage:

> That we live in the ghetto now begins to penetrate our consciousness. This ghetto clearly differs in many ways, in terms of what is still to happen and what is reality, from what we understood up till now . . . The ghetto is no longer a geographically defined district, at least not in the medieval sense. The ghetto is the "world." It has no visible sign. The sign is: being neighborless. This is the fate of the Jews: to be neighborless. Perhaps this happens only once in the world, and who knows how long it must be endured: life without neighbors.[7]

That was the message Rabbi Joachim Prinz of Berlin disseminated in April 1935, two years after the National Socialists had assumed power and terminated the German-Jewish *Lebensgemeinschaft* (co-existence). Seven months later, the rabbi raised his voice again. Responding to the Nuremberg Race Laws sanctioning the *reinliche Scheidung,* the clear parting of the ways, of Germans and Jews, he proclaimed: "The new ghetto is a life within four walls . . . It is a life without material things, without any echo, without 'life.'"[8] The spiritual caretaker and communal leader of the Berlin community sought refuge in the US, the "new world" for Jews, the "Golden Medina."

Initially, German Jews discussed at length the alternatives of home and exile, whether to stay or to leave.[9] A minority left at once: those in danger for political reasons, Zionists, and those driven out of their professions. The majority decided to stay and to adapt to the racial state. The title of Marion Kaplan's classic study, *Between Dignity and Despair*,[10] typifies Jewish life in Nazi Germany. It took a direct threat to their lives to make most German Jews realize that their ties to Germany could no longer be maintained. The November pogrom in 1938 deeply seared their consciousness and memory. Most Jews gave up the notion that they still had any right to domicile in Germany and abandoned any hope for better times, for the rapid return of democracy, and for their German-Jewish *Lebensgemeinschaft*. Panic ensued, causing mass flight.

By the autumn of 1941, almost 300,000 Jews had escaped Nazi terror, two-thirds of the Jewish population of 1933. Most of the Jews trapped in Germany still intended to leave, and desperately waited, hoping for the arrival of life-saving landing permits and visas. Thousands of applications lay unprocessed on desks in London, Washington or other cities in the "free world" that had already closed their doors to immigrants. The assumption, or the old accusation, that German Jews felt unable to bid farewell to a country that they and their ancestors had lived in for generations and where they had felt at home, falls into the realm of historical legend.

The neighbors to whom Joachim Prinz referred in 1933 played their part in the program of the "final solution," at all stages, at different levels, and with an array of motivations. The perpetrators who performed relevant functions within the Nazi machinery of destruction, as a rule with great efficiency, came from all strata of society. Next to the architects and executors of the anti-Jewish policy, representing state, party, the SS, and other institutions, stood the large cohort of *Volksgenossen* (national comrades), who gave vent to their Jew-hatred in public. Their aggression manifested itself in a series of assaults and attacks, as well as in widespread denunciations. The wave of denunciations reached a peak twice—first after the November pogrom, and then at the beginning of the deportations when Jews attempted to escape by going underground. House and block wardens, shopkeepers and passersby in general, and neighbors in particular, hastened to denounce Jews as *Volksfeinde* (enemies of the people). Once the race war was unleashed in September 1939, an army of officials embarked on their journeys *zum auswärtigen Einsatz* (for deployment abroad). Many of them carried, along with their campaign kit, not only a predisposition to racial ideology, but also first-hand experience gained in the exclusion, expropriation, and expulsion of German and Austrian Jews. Both elements encouraged and assisted them in implementing, beginning in 1941, the "final solution" in conquered territories. It occasionally happened that Nazi killers met German and Austrian Jews in ghettos, at killing pits, or in camps, and remembered that they had once lived with them in the same neighborhoods and had grown up together. When in June 1941, in the Lithuanian border village of Garsden, 201 Jews were shot by a mobile killing unit sent from nearby Memel, one victim, a Jewish refugee, recognized a marksman. Before he was shot, he addressed his former friend and neighbor: *"Gustav, schiess gut!"*[11] The man's marksmanship was poor. Other policemen had to step in and finish off the former Memel neighbor.

Individual acts of solidarity and support occurred with public gestures of compassion and regret, consternation, and indignation. The National Socialists castigated such people as *Judenfreunde*, "friends of Jews." Their number is not known. There are also no statistics to disclose the number of courageous women and men who attempted to save Jews. Risking their own lives and acting in secret, these people encountered tremendous difficulties in the face of limited resources and the hostility displayed by neighbors. By the year 2000, Yad Vashem, Israel's "Martyrs' and Heroes' Remembrance Authority," found no more than 342 Germans who, after lengthy and thorough investigation, were honored as "Righteous Among the Nations."[12] Clearly, the number of "Righteous Germans" must have been much higher. Between 10,000 and 12,000 Jews were in hidden in Germany; between 3,000 and 5,000 survived, and 1,403 resurfaced in Berlin. The Berlin-based Center for Research on Anti-Semitism conducted a large-scale research project on Jewish survival underground. Based on the findings, Wolfgang Benz estimates that twenty rescuers and accomplices (*Mitwisser*) were required to secure the "illegal" existence of one Jew.[13] If this assumption is correct, then more than 200,000 "ordinary" Germans must have been involved in the rescue of Jews.

The vast majority of Germans responded to the persecution of the Jews with indifference, large sections even responded with approval. When exclusion, expropriation, and expulsion took place in full public view, they did not trigger any spontaneous and massive protests. On the contrary, the National Socialists could rely on a broad anti-Jewish consensus in the population.[14] Combined with the support of the ruling elites, it enabled and encouraged them to gradually implement the program of the "final solution." The strongest form of public protest found its expression in a late, spectacular demonstration. In February 1943, in the Rosenstrasse in Berlin, a group of German women succeeded in securing the release of their Jewish husbands who had been rounded up as forced laborers in the course of the *Fabrik-Aktion*.[15] The successful outcome of this late protest suggests that if similar actions at an earlier stage had been carried out throughout Germany, they might have halted the increasingly destructive course of the German anti-Jewish policy.

Nazi persecution and social behavior succeeded in transforming Jews into targets for annihilation well before the regime's *Judenpolitik* reached the stage of genocide. Indeed, some 10,000 had decided to take their own lives, as suicide became for some the ultimate refuge, an act of both despair and defiance.[16] Marion Kaplan argues: "The social death of Jews and German indifference to their increasingly horrific plight were absolute prerequisites for the 'final solution.'"[17] Indeed, greatly reduced in numbers and with a preponderance of older people, separated from their families and without neighbors, stripped of all rights and pauperized, undernourished, and exhausted, conscripted into forced labor and denied freedom of movement, herded together in segregated living quarters and marked with the yellow star, the Jews trapped in Germany had become on the eve of deportation a pariah caste that society saw only as a burden and that the Nazi state could dispose of as it saw fit. Public silence reigned virtually undisturbed as 134,000 German Jews were taken from their final living quarters and loaded onto trains that would take them to the extermination sites. *Judenhäuser, Judensiedlungen,* and *Juden-Sammelstellen* (Jews' collection points) were the last stages for Jews in Germany before death.

German Jews knew of these practices only through history. When, in the eighteenth century, enlightened rulers had lifted the medieval restrictions on housing and movement, on dress and professions, Jews hastened to enter the gentile world, quickly leaving behind their *Ghettokultur* (ghetto culture) and *Ghettomentalität* (ghetto mentality). Many responded with anger or ridicule, especially in the "golden age" of their German-Jewish *Lebensgemeinschaft* during the Wilhelmine Empire and Weimar Republic, when both non-Jews and fellow Jews reminded them of their former ghetto existence. Migration movements had changed the landscape of their residential areas.[18] Many Jews had moved from rural areas to the cities, a trend which decreased the number of small Jewish communities and increased the concentration in cities and in certain urban districts. This trend intensified after 1933. In the face of open hostility, numerous rural Jews left their homes, either emigrating or moving into major centers and seeking Jewish companionship and assistance.[19] In 1933, some 525,000 Jews lived in Germany, spread over 2,000 towns of different sizes, and belonging to more than 1,600 official Jewish communities. More than half resided in ten major cities with populations over 100,000.[20] One in five still lived in a rural setting. By 1937, when the number of Jewish communities had decreased to 1,349, 85 percent of all Jews belonged to fifty-two of them.

Long before the National Socialists took power, race fanatics had demanded that Jews once again be confined to ghettos and be stigmatized with special badges. Such calls continued after 1933, when the first steps were taken to exclude Jews from social life and to dissolve personal relationships between Jews and Germans. In the face of growing hostility and in a period of acute housing shortage, Jews encountered difficulty in finding rental accommodation. Housing cooperatives pressured Jewish members to sell their row houses or apartments.[21] After the Nuremberg Race Laws in 1935, they were expelled from large municipal housing estates. In early 1938, the racial state saw no further need to support Jews with rental assistance.[22] In Berlin, a large low-rent housing company ordered the registration of all of its Jewish tenants and terminated most of their leases.[23] Economic hardship forced many Jews to leave their spacious dwellings and to search for smaller, less expensive apartments. Some families were constantly on the move, openly harassed or chased away from their current lodging. In many places, landlords were unwilling to sign leases with Jews or were eager to terminate their rental contracts. The landlords could rely on local courts, which "interpreted the tenant protection law of the Weimar Republic *against* Jewish tenants or even declared [it] invalid for them."[24] At a grassroots level, a bombardment of anti-Jewish symbols and attacks targeted the Jews, as Jürgen Matthäus has shown, for their economic, legal, and social stigmatization.[25] Towns and villages set up signposts with inscriptions "*Juden unerwünscht*" (Jews not welcome!), or placed signs on benches or at the entrance to swimming pools or other public venues, with the slogan "Only for Aryans!" Seaside resorts, following the traditional pattern of *Bäder* anti-Semitism, banned the entry of Jews.[26]

Brochures attracted visitors with the owners' claims of recreational areas already "free of Jews." In many places, Nazis staged noisy demonstrations in front of Jewish homes and shops demanding the departure of the inhabitants or owners. *"Juden raus!"* (Jews out!) was a popular slogan that called for their expulsion. *"Juda verrecke!"* (death to the Jews!) indicated the aim of the murderous campaign. Texts, photographic images, and caricatures displayed on billboards, posters, and, in *Stürmer-Kästen,* the showcases of the *Stürmer* weekly, disseminated this anti-Semitic symbolism. Jews and their *Judenfreunde* (non-Jewish friends) were pilloried to punish and degrade them, and to deter neighbors from maintaining contact with them. Together with the flood of anti-Jewish pamphlets and speeches, this anti-Semitic violence isolated, dehumanized, and demonized the Jew and created the image of a *Volksfeind* (enemy of the people), a *Rassenfeind* (enemy of the ["Aryan"] race) who, as the *Todfeind* (mortal enemy) of the German people and of the "Aryan" master race, had to be eliminated.

The *Anschluss* of Austria in March 1938 formed the prelude to the expulsion of Jews from their homes and apartments. The strategic planners of the "final solution" designed a "Viennese Model" that accelerated the exclusion, expropriation, and expulsion of the Jews.[27] "Boot the Jews out of the good cheap apartments!" This was only one of the popular slogans heralding the beginning of the exclusion of Jews from the housing market in the Greater German Reich.[28] Within a short period of time, thousands of Jews were evicted and herded together in temporary housing estates. Barrack camps, classified as *Arbeitslager* or *Selbsterhaltungslager* (workcamps or self-maintenance camps), sprang up like mushrooms, incarcerating the first Jews conscripted to forced labor.[29] In some places, Jewish families were taken from their homes and escorted to railway stations to be dumped across the Reich border. This procedure soon became standard practice. In a strategy paper, "Treatment of Jews in Berlin," compiled by the Gestapo in May 1938 and presented to Joseph Goebbels,[30] the issues of stigmatization and ghettoization were addressed. The Gestapo officials favored the idea of marking Jews as a "desirable," even "absolutely necessary," step for the implementation of "certain measures." Less optimistic were the views on ghettos. Under the heading *Zuzug,* referring to the arrival and settlement of Jews in Berlin, the introduction of police permits was suggested in order to regulate and restrict the numbers of unwanted Jews. Permission was restricted to those preparing for their emigration, since those people needed only a temporary residence permit.[31]

The establishment of ghettos was regarded at that point as "impractical." Police permits, however, could be used to prevent Jews from taking up residence in certain districts. It was hoped that, in the long term, through this exclusion and the concentration of Jews in other districts, a "kind of ghetto" would be created, a ghetto incarcerating those who were unwilling or unable to emigrate.

Besides the "experts" in Jewish matters in the SS, other Nazi leaders quickly emerged as key players in destroying the cohabitation of Germans and Jews. Albert Speer played a pivotal role in this process. Installed by Hitler as General Building Inspector, he was entrusted with the mammoth task of redeveloping Berlin as *Germania*, the future metropolis of the Great Germanic Empire that was to be *judenfrei*.[32] In September 1938, he presented his plan for a *Judensiedlung* to be built on the outskirts of Berlin. The project foresaw the construction of 2,700 *Kleinwohnungen* (small dwellings) to accommodate Jewish families. The intent of the project was to evict these families from 2,500 *Grosswohnungen* (large dwellings) located in the city center and on prime real estate. Speer hoped to gain economic advantages from the "exchange" (*Austausch*), the removal and relocation of Jews, both in the housing market, and in the acquisition of open space for his city planning. The project failed. The events of the November pogrom offered him and his staff new possibilities in the appropriation of Jewish homes. The end of November 1938 saw not only the establishment of the right of first refusal in the selling of the properties, but also the decision about which Jewish properties were to be leased and which were to be sublet.[33] Speer wasted no time using this authorization and, in a number of *Grossaktionen* (major campaigns), acted promptly to drive the Berlin Jews from their properties. All of the personal information recorded—the names and addresses of the evicted, who were now placed in *Judenhäuser*—was handed over to the Gestapo for rapid "round ups" and later for "resettlement" in the East.

The elimination of the cohabitation of Germans and Jews was on the agenda of the top-level meeting convened at Göring's headquarters in Berlin on 12 November 1938. The Nazi leaders took stock of what the pogrom had unleashed, and talked about the post-pogrom strategy.[34] There was a general consensus to speed up and complete the processes of exclusion, expropriation, and expulsion of the Jews. Three years later, at the Wannsee Conference, the decision-makers talked about the results in Germany, and then about strategies to complete the "final solution" in Europe. In November 1938, there were still opposing views expressed when the issues of ghettos and badges were raised. Reinhard Heydrich, on his way to expanding his jurisdiction over anti-Jewish policy, proposed the introduction of a *bestimmtes Abzeichen* (special badge), and emphasized the advantage of public stigmatization—the surveillance "by the vigilant eye of the population." Göring, obviously taken by surprise, exclaimed: "A uniform!" Heydrich repeated: "A badge." Göring responded by proposing his idea: "My dear Heydrich, you will not be able to avoid having ghettos in the cities on a really big scale. They will have to be established." Heydrich responded: "From a police point of view, I think, a ghetto, in the form of a completely segregated district with only Jews, is not possible. We would have no control over a ghetto where the Jew gets together with all of his tribe. It would be a permanent hideout for criminals and [a source] of epidemics."[35]

Once the decision was made in November 1938 to terminate the cohabitation of Germans and Jews, preparations commenced for the relocation and concentration of Jews. As in other areas of Nazi Jewish policy, the decision-making processes followed the patterns of what Hans Mommsen once termed "cumulative radicalization."[36] Jürgen Matthäus has introduced the term "controlled escalation"[37] as a concept to describe the transition from persecution to genocide. Indeed, "control" and "escalation" were characteristic features of the *Entjudung* of the housing market. After the November pogrom, guidelines were issued from the "center," via clear channels of command, to the "periphery," to local communities where the Jews were to be driven out from their homes, relocated, and isolated. The instructions from "above" clearly stated that the *Wegschaffung*, the removal of Jews, had to be carried out "inconspicuously," "systematically," "gradually," and should be "free of trouble," in the interest of "public security and order."[38]

The first step involved the eviction of Jews renting large apartments in "Aryan" buildings and their removal to smaller flats located, if possible, "under one roof." Secondly, Jewish-owned buildings were selected and transformed into *Judenhäuser*. They were earmarked for later "Aryanization." In other words, once the *Judenhäuser* had fulfilled their function, the final *Entjudung* of the housing market was to complete the entire process of "Aryanization." The third step involved encouraging "Aryans" residing in Jewish-owned buildings to move into "Jew-free" houses. Since these "Aryans" enjoyed tenant protection, the Nazis appealed to their *gesundes Volksempfinden* (concern about health of the people), or strongly advised them in the name of "public sentiment" to leave the *Judenhaus*. Finally, many types of Jewish-owned buildings were converted to provide alternative accommodation for the evicted Jews. They included not only private homes, apartments, and boarding houses, but also buildings belonging to the Jewish community, such as kindergartens and schools, nursing homes and hospitals, offices and halls, prayer rooms, and even funeral parlors.[39]

Hitler approved the removal strategy, designed in the aftermath of the November pogrom, and left it to Göring to convey his "wishes" and "directives" to the inner core of the party, the Gauleiters (district leaders), and to encourage them to follow the orders of the Führer. On 6 December 1938, they were told that no ghetto was to be established, no badge introduced, no general *Judenbann* imposed, and no forced labor camps—as demanded by Austrian Nazi leaders—to be set up.[40] Instead, every effort was to be made to force Jews out of Germany and to confine any remaining Jews in a ghetto without walls—until, as Göring put it, *das Stichwort gegeben wird* (the specific command or "key word" was uttered) for the "Aryanization" of the *Judenhäuser*. The guidelines were sent to the relevant Reich ministries to prepare a new *Sonderrecht* (special right) to legalize the termination of cohabitation of Germans and Jews. Göring's instructions of 28 December 1938 contained the following message:

> Wherever rental conditions permit, the Jews are to be placed together in one building. For this reason the Aryanization of Jewish-owned homes will be the last step—completing the *Gesamtarisierung* [total "Aryanization"]. Only in individual cases, provided that there are compelling reasons, can they be Aryanized at an earlier stage.[41]

In April 1939, the "Law Concerning Tenant Relations with Jews"[42] sanctioned the termination of the cohabitation of Germans and Jews. The first implementation order followed suit.[43] Any and all protection for Jewish tenants was declared null and void. Jews could be evicted only on the condition that alternative accommodation in Jewish-owned buildings was guaranteed; this requirement ensured that Jews put out on the street would not become a burden on the welfare services for the homeless. In many places, Jews were forced to meet the cost of improvements and repairs requested by the new tenant. Henceforth, Jews were permitted to sign leases only with other Jews. Jewish landlords were obliged to accept Jews as tenants or subtenants "at the request of the local authorities." It was up to the municipalities to place several Jewish families in one *Judenhaus*, "forcibly, if necessary." One basic principle was reconfirmed: the selection of *Judenhäuser* was not to lead to the establishment of ghettos. The law prescribed the registration of all living spaces, whether vacant or occupied and whether rented to Jews or to Germans. Furthermore, every eviction, letting, and change of residence required the permission of the authorities.[44] Later, these housing records—together with the *Judenkarteien* (catalogues containing Jews' registration cards)—were to facilitate the "round ups" of the Jews for deportation.

Journalists were on the alert to report the successful *Entjudung* of German homes, neighborhoods, and districts. Jurists commented on the new *Sonderrecht*. Within their vocabulary, the familiar terms of Nazi propaganda and Nazi policy dominated. A legal opinion, published in 1940, reads: "It contradicts all National Socialist sentiment about law when German *Volksgenossen* have to live with Jews together under one roof. A true *Hausgemeinschaft* (housing community), as part of the *Volksgemeinschaft* is only tenable between people of the 'same kind' and 'blood.'"[45] In the "official language," a word appeared that did not exist in the German language; as it was invented by bureaucrats, it remains untranslatable. *Entsiedelter Jude*,[46] a Jew "de-settled," forms an expression that transcends the meanings of "resettled" or "relocated," "evicted" or "displaced," or even "uprooted." The symbolic meaning connotes the final exclusion from society or the "uncompromising removal" of the Jew. The term *Entsiedelter Jude* was a file heading on a form required to process the belongings left in Jewish homes that had been "vacated."[47]

Regulations, proclamations, and registrations triggered the first wave of evictions in the early summer of 1939. The speed and form of the relocation and concentration of the Jews varied from place to place, depending on the specific conditions prevailing at the "periphery." Several municipalities had already gained first-hand experience in concentrating certain Jewish groups in separate locations, such as ill and needy clients of the Jewish welfare services. These local actions commenced in 1937 and foreshadowed, as Wolf Gruner argues,[48] the establishment of *Judenhäuser*. As in other areas of Nazi anti-Jewish policy, local authorities were given some leeway for initiative; for example, some used more radical measures and, in doing so, competed with other cities, towns, and villages in their efforts to be the first to make their residential areas *judenfrei*. The task required a considerable amount of administrative work, involving numerous Nazi institutions, agencies, and departments. Local councils, and especially housing offices, worked in close cooperation with Gestapo officials and party functionaries, as well as with landlords, real estate agents, and other Nazi representatives.

The Nazis drew Jewish organizations into their re-housing program. As in other areas involved in the persecution—emigration, welfare, forced labor, distribution of food and other goods, stigmatization, and deportation—officials of the Reichsvereinigung and Kulturgemeinden were compelled to assist in conveying the Nazi orders and in implementing the housing policy. In major cities, special Housing Advisory Boards were set up to keep the records, to draw up lists, and to organize the relocation of homeless Jews into *Judenhäuser*. Dr. Martha Moses, head of the housing department of the Jewish community in Berlin, recalls the procedures:

> The Jewish community was always informed of the apartments to be vacated and the appointed date. Through the land register, the Housing Advisory Board was able to trace both Jewish property owners and the Jewish tenants living in these buildings, where tenants forced to give up their apartments had to be re-accommodated as subtenants. This was done with all possible sensitivity. The professions of the parties concerned, their family status, the residents' state of health and the sanitary condition of the building were all taken into consideration. Given the relatively large Jewish ownership of property in Berlin, the procedures went quite smoothly . . . If the parties could not agree on a subletting fee, the Housing Advisory Board stepped in. Such differences of opinion were rare, however. The parties involved settled down to a peaceful coexistence. A different state of affairs prevailed in Vienna . . . [w]here the Jews were herded together in a very small number of apartments . . . , widespread misery, illness and infestation resulted.[49]

Everywhere, inmates of *Judenhäuser* were repeatedly warned to follow official instructions. Precise records of rents and subletting fees had to be maintained. Inspections of "vacant areas" could be undertaken only with official authorization. House keys were to be kept in an agreed location, to allow inspectors access at any time. Later, when the inmates had been deported and the doors were locked and sealed by the Gestapo, the keys were deposited at the local police station. Inspectors then appeared to compile a comprehensive report. The instructions, given by the Vermögensverwertungsstelle (Property Utilization Office) of the Finanzamt (Tax Office) in Hamburg, reveal the procedure. All items found were recorded, then compared with the property declarations the inmates had filled out and signed prior to their deportation. Bank books and securities, valuable goods such as precious metals, mints or stamps, furs and woolens, cultural objects and books in Hebrew, works of art and military medals, business papers and other relevant documents, gramophones and records were taken away, to be processed for auction or distribution. Soap and detergent were also confiscated. Rotten food had to be destroyed on the spot. Family photos and letters were also burned in ovens. The Nazi officials did not remove items that did not belong to the Jews; they merely recorded these objects, such as lamps and stoves. Before Germans were permitted to move into a vacated *Judenhaus*, officials of health and housing departments inspected the empty place to arrange the disinfection of rooms, kitchen, and bathroom, and to decide whether repairs or improvements were required. The local authorities refused to cover these costs.[50]

In September 1941, the Nazis introduced the large six-pointed yellow badge, a powerful symbol that had been part of the history of Jew-hatred since medieval times.[51] Some Jews tried to hide the star in public. A few wore the patch with pride and dignity, remembering the famous call from Robert Weltsch shortly after the anti-Jewish boycott of April 1933: "The yellow badge—wear it with pride!"[52] In September 1941, all Jews felt the stigmatizing effect of the humiliation and rejection that the star represented. Victor Klemperer, living in a *Judenhaus* in Dresden, records in his diary: "Since the Star of David, which is due to arise on Friday, 19th September, things are very bad. Everyone's attitude changing by turns, mine included: I shall go out proud and dignified—I shall shut myself in and not leave the house again."[53] After the war, he recalls in his notebook: "After the introduction of the *Judenstern* it really did not much matter anymore whether *Judenhäuser* were dispersed or formed their own quarter, every *Sternjude* (Jewish wearer of the star) carried his own ghetto with him like a snail its shell."[54]

The yellow star signaled the beginning of the mass deportations to the East. Six months later, in April 1942, another stigma similar to the *Judenstern* was introduced and it marked all *Judenhäuser*: a black star printed on white paper was to be displayed next to the entrance door or nameplates of inmates. Reinhard Heydrich was confident "that now there is not further possibility of concealment."[55] Indeed, as he had predicted after the November pogrom, the colorful symbols of identification and stigmatization attracted the attention of the public and allowed surveillance by the "vigilant eyes of the population."[56] Within their neighborhoods, Germans could see the last remaining Jews and recognize their segregated living quarters, especially young Germans who, in many places, continued to insult and abuse Jewish youngsters wearing the star.

FIGURE 5.1.: Jews from Hattingen, who were deported on 28 April 1942, lived for almost one year in an empty rifle factory that had served as a "Jewish House" (Judenhaus). To the right and above, one sees the Jewish star designating the building as a Judenhaus. *Courtesy*: Stadtarchiv Kerpen.

FIGURE 5.2.: Until their deportation in 1942, the Jews of Kerpen were forced to live in a "Jewish House" (*Judenhaus*) on Hindenburgstrasse. On 18 July 1942, the last thirty-one Jews in Kerpen were deported from here. *Courtesy*: Stadtarchiv Kerpen.

Judenhäuser also served as convenient holding and assembly centers for those *Sternträger* who were moved by the Gestapo from rural areas into larger cities as part of the preparations for deportation. Jews from North Hesse were brought to Kassel and were housed at five collection points that were classified as *Sammelunterkünfte* (collective accommodations) or *Sammellager* (collective camps).[57] A horticultural college in Ahlem confined Jews from Hannover and neighboring villages.[58] In May 1941, the Gestapo in Bonn transformed a confiscated Benedictine Monastery, Zur ewigen Anbetung (At the Place of Eternal Adoration), into a large *Judenhaus*. Three collection points were set up in nearby Cologne. In Frankfurt am Main, the Grossmarkthalle, located at the main railway station, functioned as a central place for the arrival and departure of Jews from the city and its surroundings.[59] Jews in Franconia were brought to Nuremberg, Würzburg, and Kitzingen. In Berlin, five Jewish buildings were required to process the final removals—a synagogue, a rabbinical meeting center, an orthodox community center, a home for the aged, and a hospital. Mario Offenberg has described each of these collection points as a *Zwischenstation,* "a stopover between home and rail carriage . . . an extraterritorial—though generally known—outpost of the death camps in the midst of Berlin."[60]

In view of the forthcoming mass deportations and introduction of general forced labor, several cities and communities adopted the Austrian model by setting up *Judensiedlungen*. The Ulm city council set about ridding the city of its Jews as quickly as possible.[61] A dilapidated castle in Oberstotzingen offered the solution. The council was prepared to spend 6,000 to 10,000 Reichsmarks on necessary renovations, mindful of the effects the removal of Jews had on its housing market. Officials had calculated that the cost of clearing *Judenhäuser* and renovating the castle was much lower than the construction of new dwellings. In Essen, Jews were taken to Hollbeckshof, a camp erected on the site of a former coal mine. Nine barracks awaited them, each fifty meters by fifteen meters, divided into small rooms. Fifteen inmates shared one room. In Cologne, 2,000 Jews were crammed into barracks constructed for Russian prisoners of war during World War I.[62] In November 1942, when the city of Dresden was declared *judenfrei,* the remaining 279 Jews were incarcerated in seven newly established huts at Hellerberg.[63] The camp was set up just outside the city but adjacent to the Zeiss Ikon's Göhle plant, which urgently required *Rüstungs-Juden* (armament Jews) for the manufacture of fuses for the navy. More than 300 Jews were housed in one wing of the Vincentine Convent in Berg am Laim, Munich. The Nazis referred to this detention center as a *Heimanlage* (housing estate), a model soon to be refined for the establishment of an "old people's ghetto" in Theresienstadt. They also praised their second *Judensiedlung* as a "model . . . for emulation" by other such developments.[64] It was a camp constructed by Jewish forced labor on a 14,500 square meter site in Milbertshofen, seven kilometers from the city center. By October 1941, eighteen wooden barracks designed to accommodate a maximum of 1,100 inmates were ready for occupation. The number was soon exceeded and eventually reached 1,374.

From *Judenhäuser, Juden-Sammelstellen*, and *Judensiedlungen*, German Jews set out on the last stage of their journey to the forced ghettos and death factories in the East after enduring departure procedures marked by thoroughness, humiliation, and terrorization. Once they had crossed the border, the Denaturalization Law of November 1941 came into effect to legalize the automatic confiscation of property from all Jews permanently removed from Germany.[65]

Judenhäuser and *Juden-Sammelstellen* existed until the collapse of Hitler's regime in 1945. Serving as temporary detention centers, they also housed a diverse group of people who had lived among Germans and Jews, in a German-Jewish milieu. There was no longer a place for these people in the German "Housing Community" and "Folk/People's Community," and therefore they had to be eliminated. Never-ending debates focused on the classification and treatment of the so-called *Mischehen* (mixed marriages) and *Mischlinge* (mixed breeds), groups that grew out of the processes of Jewish emancipation, acculturation, and assimilation. In the end, the status the Nazis allocated to them meant life or death to them. Beate Meyer's pioneering studies have revealed the Nazi policies pursued against these unwanted groups and have shed light on the ways in which their daily lives were marked by constant anxiety and fear.[66]

Initially, the *Sonderrecht* of 1939 sanctioning the termination of the cohabitation of Germans and Jews incorporated only "non-privileged" *Mischehen*. Local communities hastened to drive them out of their homes, intending not only to concentrate and control them, or to boost the housing market, but also—and above all—to break up their marriages within the confined space of the *Judenhäuser*. Since the National Socialists were reluctant to introduce forcible divorce, they hoped that under increased pressure, one of the spouses would seek "voluntary" divorce. Separation and divorce rescinded the privilege granted to the Jewish partner. They were removed from *Judenhäuser* and deported to the East. The same applied to Jewish widowers whose partners had died. An example of what life was like during these times can be found in the words of the victims, such as in the diaries of Victor Klemperer, a Jew in Dresden. As early as May 1940, the Klemperers were forced to vacate their home in Dresden. The diaries describe the long harrowing journey through several *Judenhäuser,* depicting daily life in ghettos without walls.

From 1942 on, "privileged" *Mischehen* and *Mischlinge* were herded into *Judenhäuser*—in some places they also became known as *Mischehenhäuser* (mixed marriage houses). Once Jews had received the eviction order, they had to apply for a room. A few dared to protest, but to no avail. In Hamburg, a Jew wrote a letter to the authorities: "I have made no application whatsoever, but I am being forcibly moved into a single room."[67] A non-Jewish spouse refused to vacate her home, announcing that her husband would commit suicide.[68] In September 1942, a Jewish husband sent a special request to the authorities:

> My wife, who is suffering a nervous breakdown because of the anti-Jewish laws, will not and cannot live in a mixed Jewish milieu, and wants to stay in her flat with my agreement. I therefore request that I alone be accommodated in a furnished room, since I have neither furniture nor a bed. [69]

The request fell on deaf ears. When the wife applied for divorce, the husband endorsed her decision and moved into a *Judenhaus.* Soon afterwards he was called up for deportation and was murdered in the East.

The Nazis did not succeed in confining all *Mischehen* in *Judenhäuser.* What they achieved was an intensification of the pressure, especially on the non-Jewish spouses, to seek divorce. Based on the figures in Hamburg and fragmentary data from other regions, Beate Meyer estimates that the general divorce rate increased from 10 to 20 percent.[70] This increase also reflects the readiness of the courts to hand down verdicts as quickly as possible, in order to secure the immediate incorporation of the divorced Jew into the process of the "final solution." The same pressure, however, kept the vast majority of the German Jewish families together, for the sake of the Jewish partner and the "half-Jewish" children. From 1944, some local Gestapo officials hastened to clear their regions and *Judenhäuser* of *Mischehen* and *Mischlinge* by deporting Jewish and non-Jewish spouses and "half-Jews" to Theresienstadt. The vast majority survived—unlike the situation in the conquered territories in the East, where the executors of the "final solution" introduced forced divorce and, if this offer of survival for the non-Jewish spouse was rejected, then murdered entire families.[71]

There are no statistics that indicate the exact number of Jews, those in *Mischehen*, as well as *Mischlinge*, incarcerated in *Judenhäuser* and *Mischehenhäuser*. Avraham Barkai suggests that by early 1943 almost all Jews and "half-Jews" lived in *Judenhäuser* or camps.[72] When, in 1945, the inmates of *Judenhäuser* were liberated, almost all of them were Jews protected by a non-Jewish partner. There were 800 found in the Jewish hospital in Berlin, some 650 survived in Hamburg, fifty in Dresden, and a handful in other smaller cities. Most of the former Jewish homes lay in ruins. It often took some years before they were rebuilt, and even longer before the question of ownership was resolved.

From the first, Jewish homes were in high demand. The seizures were driven not only by ideological forces, but also by material interests. An army of Germans queued to stake their claim as tenants or buyers, together with a host of others seeking to benefit from the expulsions. The best sites were seized by the central command of the Nazi regime. Strategically well-positioned sites were earmarked for clearance, especially in Munich and Berlin, where they hindered Albert Speer's monumental redevelopment designs. In addition, buildings were required to accommodate the *Abriss-Mieter*, the German tenants also evicted from their apartments to make room for the construction of the massive edifices, which were to symbolize the glory and power of the thousand-year Reich. With the outbreak and spread of the war, the acute housing crisis reached catastrophic proportions. Jewish homes were also required to accommodate the growing number of *Ausgebombte* (air raid victims), the *Kriegsversehrte*, returned soldiers with serious injuries, and finally *vertriebene* Germans, or ethnic Germans displaced through war.

There were a few Germans who responded to the *Entjudung* of the housing market with disapproval. Landlords occasionally refused to turn Jewish tenants out into the streets. "Aryan" tenants ignored the appeals of the Nazis and stayed in Jewish-owned buildings. Some "Aryans" tried to relieve the plight of the Jews crammed into *Judenhäuser* and *Judensiedlungen*. They offered their services as suppliers of extra food and other valuable, almost unattainable, items, or they served as couriers conveying greetings and messages to relatives and friends who were inaccessible. Others went even further, urging Jews to go into hiding and then securing their "illegal" existence on the "Aryan" side. These "Righteous Neighbors" were vastly outnumbered by those scrambling to stake a claim to Jewish homes. But once the decision for deportation had been made at the "center," and clear guidelines handed down, pressure at the "periphery" increased to speed up the process of *Entjudung*. Under the heading "The Jews and the Housing Shortage," a report from the Lübeck NSDAP in October 1941 states:

> The housing problems in the district of Lübeck . . . can only be described as catastrophic. It has, for example, not escaped our attention that the local police station here has more than 200 families on record as occupying unsatisfactory living quarters, some of which are totally unsuited for human habitation . . . On the other hand, some of the Jews still occupy highly desirable quarters. It should be considered whether these unpleasant creatures should not be deported to the east and disappear from the towns in our area once and for all.[73]

Initially, the *Entjudung* of the housing market provided over 2,000 cities, towns, and villages with a welcome addition to their real estate. By 1942, the Viennese had been offered some 70,000 dwellings. In Berlin, the Nazis seized more than 30,000 homes, in Munich about 3,000, and in Düsseldorf, 700. Moreover, the seizure of Jewish homes provided a low-cost reserve to satisfy the expectations and greed of Nazi leaders and institutions, *Parteigenossen* (members of the NSDAP—Party comrades) and *Volksgenossen* or *Genossen* (comrades of the Party and the Folk). The experiences gained and the profits made encouraged the Nazis to continue the pillage throughout Europe. Waging a racial war enabled them not only to rule and to exploit the conquered countries, but also to eliminate the Jews once and for all through the "final solution." The acquisition of Jewish homes, however, was far outweighed by the massive loss of housing incurred in the Allied air raids. Frank Bajohr has shown that in Hamburg prior to September 1942, only 900 families were presented with Jewish homes. Considering that 1,200 dwellings were vacated while 260,000 homes were destroyed, the proportion of Jewish homes allocated made up less than one percent of the total housing shortfall.[74]

The surrender of their homes affected the Jews deeply. They were forced to uproot themselves from places they had lived in for years, often for generations. In the early years of Hitler's rule, they had at least been able to escape public anti-Semitic violence by withdrawing into the relative security of their homes. This refuge was no longer available. The loss gave rise to the growing feeling of homelessness. Plagued by homesickness after their evictions, some Jews made pilgrimages back to their old addresses, to gaze at their old apartments and houses from outside. Years later, those who had found sanctuary in exile and returned to Germany to search for their old homes, schools, and the cemeteries where relatives and friends had been buried echoed such feelings of sorrow and anguish. The poet Gertrud Kolmar, driven from her cozy country home near Berlin in early 1939, referred to a "paradise" she had lost in Finkenkrug. It was a "paradise" without neighbors. In a letter to her sister she wrote: "I became homesick for Finkenkrug. I did not like the people there—on the contrary—but I loved the meadows, the forest . . . the animals, the flora."[75] After six months spent living in a *Judenhaus* in the Berlin district of Schöneberg, she wrote her sister again: "I just cannot seem to develop some sort of relationship, whether tolerable or intolerable, to this area. I feel as strange here now as I did the first day." In another letter weeks later she confessed:

> Occasionally I would like to take my hat and coat and go far away. Now I think more than ever that I should go to Finkenkrug once snow has fallen, and go out in the moonlight the way I used to and tramp through the forest.[76]

With the eviction from their homes came the abandonment of familiar pieces of furniture and household items, books and pictures, along with the memories of childhood and schooldays, of profession and family. Belongings for which there was no place in the new, small, room in the *Judenhaus*, were given away for almost nothing, placed in storage, or given to trustworthy neighbors. As it often turned out after the war, in Germany and other countries, their belongings no longer existed when they attempted to claim them from those same neighbors, or they surfaced on the black market. Sometimes, when the "evacuation" order arrived, and comprehensive declaration forms had to be filled out, Jews no longer had possessions sufficient for the 50kg allowance as hand baggage on the last journey. The final belongings were removed upon arrival at the execution sites or gassing installations, or even after the murder. The items—ranging from glasses to artificial limbs, from clothing and hair, to spare change and gold fillings—were registered and stored, distributed and recycled.

Moving into *Judenhäuser* involved an adjustment to new heterogeneous communities and survival in wretched physical and psychological conditions. Jews who had retained the privilege of temporary residence in their own apartments had to take in new housemates: unmarried or divorced individuals, married couples, or families with children. Often confined in one room within a crowded apartment under one roof, or herded together in halls, sharing joint kitchens, washing, and toilet facilities, there was hardly any space left for movement, let alone privacy. Overcrowding and competition for shared facilities often gave rise to irritability and nervousness, tensions, and conflicts among inmates. In September 1941, on the eve of mass deportations, the Gestapo had instructed local authorities: "The Jews are to be assigned only the dirtiest and worst accommodation, whilst current sanitary regulations must be observed. Care should also be taken that not all houses are adjacent [in light of] the ban on ghettoization. The Jewish living space thus vacated is to be made available to those of German blood, without causing expense to the Reich or local councils."[77] In most places, poor hygienic and sanitary conditions prevailed, and, in time, deteriorated, since the local councils saw no reason to maintain these temporary Jewish housing estates properly or to supply them with sufficient fuel, essential for heating and for the supply of warm water.

The Liebmanns, an elderly couple, found refuge in a room in a Jewish boarding house on Munich's Akademiestrasse. One visitor recalled:

> The living area ... was quite uncomfortable. Not that it was dirty or even untidy ... But the innumerable cases, cardboard boxes and small chests, wardrobes and cupboards piled on top of each other, took up every inch of space and stood in the way. The furniture they hadn't known what to do with after being driven out of their previous home had been stored with a removal firm; there was no place for it in the furnished room in the *Pension*. Everything that they had previously kept in drawers and cupboards—clothes, underwear, shoes, books, all their painting and drawing materials—was packed away in this pile of parcels and boxes. Alexander Liebmann referred to his new residence ironically as the "night refuge." One day, with tears in his eyes, he showed me his German war decorations, and asked me the question: "And suddenly I am 'not supposed to be a German any more'?"[78]

Joel König visited his parents in Berlin at the beginning of 1940. They had sublet the apartment of a former Jewish businessman, close to the Hansaplatz:

> The one and a half rooms ... were so cramped that one literally had to worm one's way between the furniture. Titian's *Lavina* gazed at us from the corner of the room where mother cooked lunch on a

primus stove. There was not enough coal to keep the room warm. My father had a flannel blanket draped about his shoulder, and tried to stay close to the lukewarm stove. Despite the cramped conditions and the cold, my parents were happy to have this apartment.[79]

Ruth Klüger recalls the dark, insect-ridden room she shared with her mother: "You turn off the light and imagine the bugs crawling out of the mattress. Then you get bitten, turn on the light and wail loudly, because the disgusting vermin are actually walking around in the bed."[80] Theodor Tuch describes the situation in Hamburg:

> All Jews must now live in buildings that belong to a Jew, mostly in the Grindel area. Whole districts of the city are *judenfrei*. Usually, people in one or two rooms. Dora, for example, moved in with Paul's mother-in-law. The room is about 3 by 4 meters. You can work out for yourselves how much freedom of movement they have. Sleeping, eating, washing. Pick up the bed cushions, but where can they be stored? . . . In the kitchen, the washing is drying. Four wardrobes stand in the narrow hall, holding the remains of those possessions, which the people were allowed to keep. Everything had to be auctioned off.[81]

There were *Judenhäuser* that were even more wretched. In Hannover, almost 100 Jews were crammed into a house in Bergstrasse 8 known as the "old synagogue." An inmate, deported to Riga in December 1941, who survived the Holocaust, remembers the distress and suffering caused by lack of space:

> So many people were packed into the hall that there was only a tiny path left between the beds. Everyone had to climb over neighbors to reach his or her bed. There was a gallery—occupied too. From there one could see what was going on the ground floor. Men, women and children all mingled together. The sanitary conditions defy description. There were no tables or chairs. Life took place on beds. The mood among the inmates was one of deep despair. Some committed suicide. As women we suffered more than men, the more since [there was no other way] we had to undress and wash ourselves in the presence of men.[82]

Conditions were also agonizingly cramped in the *Judenhaus* located in Ohestrasse 8/9, which had once served as the main office of the Jewish welfare service, as well as a soup kitchen and crèche. "Two hundred Jews were confined to sections marked off by blankets . . . It was like a terrible refugee camp." Also in Hannover, one hundred and fifty men, women, and children were incarcerated in the funeral parlor of the Jewish cemetery. "Squeezed together like sardines, they had to vegetate in one room filled with iron beds."[83]

In Berlin, the Gestapo converted the old synagogue at the Grosse Hamburger Strasse 26, built in 1829, into a *Sammelstelle* (assembly camp) from which thousands of Jews were shipped to the East. Martin Riesenburger recalls:

> The building was a prison—with iron bars at the window and guards posted at the gates. Large searchlights were set up in front and the rear of the building to prevent any escape. Herded together like cattle—kept on the floor—the elderly and the young, men, women and babies had to wait till they were finally called up for the final barbaric removal—professors, doctors, lawyers, prominent artists—a never-ending death march of the condemned. [84]

One of the largest *Judenhäuser* emerged in Berlin. When in June 1943 the Reichsvereinigung was liquidated and Germany's capital declared *judenfrei* (free of Jews), the hospital in the Iranische Strasse continued to offer—under the control of the Gestapo—a confined last space for Jewish life. The vast complex of buildings contained a medical ward and administrative center, a prison for Jews caught in hiding, and a *Sammelstelle* (assembly camp) for "privileged" Jews, a total of 800 occupants, almost entirely composed of spouses of *Mischehen* and *Mischlingen,* and a handful of foreign Jews. The statistician Bruno Blau, a patient at the hospital until the liberation in 1945, describes the final days of what he terms the *Krankenhaus Ghetto* (hospital ghetto):

> Cut off from the world, without freedom of movement, exposed to all the dangers of the terrible war, 800 Jews lived through these days and awaited the dawning of a new era; filled with hope and longing, how they looked forward to liberation; knowing that salvation was coming, how gladly they took upon themselves every trouble and hardship—nowhere else could that be experienced with the same intensity as in the Berlin hospital ghetto. For in no other place were as many Jews crowded together as here, where all the institutions that either positively or negatively affected the continued existence of Jews in Germany could also be found, where everyone without exception was inspired by one and the same thought, where on everyone's lips— whether voiced or not—there lingered the one anxious question: Is the end near? When will it come? Will I live to see it! . . . When we

finally came out of our live entombment into the light of the day, the Nazi nightmare was over . . . First we took off the Yellow Star, and the compulsory Jewish middle names disappeared. Once again the Jews were human beings.[85]

Whenever *Sternträger* left the German ghettos without walls, they not only encountered manifold barriers restricting their movements, but they were also exposed to a hostile environment in which they experienced the most profound dehumanization and ostracism. Curfews closed the door of their living quarters from dark to dawn. The strain of traveling became an integral part of everyday life. Motor vehicles and driving licenses had already been confiscated after the November pogrom in 1938. Bicycles were requisitioned in 1942. *Sternträger* could use buses or trams, underground trains, or municipal railways only if they had a special pass. This privilege was granted for forced laborers if the distance from home to work was more than seven kilometers, or over an hour's walk. They were allowed to sit on public transport only when all Germans had found a seat. Enforced detours were frequent, as Jews could not travel through designated roads, squares, and parks. They were not permitted to enter public phone booths, and restrictions were imposed on shopping. Seeking refuge during allied bombardments in air raid shelters was in most cases not allowed. In addition, public space was no longer available for recreation and play, especially for Jewish children.

Confined within ghettos without walls, the Jews lived a life on borrowed time. The waiting, the uncertainty, and the fear of being evicted again and "evacuated" to the East became torturous for many, as did the fear of attacks by fanatical anti-Semites. *Judenhäuser* were preferred targets for members of the party or Gestapo officials bent on showing their hatred of the Jews in acts of brutality. *Kontrollgänge,* inspections or "spot checks," provided the perfect excuse for molestation, looting, and ill-treatment. Marion Kaplan has described the daily life of German Jews under Nazi rule, and concluded that the remaining Jews, trapped in Germany, created on the eve of their deportation and murder "a community of connection and concern, some even finding a new 'extended family'":

> Holding on to their bourgeois values and way of life was a matter of integrity and identity, or a resistance against "Aryan" dehumanization. Jews shared and bartered food with each other, consoled each other after the arrest of friends and family members, gave gifts and

services. No longer integrated into German neighborhoods . . . most "full" Jews were spared much of the public enmity they had previously faced and could aid and comfort each other.[86]

Jewish youngsters found the strength to resist. Banned from schools and conscripted into forced labor, some attempted to break out of the cycle of demoralization and isolation. They listened to banned gramophones and forbidden music, organized social and cultural gatherings, and enjoyed the brief moments of dancing and dating. In the *hachschara*, agricultural retraining camps described by the Nazis as "living communities for Jewish forced laborers" and liquidated in 1943, Jewish and Zionist ideals survived and found expression in the will to emigrate and the longing for a new life in *Eretz Israel* (the Land of Israel, or Palestine at the time). In 1942, a Zionist youth group by the name of Chug Halutzi (Pioneer Circle), comprising some forty members, escaped into the Berlin underground. Groups were also formed in factories and firms. In many cases, social barriers had to be to overcome before new friendships could be made. This problem was most severe for young Jews who had grown up in middle- and upper middle-class environments. As forced laborers, they made their first-ever contacts with their companions-in-suffering from working-class backgrounds. Most of the members of the Herbert Baum Group, the largest Jewish Communist resistance organization in Germany, were recruited from the two "Jewish departments" of the Siemens plant in Berlin. Their spectacular, abortive sabotage attempt against the Nazi exhibition, "The Soviet Paradise," in May 1942 represented the highpoint of their anti-Fascist resistance. The Gestapo and the People's Court put a rapid end to the existence of the group.[87]

Some German Jews sought refuge from the onslaught in the Jewish faith. In many places, prayer services continued, first in communal offices under the control of the Gestapo, then in secrecy and in private circles. Fräulein Rabbiner Jonas, Germany's first woman rabbi, shared a room with her mother in a Berlin *Judenhaus*. She continued her rabbinical services both within the Jewish community and in a German armament factory in which she was deployed as a forced laborer. She gave her last sermon in October 1942. Soon afterwards she was deported to Theresienstadt and murdered.[88] Rabbi Martin Riesenburger, protected by his non-Jewish wife, continued to bury the dead in the Weissensee cemetery until liberation. In June 1943, he performed a Jewish wedding, probably the last in Germany. The groom was aged 40, the bride 37. A few days later, the couple was deported to the East. Riesenburger compiled a calendar containing the dates of the Jewish festivals. Handed over to fugitives, the list of dates helped them to keep the rhythm of Jewish life. Some of them survived in secret locations in the cemetery. Riesenburger also knew that Jews who had died in hiding were not only brought at night to the cemetery, but also to secluded places at the outskirts of Berlin to be buried. Those Germans who had attempted to save the Jews and then had to carry out their burials remembered the exact locations, to ensure that one day, a burial according to Halachic ruling could be performed.[89]

Only 8,000 German Jews returned out of the 134,000 who had been dragged from their last refuges and loaded on to the trains. When they embarked on their journeys to the East, they had already experienced ostracism and banishment and a total expulsion from society. There was a further awareness that many took with them on their way to the murder and burial sites, the consciousness that they had been forced into a Jewish community united by a common fate and shared suffering. Else Behrend Rosenfeld witnessed the animosities and tensions among 320 Munich Jews from many walks of life, incarcerated in the *Heimanlage,* the barracks at Berg am Laim, and she recalls the creation of a "true community":

> Orthodox and Liberals, those baptized as Catholic and Protestant, the formerly rich and poor, the highly educated and those from very simple social circles had to live and get along with each other. And, naturally, not everyone demonstrated good will. We did our best, and then it became clear . . . that we had been successful: In Berg am Laim we had become a true community.[90]

Scholars have offered different names to define this "true community."[91] H.G. Adler and many others refer to a *Zwangsgesellschaft*, a community kept together by force. Wolf Gruner adds an adjective, describing it as a *geschlossene* (closed) *Zwangsgesellschaft*.[92] Widespread and often quoted is the notion of *Schicksalsgemeinschaft,* a community formed by destiny. Avraham Barkai points to what he calls "Pariah Existence and Resignation to Fate."[93] As noted previously, Marion Kaplan emphasizes the notion of "social death."[94] Whatever term one chooses to specify for the nature of this residual group of German Jewry, made homeless in Nazi Germany and, since the beginning of the war, prevented from seeking refuge in exile, it shared the fate of their co-religionists in countries conquered by the National Socialists, in Lodz and Warsaw, Riga and Kovno, Minsk and Izbica, Chelmno, Treblinka and Sobibor, Maidanek and Auschwitz-Birkenau, Theresienstadt, and other, smaller murder sites of the "final solution."

Ghettoization and forced labor deployment in Germany were no more than temporary reprieves. Both fulfilled two relevant, interrelated functions. *Judenhäuser* and *Judensiedlungen* served as a means to exclude Jews from society and to include them—temporarily—into a new "Jewish" place, a segregated Jewish living quarter.[95] This function was assigned to all ghettos set up by the Nazis in the occupied territories, be it in the form of a hermetically sealed ghetto, a "semi-open," or an "open" ghetto. *Judenkommandos* and *Judenabteilungen* served as a means to absorb an army of impoverished and jobless German Jews into the production process, and to include them as forced laborers in the Nazi war economy, in "self-contained" units, "separated from the main body of workers."[96] The gradual liquidation of *Judenhäuser* and *Judensiedlungen* commenced once the decision was made to remove the inmates for murder. Forced laborers were incorporated into the program of the "final solution" as soon as, often even before, replacements, in the shape of other non-Jewish forced laborers, could be found for them. The removal of Jews, both from their segregated homes and from their workplaces, eased neither the acute and growing housing crisis nor the shortage of workers, a situation described by experts since 1939 as "anarchy" in the labor market. Within the Nazi system, based on racial hatred and mass murder, ghettoization and forced labor were only steps along the path to genocide.

A few years ago, an artist, Gunter Demnig, conceived a remarkable idea. He designed a small stone, made of concrete and covered by a brass plate. The plate contains the name of a Jew or of another victim of Nazi terror, alongside the dates of birth and death. The stone is placed in the ground at places where the victim had once lived, committed suicide, was deported, or escaped into hiding. These public *Stolpersteine* ("stumbling blocks") are now keeping the memory of the fate of Jews and other victims alive, at least for the new neighbors now living there and any visitors who may come.[97] More than 7,000 public memorials, dispersed over 130 sites, have been set up. It can be assumed that for some Germans and for other people, these *Stolpersteine* have become an offensive reminder of events that they would prefer to bury once and for all. This applies above all to neighbors like those to whom Joachim Prinz referred in 1935.

Notes

1. For assistance in producing this article, I should like to extend my warmest thanks to my friends and colleagues Dr. Beate Meyer (Hamburg), Dr. Jürgen Matthäus (Washington, DC), and Lucy Davey (Sydney), and to my beloved wife Jane Sydenham-Kwiet.

2. Jan T. Gross, *Neighbors. The Destruction of the Jewish Community in Jedwabne, Poland* (Princeton: Princeton University Press, 2001). Gross's revelations sparked a heated controversy both in Poland and abroad, disagreements that continue to this very day. See Dariusz Stola, "Jedwabne: Revisiting the evidence and nature of the crime," in *Holocaust and Genocide Studies* 17 (2003): 139–152; Antony Polonsky and Joanna B. Michlic, eds., *The Neighbors Respond: The Controversy over the Jedwabne Massacre in Poland* (Princeton: Princeton University Press, 2003); Marek J. Chodakiewicz, *The Massacre in Jedwabne, July 10, 1941: Before, During, After* (New York: Columbia University Press and East European Monographs, 2005).
3. Adolf Hitler to Adolf Gemlich, 16 September 1919, in *Hitler. Sämtliche Aufzeichnungen 1905–1924*, eds. Eberhard Jäckel and Axel Kuhn (Stuttgart: Deutsche Verlagsanstalt, 1980), 88–90.
4. Frank Bajohr, "'The Folk Community' and the Persecution of the Jews," in *Holocaust and Genocide Studies*, 20 (2006): 192.
5. Avraham Barkai, "Im mauerlosen Ghetto," in *Deutsch-jüdische Geschichte der Neuzeit*, Vol. 4: *Aufbruch und Zerstörung 1918–1945*, ed. Michael A. Meyer (Munich: Beck Verlag, 1997), 319–349.
6. Saul Friedländer, *Nazi Germany and the Jews: The Years of Persecution, 1933–1939* (New York: HarperCollins, 1997), 113–144.
7. *Jüdische Rundschau*, 17 September 1935, quoted from Gudrun Schwarz, *Die nationalsozialistischen Lager* (Frankfurt am Main: Fischer Verlag, 1996), 41.
8. *Jüdische Rundschau*, 5 November 1935, quoted from Volker Dahm, "Kulturelles und geistiges Leben," in *Die Juden in Deutschland 1933–1945. Leben unter nationalsozialistischer Herrschaft*, ed. Wolfgang Benz (Munich: C. H. Beck, 1988), 157.
9. Konrad Kwiet, "To Leave or Not to Leave. The German Jews at the Crossroads," in *November 1938: From Reichskristallnacht to Genocide*, ed. Walter Pehle (Oxford: Berg Publishers, 1991), 139–153.
10. Marion A. Kaplan, *Between Dignity and Despair. Jewish Life in Nazi Germany* (New York: Oxford University Press, 1998).
11. Quoted from Jürgen Matthäus, "Jenseits der Grenze. Die ersten Massenerschiessungen von Juden in Litauen (Juni–August 1941)," in *Zeitschrift für Geschichtswissenschaft* 44 (1996): 116.
12. Yad Vashem, Righteous Among the Nations (per Country and Ethnic Origin), 1 January 2001.
13. Wolfgang Benz, ed., *Überleben im Dritten Reich. Juden im Untergrund und ihre Helfer* (Munich: C.H. Beck, 2003); see also Beate Kosmala and C. Schoppmann, eds., *Überleben im Untergrund: Hilfe für Juden in Deutschland 1941–1945* (Berlin: Metropol, 2002), as well as the study by Mark Roseman, *The Past in Hiding* (New York: Metropolitan Books, 2001).
14. See Bajohr, "The Folk Community," 183. See also Götz Aly, *Hitlers Volksstaat: Raub, Rassenkrieg und Nationaler Sozialismus* (Frankfurt am Main: Fischer Verlag, 2005).
15. Nathan Stoltzfus, *Resistance of the Heart: Intermarrige and the Rosenstrasse Protest in Germany* (New York: W.W. Norton, 1996). After the release of Margaretta von Trotta's film *Die Rosenstrasse*, a heated debate erupted both in Germany and abroad that was centered on the filmmaker's reconstruction and interpretation of this historic event. See Beate Meyer, "Geschichte im Film. Judenverfolgung, Mischehen und der Protest in der Rosenstrasse," *Zeitschrift für Geschichtswissenschaft*, 52

(2004): 23–36; Wolf Gruner, *Widerstand in der Rosenstrasse. Die Fabrik-Aktion und die Verfolgung der "Mischehen"* (Frankfurt am Main: Fischer Verlag, 2005).
16. Konrad Kwiet, "The Ultimate Refuge: Suicide in the Jewish Community under the Nazis," *Leo Baeck Institute Yearbook* 29 (1984): 135–167.
17. Kaplan, *Between Dignity and Despair*, 229.
18. Steven M. Lowenstein, "The Beginning of Integration: 1780–1870," in *Jewish Daily Life in Germany, 1618–1945*, ed. Marion Kaplan (New York: Oxford University Press, 2005), esp. 95f.
19. Avraham Barkai, "'Volksgemeinschaft,' 'Aryanization' and the Holocaust," in *The Final Solution. Origins and Implementation*, ed. David Cesarani (New York: Routledge, 2004), 41.
20. Trude Maurer, "From Everyday to a State of Emergency: Jews in Weimar and Nazi Germany," in Kaplan, *Jewish Daily Life*, 273.
21. Ibid., 275.
22. *Reichsgesetzblatt* I, 342, Verordnung über Mietbeihilfen, 30 March 1938.
23. Friedländer, *Nazi Germany*, 260.
24. Maurer, "From Everyday," 275.
25. Jürgen Matthäus, "Antisemitic Symbolism in early Nazi Germany," *Leo Baeck Institute Yearbook* 45 (2000): 183.
26. See the study by Frank Bajohr, *"Unser Hotel ist judenfrei." Bäder-Antisemitismus im 19. und 20. Jahrhundert* (Frankfurt am Main: Fischer Verlag, 2003).
27. See Hans Safrian, "Expediting Expropriation and Expulsion. The Impact of the 'Vienna Model' on Anti-Jewish Policies in Nazi Germany in 1938," *Holocaust and Genocide Studies*, 14 (2000): 390.
28. See Gerhard Botz, *Wohnungspolitik und Judendeportation in Wien 1938 bis 1945. Zur Funktion des Antisemitismus als Ersatz nationalsozialistischer Sozialpolitik* (Vienna: Geyer, 1975).
29. See Wolf Gruner, *Zwangsarbeit und Verfolgung. Österreichische Juden im NS-Staat 1938–45* (Innsbruck: Studien Verlag, 2000).
30. Wolf Gruner, "'Lesen brauchen sie nicht zu können...' Die Denkschrift über die Behandlung der Juden in der Reichshauptstadt auf allen Gebieten des öffentlichen Lebens vom Mai 1938," *Jahrbuch für Antisemitismusforschung* 4 (1995): 305–341.
31. Ibid.
32. Susanne Willems, *Der entsiedelte Jude. Albert Speers Wohnungsmarktpolitik für den Berliner Hauptstadtbau* (Berlin: Edition Hentrich, 2000), 71–87.
33. Ibid., 87, Letter Göring to Speer, 26 November 1938.
34. Stenographische Niederschrift, 12 November 1938, Nuremberg Document, PS-1806.
35. Ibid.
36. Hans Mommsen, "Die Realisierung des Utopischen: Die 'Endlösung der Judenfrage' im Dritten Reich," *Geschichte und Gesellschaft* 9 (1983): 381–420. For the debate see Christopher Browning, "The Decision Making Process," in *The Historiography of the Holocaust*, ed. Dan Stone (New York: Palgrave Macmillan, 2004), 173–196.
37. Jürgen Matthäus, "Controlled Escalation. Summer 1941 and the Holocaust in the occupied Soviet Union," *Holocaust and Genocide Studies* 21 (2007): 218–242.
38. Wolfram Selig, *Richard Seligman. Ein jüdisches Schicksal. Zur Geschichte der Judenverfolgung in München während des Dritten Reiches* (Munich: Stadtarchiv, 1983), 60.

39. Ibid.
40. Susanne Heim and Götz Aly, "Staatliche Ordnung und 'organische Lösung.' Die Rede Görings über die Judenfrage vom 6. Dezember 1938," *Jahrbuch für Antisemitismusforschung* 2 (1993): 378–404.
41. Anordnung no. 1/39g, 28 December 1938, Nbg.Doc. PS 069.
42. Gesetz über Mietverhältnisse mit Juden, 30 April 1939, published in Willems, *Der entsiedelte Jude*, 138–139. See also Karl Christian Führer, "Mit Juden unter einem Dach? Zur Vorgeschichte des nationalsozialistischen Gesetzes über Mietverhältnisse mit Juden," *1999: Zeitschrift für Sozialgeschichte des 20. und 21. Jahrhunderts* 1 (1992), 5161.
43. Durchführung des Gesetzes über Mietverhältnisse mit Juden, 4 May 1939, in *Das Sonderrecht für die Juden im NS-Staat*, ed. Joseph Walk (Heidelberg: Müller Juristischer Verlag, 1981), 293.
44. Ibid.
45. Quoted from Angela Schwarz, "Von den Wohnstiften zu den 'Judenhäusern,'" in *Kein abgeschlossenes Kapitel: Hamburg im "Dritten Reich,"* ed. Angelika Ebbinghaus and Karsten Linne (Hamburg: EVA Europäische Verlagsanstalt, 1997), 235.
46. Used as the title of Susanne Willems' comprehensive study on Speer's housing policy in Berlin, see Matthäus, "Controlled Escalation."
47. See Willems, *Der entsiedelte Jude*, 18.
48. Wolf Gruner, *Öffentliche Wohlfahrt und Judenverfolgung. Wechselwirkungen lokaler und zentraler Politik im NS-Staat (1933–1942)* (Munich: Oldenbourg, 2002), 112f., 193–198. See also Gai Miron, Jacob Borut, and Rivka Elkin, *Aspects of Jewish Welfare in Nazi Germany* (Jerusalem: Yad Vashem, 2006), 20.
49. Quoted from H.G. Adler, *Der verwaltete Mensch. Studien zur Deportation der Juden aus Deutschland* (Tübingen: Mohr/Siebeck, 1974), 46f.
50. Instructions by the Oberfinanzpräsident Hamburg, 3.8.1942, in *Die Verfolgung und Ermordung der Hamburger Juden 1933–1945. Geschichte, Zeugnis, Erinnerung*, ed. Beate Meyer (Göttingen: Wallstein Verlag, 2006), 44.
51. Konrad Kwiet, "Nach dem Pogrom: Stufen der Ausgrenzung," in Benz, *Juden in Deutschland*, 614–631; see also Jens J. Scheiner, *Vom Gelben Flicken zum Judenstern? Genese und Applikation von Judenabzeichen im Islam und christlichen Europa (849–1941)* (Frankfurt am Main: Peter Lang Europäischer Verlag der Wissenschaften, 2004).
52. Years later, Weltsch distanced himself from his front-page article in the *Jüdische Rundschau*, which was written as a response to the Nazi assault. He urged the Jews to transform the stigma into a Jewish symbol of pride and to accept and strengthen Jewish identity.
53. Victor Klemperer, *I Shall Bear Witness: The Diaries of Victor Klemperer, 1933–1945*, 2 vols. (London: Weidenfeld & Nicolson, 1998), 413.
54. Victor Klemperer, *The Language of the Third Reich: LTI. Lingua Tertii Imperii: A Philologist's Notebook* (London: Continuum, 2000), 168.
55. Quoted from Kwiet, "Nach dem Pogrom," 618.
56. Stenographische Niederschrift, 12 November 1938, Nuremberg Document, PS-1806.
57. See Schwarz, *Die nationalsozialistischen Lager*, 45.
58. Marlis Buchholz, *Die hannoverschen Judenhäuser. Zur Situation der Juden in der Zeit der Ghettoisierung und Verfolgung, 1941 bis 1945* (Hildesheim: A. Lax, 1987).

59. Ute Daub, "Die Stadt Frankfurt am Main macht sich 'judenfrei.'" Zur Konzentrierung, Verbannung und Ghettoisierung der jüdischen Bevölkerung zwischen 1938 und 1943," in *Nach der Kristallnacht." Jüdisches Leben und antijüdische Politik in Frankfurt am Main 1938–1945*, ed. Monica Kingreen (Frankfurt am Main: Campus, 1999), 319–355.
60. Mario Offenberg, *Adass Jisroel. Die jüdische Gemeinde in Berlin (1869–1942). Vernichtet und Vergessen* (Berlin: Museums-Pädagogischen Dienst Berlin, 1986), 222.
61. Heinz Keil, *Dokumentation über die Verfolgung der jüdischen Bürger von Ulm/Donau* (Ulm: Stadt Ulm, 1961), 237.
62. Kaplan, *Between Dignity and Despair*, 155.
63. See Beate Meyer, "Der 'Eichmann von Dresden,'" in *Deutsche, Juden, Völkermord. Der Holocaust als Geschichte und Gegenwart*, ed. Jürgen Matthäus and Klaus-Michael Mallmann (Darmstadt: Wissenschaftliche Buchgesellschaft, 2006), 274–291.
64. Peter Hanke, *Zur Geschichte der Juden in München zwischen 1933 und 1945* (Munich: Buch und Kunstantiquariat Wölfle in Kommission, 1967), 339. See also Ulrike Härendel, *Kommunale Wohnungspolitik im Dritten Reich. Siedlungsideologie und Kleinhausbau und "Wohnraumarisierung" am Beispiel Münchens* (Munich: Oldenbourg, 1999); Ulrike Härendel, "Der Schutzlosigkeit preisgegeben: Die Zwangsveräußerung jüdischen Immobilienbesitzes und die Vertreibung der Juden aus ihren Wohnungen," in *München arisiert. Entrechtung und Enteignung der Juden während des Nationalsozialismus*, ed. Angelika Baumann and Andreas Heusler (Munich: C.H. Beck, 2004), 105–126.
65. See Martin Dean, "The Development and Implementation of Nazi Denaturalization and Confiscation Policy up to the Eleventh Decree to the Reich Citizenship Law," *Holocaust and Genocide Studies* 16 (2002): 217–242.
66. See Beate Meyer, *"Jüdische Mischlinge." Rassenpolitik und Verfolgungserfahrung 1933–1945* (Hamburg: Dölling & Galitz Verlag, 1999).
67. Quoted from Beate Meyer, "Verfolgung und Verfolgungserfahrung 'jüdischer Mischlinge' in der NS-Zeit," Dissertation University of Hamburg 1998, 78.
68. Ibid., 80.
69. Ibid.
70. Ibid., 73
71. See Konrad Kwiet, "Forced Labour of German Jews in Nazi Germany," *Leo Baeck Institute Yearbook* 35 (1991): 394.
72. Avraham Barkai, *Vom Boykott zur Entjudung. Der wirtschaftliche Existenzkampf der Juden im Dritten Reich 1933–1943* (Frankfurt am Main: Fischer Verlag, 1988), 182.
73. Institut für Zeitgeschichte (IfZ), MA 138, *Stimmungsbericht* der NSDAP *Kreisleitung*, Lübeck, October 1941.
74. Frank Bajohr, "Die Deportation der Juden: Initiativen und Reaktionen aus Hamburg," in Meyer, *Die Verfolgung und Ermordung*, 34.
75. Letter G. Kolmar to her sister H. Wenzel, 13 May 1939, in Johanna Woltmann, ed., *Gertrud Kolmar Briefe* (Göttingen: Wallstein, 1997), 33. Gertrud Kolmar never returned to Finkenkrug. At the end of February 1943—in the wake of the *Fabrik-Aktion*—she was arrested as a forced laborer and deported to Auschwitz-Birkenau, where she was murdered a few days after her arrival.
76. Ibid.

77. Quoted from Adler, *Der verwaltete Mensch*, 47. Letter Gestapo Düsseldorf to local council in Kleve, 18 September 1941.
78. Karl Wieninger, *In München erlebte Geschichte* (Munich: Stromberger, 1985), 64.
79. Joel König, *Den Netzen entronnen, Die Aufzeichnungen* (Göttingen: Vandenhoeck & Ruprecht, 1967), 164.
80. Quoted from Kaplan, *Between Dignity and Despair*, 154.
81. Ursula Randt, "Theodor Tuch: An meine Tochter. Aufzeichnungen eines Hamburger Juden 1941/1942," *Bulletin des Leo Baeck Instituts* 70 (1985): 20f.
82. Quoted from Buchholz, *Die hannoverschen Judenhäuser*, 101, 138.
83. Ibid., 138.
84. Martin Riesenburger, *Das Licht verlöschte nicht. Ein Zeugnis aus der Nacht des Faschismus*, ed. Andreas Nachama and Hermann Simon (Berlin: Edition Hentrich, 2003), 58.
85. Quoted from Monika Richarz, ed., *Jewish Life in Germany. Memoirs from Three Centuries* (Bloomington: Indiana University Press, 1991), 471.
86. Ibid., 155.
87. See Konrad Kwiet and Helmut Eschwege, *Selbstbehauptung und Widerstand. Deutsche Juden im Kampf um Existenz und Menschenwürde 1933–1945* (Hamburg: Christians Verlag, 1986). On the latest stage of research see Arnold Paucker, *German Jews in the Resistance 1933–1945. The Facts and the Problems* (Berlin: Gedenkstätte deutscher Widerstand, 2005).
88. See Elisa Klapheck, *Fräulein Rabbiner Jonas. The Story of the First Woman Rabbi* (San Francisco: Jossey-Bass, 2004).
89. Riesenburger, *Und das Licht verlöschte nicht*, 67.
90. Hans Lamm, *Von Juden in München, ein Gedenkbuch* (Munich: Ner-Tamid-Verlag, 1959), 385f.
91. Apart from H.G. Adler's monumental study on the deportation of German Jews, *Der verwaltete Mensch*, see also his earlier book, *Theresienstadt 1941–1945. Das Anlitz einer Zwangsgemeinschaft. Geschichte, Soziologie, Psychologie* (Tübingen: Mohr/Siebeck, 1960).
92. Gruner, "Lesen brauchen sie nicht zu können," 306.
93. Also the subtitle of his book chapter in Meyer, *German-Jewish History*, 334.
94. Kaplan, *Between Dignity and Despair*, esp. 5, 150f.
95. See Tim Cole, "Ghettoization," in Stone, *The Historiography of the Holocaust*, 65–87.
96. Kwiet, "Forced Labour," 392.
97. Interview Beate Meyer with Gunter Demnig, "'Ein Mensch ist erst vergessen, wenn sein Name vergessen ist.' Die Aktion Stolpersteine," in Meyer, *Verfolgung und Ermordung*, 167–173.

Chapter Six

BETWEEN SELF-ASSERTION AND FORCED COLLABORATION
The Reich Association of Jews in Germany, 1939–1945

Beate Meyer

IN JULY 1945, THE CHIEF of Police of Greater Berlin dissolved the Reichsvereinigung der Juden in Deutschland (Reich Association of Jews in Germany).[1] Berlin Jews, who had survived the Holocaust, reported to the Soviet occupation authorities and denounced the last head of the organization, Walter Lustig, as a Nazi collaborator. Lustig was arrested by Soviet soldiers and killed.[2] In September 1945, the Allied Control Commission outlawed all Nazi organizations, including the Reichsvereinigung.[3] Thus, with the end of the Third Reich, the last remaining Jewish organization in Germany was banned as a Nazi institution.

This ban marked the end of the vicissitudes of German-Jewish organizations in the Nazi state. Various societies, groups, and local Jewish communities (*Gemeinden*) had come together to form the Reichsvertretung der deutschen Juden (Reich Representation of German Jews) in 1933—changed to the Reichsvertretung der Juden in Deutschland (Reich Representation of Jews in Germany) in 1935—and had cooperated in this umbrella organization until 1938. The executive boards and committees of the Reichsvertretung reflected the nature, interests, and goals of the various organizations within German Jewry. This umbrella organization saw itself as representing the interests of the Jews and as serving as a mouthpiece for the entire Jewish community in Germany in its dealings with the Nazi state.[4] By the end of 1938, however, the Reichsvertretung was no longer functional because the official Jewish communities (*Gemeinden*) had lost their status as public bodies as they were forced to become private associations; in the autumn of 1938, the Nazi state formally dissolved the various Jewish organizations that had been members of the Reichsvertretung. Jewish functionaries rushed to establish a successor organization to represent the remaining Jews in Germany, announcing its establishment in February 1939.[5] In the same period, the idea that a Jewish organization was an essential element in the implementation of the Nazis' anti-Jewish policies had prevailed within the Sicherheitsdienst (Security Service, or SD) of the SS, the Nazi authority that had taken control of the regime's Jewish policies in the aftermath of the November 1938 pogrom.[6] The result was the establishment of the Reichsvereinigung der Juden in Deutschland in February 1939 and its establishment by law in July of that year.[7] Both sides, the SD and the German Jews, expected the Reichsvereinigung to become a useful tool in the promotion of their respective interests.

The organization was directly subordinate to the Reichssicherheitshauptamt (Reich Security Main Office, or RSHA). The Reichssicherheitshauptamt installed the same functionaries that had worked in the Reichsvertretung: Leo Baeck, Otto Hirsch, Julius Seligsohn, Paul Eppstein, to name just a few. Serving as department heads one step down in the hierarchy were numerous women, such as Martha Mosse, Cora Berliner, Hannah Karminski, and Paula Fürst.[8] But the apparent similarities between the Reichsvertretung and the Reichsvereinigung concealed a rapid process of transformation that gained momentum in the years that followed.[9] Rather than consisting of local Jewish communities and a broad spectrum of Jewish organizations, the members of this new umbrella organization were now individuals who were deemed Jews according to the Nazi regime's "racial" definition. For them, membership was mandatory. All foundations, associations, and societies, as well as the smaller Jewish communities, lost their independence, were integrated into the Reichsvereinigung, and, most significantly, were forced to relinquish their assets, effectively securing centralized access to this property for the Nazi state. The chief tasks that remained in the domain of the Reichsvereinigung were facilitating emigration and serving the needs of those Jews who remained in Germany, specifically in the spheres of education, vocational training, and public welfare. The organization was by no means free to fulfill these tasks independently, but was instead subject to detailed rules and instructions.

The work of the Reichsvereinigung can be divided into three phases: from 1939 to October 1941, it was involved in the "enforced emigration" of the Jews from Germany; from October 1941 to June 1943, the Reichsvereinigung increasingly became an instrument of the RSHA and the Gestapo in organizing deportations of German Jews to the East; and in the summer of 1943, upon completion of the deportations, the Reichsvereinigung was officially dissolved, but continued *de facto* to exist as it cared for the needs of Jews who were married to non-Jewish partners.

The "Enforced Emigration" (1939–1941)

In the first phase of the life of the Reichsvereinigung, which lasted from 1939 to the fall of 1941, the interests of the Nazi state and those of the Jewish organization coincided in one central aspect, namely, the efforts to facilitate mass Jewish emigration. While the Nazi state plundered the Jews financially, harassed and arrested them, and tormented them in concentration camps, Jewish leaders feverishly sought any legal, as well as—from the perspective of the countries of immigration—illegal means to aid the emigration of Jews from Germany. They appealed to well-to-do emigrants to cover the emigration costs of the less wealthy, to those who had already left for donations from their blocked German bank accounts, and to foreign aid organizations for the payment of ship passages. They informed readers of the *Jüdische Nachrichtenblatt* about the few remaining opportunities for asylum in South America, the Caribbean, or Shanghai, when more sought-after countries had stopped admitting refugees. Thus, most of the people who left Germany were either relatively young, affluent, equipped with the necessary language or desirable professional skills, or had relatives abroad. Besides people who chose not to emigrate for political or emotional reasons, the majority of those who stayed behind were elderly, ill, or unable to work. Caring for these people absorbed a large part of the resources of the Reichsvereinigung, which was obliged to set up in large numbers asylums, homes, and soup kitchens.[10] The RSHA granted the larger official Jewish communities permission to continue their work as local chapters of the Reichsvereinigung. Beyond the tasks already mentioned, these local communities also continued to care for the religious needs of the Jewish population. Communities that declined in size to fewer than one thousand members were dissolved as independent organizations and incorporated into the Reichsvereinigung. By the end of 1941, fourteen regional offices of the Reichsvereinigung, the organization's headquarters in Berlin, and seventeen larger local Jewish communities were still in existence.

Although all functionaries in the Reichsvereinigung considered emigration to be their primary goal, there were great differences among them about how to pursue this aim. Larger communities wanted to negotiate directly with aid organizations and seek donations, whereas the Reichsvereinigung favored a centralized scheme under their control. In the Berlin headquarters, a group of representatives led by Paul Eppstein hoped to implement an organized scheme of emigration in cooperation with destination countries that would span a period of several years.[11] Following the failed conference in Evian-les-Bains in July 1938, however, and in particular after the war had begun and Germany's borders had been closed, this idea proved to be utopian. The Zionist organizations had set up *hachschara* sites where young people, whose physical stamina and character had been tested, were trained primarily in agriculture and the trades in preparation for emigration to Palestine. These young emigrants were to build *Eretz Israel* and fight in the Haganah for a Jewish state. According to the Zionists' plans, at least 70 percent of each transport to Palestine was to consist of people whom they considered suitable for these tasks and who were between the ages of eighteen and twenty-eight. As long as other opportunities for emigration still existed, this selection procedure was not controversial. Such alternatives, however, gradually disappeared. If the Reichsvereinigung could secure immigration certificates, then these could be used to effect the release of Jewish prisoners from concentration camps. When the only remaining immigration certificates to be had were for Palestine, demands swelled to open these transport lists to include older people and those who had not completed *hachschara*.[12] Once the war began and Polish Jews were also being rounded up, brought to concentration camps, and were dying there in great numbers, the conflict escalated further over whether it was preferable to make use of the few remaining opportunities to save German Jews rather than to save Eastern European Jews.[13]

Among the ranks of Zionists, there were controversies over other fundamental issues as well. From the outset, Austrian Jews hired agents to organize illegal immigration to Palestine. German Jews, in contrast, wanted to organize things on their own. They managed to adhere to the principle of legality until they were forced to change their strategy because no legal immigration opportunities remained. Paul Eppstein, in particular, refused to fund transports in advance that sent emigrants on unapproved routes with unseaworthy ships. There have been rumors that his colleagues spent part of their energy on misleading him with respect to the actual nature of some transports.[14] The Gestapo, in contrast, insisted on illegal emigration. When Eppstein refused to agree to a risky transport to Palestine in 1940, they arrested him and detained him for four months.[15] Following this arbitrary act by the Gestapo, Eppstein's predilection for legalism was transformed into something more like anticipatory obedience. For the purposes of this essay, these brief references to policy conflict with respect to emigration policies must suffice.[16] What is important is that German-Jewish functionaries saw themselves *simultaneously* facing emigration as well as expulsion and deportation in these transition years between 1939 and 1941.

In this period, the Nazi leadership as well as the individual Gauleiter (Nazi district leaders) repeatedly ordered that Jews be deported, purportedly either for military reasons or as part of "settlements" policies. In October 1938, 17,000 Jews of Polish origin were expelled from Germany to Poland. In further operations after the war began, Jews were brought to the Lublin District in the General Government in Poland and to Gurs in unoccupied France.[17] The Reichsvereinigung usually learned of these deportations accidentally, at the last minute, or even after the fact; their protests were generally futile. I would like to illustrate this by retracing briefly the deportation of Jews from Stettin in 1940.

On 12 February 1940, more than one thousand Jewish residents of Stettin were ordered to pack their belongings within a few hours. These orders came as a surprise, and yet the Stettin Jews had been anticipating this kind of operation from one day to the next. On 1 January 1940, the rabidly anti-Semitic Gauleiter, Franz Schwede-Coburg, and the local mayor had announced in writing to the Jews of Stettin and Pomerania that they would be obliged to move into an empty department store within two weeks. Paul Hirschfeld, a member of the board of the Stettin Jewish community, had been informed of the impending move, but he did not pass this knowledge on to the Reichsvereinigung headquarters, which learned of these occurrences from a Jewish woman who had been ordered to move. The Berlin office intervened successfully with the RSHA, which had not been in charge of the operation but subsequently did halt its implementation.

The Jewish residents of Stettin feared—quite rightly—that the Nazi Party authorities would not accept this change of plans. Indeed, a second attempt was undertaken; this time, the RSHA was included in the plans from the beginning. Heydrich announced on 30 January 1940 that the Stettin Jews would be deported shortly. Less than two weeks later, police, SS, and SA appeared and arrested all Jews, except those who were married to non-Jews. The people rounded up were deported to the Lublin District in Poland in a train transport that also included Jews from Pomerania. Many of those deported died in transit, and some 30 percent of the survivors died within six months due to inhuman living conditions.[18] The Reichsvereinigung was not informed and had no opportunity to intervene. Paul Eppstein, who was obliged to appear at the RSHA for regular meetings, pointed out "that this kind of transport seriously threatens the work of the Reichsvereinigung."[19] He was told that the RSHA was also opposed to such transports and that further operations of this kind "would presumably not occur."[20] All this was in spite of the fact that Heydrich had been involved in the decision-making process! Moreover, the Gestapo was already planning the next deportation from Schneidemühl. Apparently, the lower-ranking representatives of the RSHA with whom Eppstein negotiated were no better informed than the representatives of the Jewish organization.

There was little the Reichsvereinigung could do for the Jews of Stettin. It was only granted permission to send a representative there. With funds supplied by the Reichsvereinigung, this emissary bought the deportees' property back from the Nationalsozialistische Volkswohlfahrt (National Socialist People's Welfare Agency, or NSV), which had misappropriated it. The Reichsvereinigung's representative also organized aid for a few people who had been left behind because they were infirm or aged.[21] And, as a further result of these events, the Reichsvereinigung unseated Paul Hirschfeld, the member of the board of the Jewish community who had failed to inform the central office. As far as the deportations from Schneidemühl were concerned, the Reichsvereinigung at least succeeded in reducing the number of Jews deported to 165, fewer than originally planned.[22] But what was to prove of much greater consequence was a fundamental decision reached by the RSHA in this period, namely, that Eppstein was forbidden to undertake any action on behalf of the deported Jews once they reached their destination.[23] This principle was to remain in effect for subsequent deportations.

The functionaries of the Reichsvereinigung did, however, prevent one mass deportation. There were plans to deport the some 1,000 Jewish inhabitants of East Frisia and Oldenburg to Lublin as well. The Reichsvereinigung assured the Gestapo that they could relocate these people quickly and inexpensively and, within three weeks, found new quarters for them in Berlin, Hamburg, and Hannover.[24] For the most part, however, even before the mass deportations from Germany began, Jewish leaders were forced to witness the course of events without any opportunity to act. The Reichsvereinigung struggled to keep up with events. An attempt was made at one point to organize a silent protest. In reaction to the deportation of 6,500 Jews from Baden and the Palatinate in October 1940, Julius Seligsohn, a member of the executive board of the Reichsvereingung, called on rabbis to announce a day of fasting throughout the Reich. The day of fasting was banned and Seligsohn paid for this initiative with his life.[25]

Today, it is common knowledge that the Nazi state sought "territorial solutions" before it conceived of the indiscriminate murder of all Jews, called the "final solution." Some examples include the short-lived Lublin Reservation of 1939 and the so-called Madagascar Plan of 1940, which had intended to move large numbers of Jews from Greater Germany and from German-occupied territories in Europe to eastern Poland and to Madagascar respectively. The Reichsvereinigung was not involved in these utopian plans, but found itself confronted with them at certain points. For example, following the German attack on France in 1940, the RSHA demanded that Jewish leaders produce within twenty-four hours a plan for relocating seven and one-half million European Jews, "an opportunity of a kind that National Socialism has never before given to a Jewish organization."[26] The Jewish leaders assumed that the destination was to be Palestine. After two days, they answered that they would first have to conduct more intensive investigations. The RSHA interpreted this answer as an attempt to buy time. It confronted Paul Eppstein and Otto Hirsch with its intention, under these circumstances, to ship the Jews off to Madagascar—at the expense of the "Jewish millionaires" in the United States.[27]

Arrests of Jewish functionaries became increasingly frequent in 1940 and 1941. The case of Julius Seligsohn has already been mentioned. Seligsohn was tormented to death in the Sachsenhausen concentration camp; his colleague Otto Hirsch died in the Mauthausen concentration camp, to name only two examples. In this transition phase, Jewish functionaries were regularly permitted to travel abroad to negotiate with aid organizations, but their personal plans to emigrate were thwarted, and they were forced to relinquish their passports after each trip. Paul Eppstein's sister-in-law later aptly described a situation that was characteristic of the plight of Eppstein and others: "Paul and

Hedwig never received permission to leave Germany at the same time. One of the passports was always retained. One was always the hostage for the other."[28]

Why did Jewish functionaries return from their trips abroad? Why did they not take the opportunity to flee Germany? Of course, they could not have known how the persecution of the Jews was to end, but the situation was threatening enough as it was. In my estimation, a highly developed sense of responsibility, external coercion, and exaggerated self-confidence came together to prevent their leaving. In later accounts, not only Leo Baeck but nearly every Jewish representative was described as having wanted to put his skills to use for the remaining Jews in Germany. One of the few survivors later explained that Eppstein, for example, aimed to preserve the independence of the Jewish administration in order to prevent the worst from happening. According to Eppstein, that goal could only be realized if the Jews themselves carried out all orders in a manner that did not offer the Gestapo any excuse for taking over the administration of Jewish affairs themselves.[29] Moreover, in Eppstein's view, he himself was more or less the only person capable of fulfilling this task.

Nevertheless, many of the functionaries themselves attempted to flee when it was already too late. In February 1941, the Reichsvereinigung had applied to the American Jewish Joint Distribution Committee

FIGURE 6.1.: Paul Eppstein, member of the board of the Reichsvertretung der Juden in Deutschland, ca. 1935. *Courtesy*: Stadtarchiv Mannheim, Nachlass Paul Eppstein.

(AJDC) for visas for all of the leading German-Jewish functionaries in Germany, but these visas were no longer of any use to them.[30]

The Deportation of German Jews (1941–1943)

In October 1941, representatives of the Reichsvereinigung recorded—as a measure of the success of their work—that some 70,000 German Jews had left the country during the two years of the organization's existence. About 10,000, however, had been deported to the district of Lublin or to Gurs in France during the same period, a sign that the Reichsvereinigung had been unable to prevent the brutal dynamics of Nazi policy against the Jews from taking its course. It had achieved, at best, deferment or mitigation. Although the Nazis continued to deny it, the Reichsvereinigung leaders realized that they themselves were also trapped. When the Jewish functionaries were told in October 1941 that emigration was to be banned for all Jews, the Nazi leaders added a lie to this announcement. They asserted this ban was to hold for all members of the Reichsvereinigung, but not for its functionaries.[31]

At that time, about 73,000 Jews lived in Berlin, the capital of the Reich. This was more than one-third of Germany's remaining Jewish population. Some of the Berlin Jewish community's functionaries were ordered to report to the Gestapo in early October. They were told that a "relocation" of the Berlin Jews was to begin. The community had to cooperate, or else the SA and SS would take over.[32] After joint consultations, the executive boards of the Reichsvereinigung and the Jewish community decided—in view of the threats about the SA and the SS and "despite serious reservations"—on a strategy of cooperation. They intended to "prevent anything worse," and hoped "in this way to be able to do as much good as possible in the interest of those affected."[33] Perhaps they also expected that the chaos of the previous two years would now give way to an orderly process in which they could take part and potentially intervene. In any event, Jewish leaders assumed that only some of the German Jews would be affected by the deportations. After the partial deportation was over, the Jewish representatives could continue administering and caring for the welfare of those that remained in the community. At this point as well as later, they felt forced to accept the obligation of concealing their knowledge about the deportations from their members, especially since this order from the RSHA had been underlined with the threat of incarceration in a concentration camp.

Thus, the Berlin headquarters of the Reichsvereinigung, its regional offices, and the remaining local Jewish communities took on the tasks assigned them by the RSHA and the Gestapo. The Reichsvereinigung compiled one central file and numerous regional files. These files were used by the Gestapo as the basis for the deportation lists. At times, the Jewish functionaries also drew up lists of specific groups of people who were to be deported. In most cases, the Jews had already been drawn together in certain neighborhoods or in so-called *Judenhäuser* (Jewish houses) in the preceding years. Now the Reichsvereinigung set up *Sammellager* (assembly camps) in exhibition halls, gymnasiums, taverns, or public institutions from which the Jews were picked up for deportation. In these assembly camps, the Reichsvereinigung organized camp leadership, medical services, and food. The Reichsvereinigung informed people of their impending deportation by mail or messenger, and sent out marshals to collect their luggage. Later, Jewish marshals also had to accompany Gestapo men who picked up the Jewish deportees. Reichsvereinigung staff members assisted the deportees in filling out property lists. These lists made it easier for the German authorities to confiscate property left behind after the transports had departed. The Reichsvereinigung also appointed people to oversee the transports, collected money from the deportees to pay for the transports and transferred it to the Gestapo. Later, the Reichsvereinigung for a time assumed responsibility for postal service in and out of the ghettos and camps. This included, in the earliest phase, delivering urns with the ashes of Jewish *Schutzhäftlinge* (prisoners in protective custody) who had died.[34]

Hopes of being able to prevent the worst from occurring were fulfilled only in a few cases. In the larger cities, deportation of those who were ill was deferred (until the end of 1942).[35] The orders and guidelines for deportations sent to the Gestapo by the RSHA also stipulated that certain groups of people were to be excluded: Jews who worked in the armaments industry, people older than sixty-five, invalids between the ages of fifty-five and sixty-five, those with non-Jewish spouses, Jews of foreign citizenship, and those who had been awarded military honors in World War I.[36] If the Gestapo did not adhere to its own guidelines, then the Jewish functionaries at times protested successfully. The Theresienstadt ghetto, originally earmarked for Czech Jews, was expanded to serve as a "ghetto for the elderly" and a *Vorzugslager*, a camp for the privileged. Later, Theresienstadt became the destination for Jewish spouses and their children from mixed marriages, which had since been dissolved. After June 1942, transports with those who had been deferred rolled into the old garrison town, which was considered a "good" deportation destination. Reichsvereinigung staff filled out *Heimeinkaufsverträge* (home purchase contracts) for the elderly, as if they were buying into a nursing home and paying for it with all they owned. The Reichsvereinigung collected these sums in a central account and transferred millions of marks to an account in Prague.[37]

Limited as they were at the outset, the opportunities for the Reichsvereinigung to intervene had dissolved almost completely by the spring of 1942. This was the same period in which the program for systematically murdering the Jews in the East was being established. Following the assassination of Heydrich in May 1942 and the arsonist attack by a communist-Jewish group, the Baum Group, on an anti-Soviet exhibition in Berlin, Berlin's NSDAP Gauleiter Joseph Goebbels ordered 250 Jews shot in the nearby Sachsenhausen concentration camp. The same number was arrested in Berlin and brought to Sachsenhausen. The executive boards of the Jewish communities in Berlin, Prague, and Vienna, as well as the representatives of the Reichsvereinigung, were ordered to report to the RSHA and to stand there for hours, their faces turned to the wall. They did not receive an explanation until some time later.[38] This image of the waiting functionaries is a fitting symbol of their situation in spring 1942. Without information, without any opportunities for movement, exchange, or escape, they were condemned to wait. Their own lives were in danger, and they had no choice but to obey orders. The period in which it had been possible to negotiate or to mitigate a specific situation was over, once and for all. They had themselves become hostages.

Although the Reichsvereinigung could hardly influence the course of Nazi persecution of the Jews, it did have—for the moment—an important function in protecting its staff. Even after the deportations had begun, the organization and its many branches offered several thousand Jews the opportunity to provide evidence that they had paid or unpaid employment. This evidence protected the employees and their families from being deported. In 1942, in Berlin alone, the Reichsvereinigung had more than 1,500 employees who worked in the administration, in hospitals, schools, daycare centers, orphanages, training centers, soup kitchens, or clothing rooms.[39] When departments were dissolved, as was the case with the Kulturbund (Culture League) in September 1941, or the schools department in June 1942, the Reichsvereinigung sought to transfer these employees to other sections. Until the spring of 1943, the department that was involved in the deportations was still expanding.

Although the RSHA repeatedly pressured the organization to fire staff members, the total size of the staff declined very slowly. Finally, the RSHA forced the department heads to select "expendable" employees who were to be deported with their families. Nearly 900 people were deported.[40] Shortly thereafter, deportation expert Alois Brunner and his henchmen were sent from Vienna to Berlin and the situation escalated further. This group conducted raids in residential areas, ordered the deportation of the occupants of entire orphanages, elderly homes, etc., or all members of a certain profession. They transformed the assembly camp into a prison, and reorganized the marshals. The response to these occurrences was the first wave of Berlin Jews going underground.[41]

The top-level functionaries remained in their posts despite the fact that, as highly exposed persons, they lived in constant danger. Many had already been murdered because of alleged offenses, among them Conrad Cohn, Cora Berliner, and Paula Fürst. Some eleven thousand "armament Jews" fell prey to the so-called factory operation. Berlin Jews employed in the weapons industry were rounded up in late February and early March 1943 in factories, on the streets, and in their living quarters, and were deported.[42] The second wave of Berlin Jews went into hiding.[43]

The heads of the Jewish communities and the Reichsvereinigung were unable to react to these developments because they had been deported in January 1943. In 1942, the RSHA had warned the local Gestapo offices not to deport the highly useful Jewish leaders. One year later, it was of the opinion that their tasks had been nearly completed. According to survivor Erich Simon, the leading functionaries were brought to the "privileged camp" in Theresienstadt as a "reward for trouble-free cooperation."[44] The Nazis deceived the deportees again, as they had before with respect to the functionaries' opportunities for emigrating. When Paul Eppstein was appointed head of the ghetto in Theresienstadt, the RSHA deceived him into thinking that this was simply a continuation of his position as head of the Reichsvereinigung in Berlin. He was told he would remain on the Berlin executive board as an "absentee," maintain his residence in Berlin, and be permitted to travel there for important meetings. Eppstein never returned to Berlin.[45] Leo Baeck and other functionaries were forced to "relocate" to Theresienstadt together with Eppstein. Six months later, in June 1943, their successors, Kurt Levy and Moritz Henschel, arrived in Theresienstadt together with their families and the heads of the now-dissolved regional offices.

FIGURE 6.2.: Paul Eppstein, Elder of Jews in Theresienstadt, August/September 1944. *Courtesy*: Stadtarchiv Mannheim, Nachlass Paul Eppstein.

Once they had recovered from this rude awakening, Paul Eppstein and the other German functionaries found that in Theresienstadt they could—and according to their own understanding, were obliged to—continue their activities in the interests of those entrusted to them. This now involved assembling transports to the extermination camps on orders from the SS. The SS fixed the total number of people per transport as well as which groups were to be included and which were not. There was also a list of the Jews who were to be deported without fail.[46] The German-Jewish functionaries were now making decisions they had never wanted to make. While still in Germany, they had contributed to the Nazi regime's preparations for deportations; in Theresienstadt, they were *themselves* compiling the deportation lists. Although they were following strict orders, *they* prepared most of the lists, the people selected appealed to *them*, and *they* checked off the names before the transports left.

Until the fall of 1944, the Jewish functionaries were spared deportation as "important persons." At this point, however, the tasks that Paul Eppstein and the other members of the executive board were supposed to fulfill were finished in Theresienstadt as well. Paul Eppstein was apparently shot on 28 September 1944. Most of the others were sent to Auschwitz in the large-scale transports that left Theresienstadt in October 1944. Very few people in these transports survived.[47]

Did the Jewish functionaries know that, from October 1941 on, the deportations meant a death sentence for those involved? Perhaps, but in this early phase, German Jews were dying in large numbers as a result of the life-threatening conditions, whereas the victims of mass executions were Jews from the occupied territories in the East. By the spring of 1942, this had changed, and news had arrived that made it quite clear what was happening at the destinations of those who were deported. Most functionaries preferred not to see the terrible truth. Did they know in Theresienstadt that the people who were being transported elsewhere faced certain death? Probably. Leo Baeck, who was informed in Theresienstadt about the gas chambers in Auschwitz, decided not to pass on this knowledge in order to make the situation more bearable.[48] After the war, other survivors, such as Erich Fabian and Moritz Henschel, insisted that they had not known what was happening.[49]

The Intermediaries (1943–1945)

By June 1943, the Reichsvereinigung had become superfluous in the eyes of the Nazi regime. The only Jews remaining in Germany were some 16,600 people married to non-Jewish spouses.[50] The RSHA decreed that their affairs should be placed in the hands of the rump Reichsvereinigung, which was to organize their deportation when the marriage ended due to death or divorce. To this end, *Vertrauensmänner* (intermediaries) were appointed for the organization's headquarters and its regional offices. They were primarily Jewish physicians or lawyers who were partners in mixed marriages, had worked for the Reichsvereinigung before, and who were accepted by the Gestapo. They were obliged to negotiate with the local Gestapo, supply statistical reports on a regular basis, and complete deportees' *Heimeinkaufsverträge* for Theresienstadt. Moreover, they served as a clearing-house for all applications that spouses in mixed marriages wished to submit to the authorities. Most of these *Vertrauensmänner*, in particular Walter Lustig, the head of the Berlin office, were reputed to be willing henchmen or accomplices of the Gestapo. But there is little evidence to support this allegation. Instead, existing documents indicate that most of these men tried to follow the Gestapo's orders without exception, while at the same time attempting to protect their fellow Jews, resisting growing tendencies to centralize the administration, or trying to save their personnel from deportation. With the increasing disintegration of Nazi rule and the effects of Allied bombings, Germany's devastated infrastructure and non-existent communication channels provided the *Vertrauensmänner* with an excuse for acting on their own authority. But until May 1945, these intermediaries were subject to the control of both the Reichsvereinigung's own Berlin headquarters—which had to secure the RSHA's approval for all its activities—and of local Gestapo authorities. This meant that their room to maneuver was severely limited.[51] In February and March 1945, the RSHA ordered that the deferred Jewish spouses in mixed marriages were to be deported. Despite the fact that the end of the war was obviously imminent, the Nazi regime planned to deport the last remaining Jews from Germany. Most of those deported in these final transports and a majority of the *Vertrauensmänner* survived the Third Reich.

The lives of some *Vertrauensmänner* were in danger once again when Allied troops marched into Germany. As noted at the beginning of this paper, Walter Lustig's compliant cooperation with the Gestapo cost him his life. Other former functionaries also faced the bitter lesson that the dangerous posts they had taken on under duress—positions that had conferred upon them real or supposed power over their fellow-Jews—now proved to be disadvantageous. The occupation forces of the United States, for example, found the Jewish *Vertrauensmann* in Munich guilty of being an informer. He was sentenced to ten years of forced labor and released from prison after three years. The Dresden intermediary, who was also sentenced to several years of hard labor by a Soviet tribunal, died in a camp one year after his colleague from Munich was set free.[52]

Bureaucratic Rules as a Bulwark Against Murder?
A Few Concluding Remarks

In my opinion, H.G. Adler is mistaken when he apodictically declares that by the time the deportations began, the leading Jewish functionaries were already completely paralyzed and did not know "what they were doing."[53] Despite increasingly difficult conditions in the period between 1939 and 1941, Jewish functionaries organized emigration for thousands of Jews in order to rescue them from Nazi terror. The realization that there was nothing they could do for those who had already been deported led them to intensify these efforts. When mass deportations began in 1941, Jewish functionaries cooperated in organizing them. They hoped to regulate and thus make more tolerable what had previously been a chaotic and violent process. They assumed that a Jewish community would still exist at the end of this process, and they became increasingly co-opted by the Nazis' plans as they continued to pursue this strategy, long after they had forfeited previous minimal opportunities to influence the course of events. They continued to respect the secrecy requirement imposed by the Nazis, and struggled to obey all orders to a fault, leaving the Nazis no reason to take over these tasks themselves. In this respect, I consider Raul Hilberg's assessment to be correct, namely, that the Reichsvereinigung was a kind of Jewish Council,[54] even if the German Jews did not live in a ghetto.

Hannah Arendt's critique goes far beyond this position. In her opinion, the German-Jewish representatives were "voluntary custodians of the secrets" that the Nazis obliged them to keep and helped guarantee peace and order during the process of extermination. Without their cooperation, chaos and misery would have reigned, but the total number of victims would have been lower.[55] One can counter this position by pointing out that all of the existing documents and survivors' accounts provide some indications of the efforts made by functionaries to ward off disaster and rescue at least some of the Jews. Their concern for the Jewish community led them to adopt a strategy of cooperation.[56] Germany's Jewish population had a large portion of elderly people who depended on assistance. In my estimation, it is highly unlikely that, had the Jewish functionaries refused to cooperate, a considerably higher number of German Jews would have been able to save themselves. German Jews could neither flee to neighboring countries, nor could they have fled into the forests to join partisan groups. They lived in the midst of the German population, robbed of their financial assets, socially isolated, and controlled from all sides.

Nonetheless, Otto Dov Kulka considers the Reichsvereinigung to have been primarily a closed, pluralistic-democratic community that preserved elements of former Jewish life, such as education and social welfare activities in the midst of a totalitarian terror state.[57] Kulka's perspective on the Reichsvereinigung, however, hardly takes into account the extent of its cooperation with the Nazis in preparing the deportations, the work of German-Jewish functionaries in Theresienstadt, and the activities of the Jewish *Vertrauensmänner* from 1943 to 1945.

Why did the Jewish functionaries take on these dangerous positions that cost most of them their lives? Out of a highly developed sense of responsibility and an exaggerated level of self-confidence and because they were coerced into doing so—that is the answer supplied earlier. With what means could they confront the implementation of the "final solution"? Many high-level Jewish functionaries were lawyers and economists who had held upper-echelon positions in government administration before the Nazis came to power. The Reichsvereinigung's apparatus, with its many departments and sections, its predetermined areas of competence, its rigid structures and regulations, and its "chain of command," closely paralleled the government administration. When Eppstein was ordered to report to the RSHA, his "higher authority," he regularly took minutes of the meetings. Ignoring the humiliating forms of communication, he recorded the orders given, his own suggestions for implementing them, and the reactions of the other side. All of this was written in a language that was demonstratively matter-of-fact and bureaucratic. The complete version of these minutes went to the RSHA and the executive board of the Reichsvereinigung. Certain sections were sent as memos to the appropriate department heads or staff members. Apparently, the aim was to record in writing anything that pertained in the broadest sense to the deportations, and to deal with these matters in a manner that was transparent, comprehensible, consistent, and independent of the persons involved.

Administrative authorities normally work dependably and in accordance with the law. The Jewish functionaries followed the principles of this type of "old-style administration." They expected that such bureaucratic rules would act as a counterweight to arbitrariness, violence, and murder. That such bureaucratic rules and mass murder by no means precluded one another but might, on the contrary, form a tight bond, contradicted the personal experience of these Jewish functionaries. The National Socialists, in contrast, propagated the ideal of a "fighting administration" that was not bound by norms and the law. The RSHA was the prototypical model. Michael Wildt has referred to this kind of authority as a "new type of institution" because of its structure, which went unchecked by regulations and laws and its directors who alternatively organized the process of deportations and mass murder in the "killing fields" in the East.[58] The Reichsvereinigung's functionaries interpreted their "old-style administration" as a bulwark against the corruption, exploitation, arbitrariness, and inhumanity all around them. Even in Theresienstadt, they persevered and created an oversized administrative apparatus. The commission that compiled the deportation lists there, for example, consisted of forty-three people, all of whom held positions entitling them to participate in these decisions. But preserving an administration that functioned methodically and followed the rules proved to be a pitifully helpless strategy for averting what Dan Diner has termed the "rupture of civilization." Survivor Erich Simon later summarized his position and that of his murdered companions as follows: "Horrible, when one thinks back today, but it [the cooperation with the Nazis] happened in the interest of our people, from the perspective of the time; we believed that by cooperating we had accompanied them into a foreign situation in an orderly manner."[59]

Notes

1. Landesarchiv Berlin (hereafter LAB): Rep. 20, No. 4616–4617, Announcement of the Jewish Community in Berlin, 12 July 1945.
2. See Beate Meyer, "Gratwanderung zwischen Verantwortung und Verstrickung— Die Reichsvereinigung der Juden in Deutschland und die Jüdische Gemeinde zu Berlin 1938–1945," in *Juden in Berlin 1938–1945*, ed. Beate Meyer and Hermann Simon (Berlin: Philo Verlagsgesellschaft, 2000), 291–337.
3. Allied Control Council, Act No. 1, 20 September 1945, I.1.
4. See Esriel Hildesheimer, *Jüdische Selbstverwaltung unter dem NS-Regime. Der Existenzkampf der Reichsvertretung und Reichsvereinigung der Juden in Deutschland* (Tübingen: Mohr/Siebeck, 1994); Otto Dov Kulka, *Deutsches Judentum unter dem Nationalsozialismus. Dokumente zur Geschichte der Reichsvertretung der deutschen Juden 1933–1939*, Vol. 1 (Tübingen: Mohr/Siebeck, 1995); and Otto Dov Kulka, "The Reichsvereinigung and the Fate of the German Jews, 1938/1939–1943. Continuity or Discontinuity in German-Jewish History in the Third Reich," in *Die Juden im nationalsozialistischen Deutschland/The Jews in Nazi Germany*, ed. Arnold Paucker (Tübingen: Mohr/Siebeck, 1986), 353–363.
5. *Leo Baeck Institute* (hereafter: LBI), Jerusalem: D 52, 556/2, D 24, 556/1, Reichsvereinigung der Juden in Deutschland, Circular Letter No. 454, 3 February 1939; see also Yehoyakim Cochavi, "'The Hostile Alliance': The Relationship between the Reichsvereinigung of Jews in Germany and the Regime," *Yad Vashem Studies* 22 (1992):237 –272.
6. See Michael Wildt, *Die Judenpolitik des SD 1935 bis 1938. Eine Dokumentation* (Munich: Oldenbourg Verlag, 1995).
7. *Reichsgesetzblatt* 1939: 10. Verordnung zum Reichsbürgergesetz, 4 July 1939, 1097.
8. See Gudrun Maierhof, *Selbstbehauptung im Chaos. Frauen in der Jüdischen Selbsthilfe 1933–1943* (Frankfurt am Main: Campus, 2002).
9. See Avraham Barkai, "Von Berlin nach Theresienstadt. Zur politischen Biographie von Leo Baeck 1933–1945," in Avraham Barkai, *Hoffnung und Untergang. Studien*

zur deutsch-jüdischen Geschichte des 19. und 20. Jahrhunderts (Hamburg: Christians Verlag, 1998), 141–165.
10. See Maierhof, Selbstbehauptung, and Wolf Gruner, "Armut und Verfolgung. Die Reichsvereinigung, die jüdische Bevölkerung und die antijüdische Politik im NS-Staat 1939 bis 1945," in *Juden und Armut in Mittel- und Osteuropa*, ed. Stefi Jersch Wenzel (Cologne/Weimar/Vienna: Böhlau, 2000), 405–433.
11. See LBI, New York: AR 7171, Letter Leo Loewenstein to Ernst Noah, Martin Salomonski, Heinrich Stahl, und Hermann Stern, 20 February 1940.
12. See Yad Vashem Archives, Jerusalem (hereafter YVA): 01/226, Benno Cohn et al, "Verschiedene Informationen über die jüdische Situation in Berlin in den Jahren von 1933 bis 1940, Sitzung des Arbeitskreises von Zionisten aus Deutschland on 20 May 1958," 5.
13. See Recha Freier, *Let the Children Come* (London: Weidenfeld and Nicolson, 1961), 64–74; Yfaat Weiss, *Deutsche und polnische Juden vor dem Holocaust. Jüdische Identität zwischen Staatsbürgerschaft und Ethnizität 1933–1940* (Munich: Oldenbourg, 2000), 211–217.
14. YVA: 01/320, K. J. Ball, Illegale Aliya (!) 1939/1940 aus Hitler-Deutschland, 32.
15. YVA: 02/283, Michael Meyer, Emigration to Palestine during the War, 10.
16. The author is working on a comprehensive study on the Reichsvereinigung and the deportations. It is due to be published in 2009.
17. See Wolf Gruner, "Von der Kollektivausweisung zur Deportation der Juden aus Deutschland (1938–1945)," in *Die Deportation der Juden aus Deutschland. Plaene—Praxis—Reaktionen*, ed. Birthe Kundrus and Beate Meyer (Göttingen: Wallstein, 2004), 21–62.
18. See Wiener Library, London: P. III.c.No. 622, Evakuierung der Juden aus Stettin, 1 September 1940. For the living conditions in the Lublin district, see Robert Kuwalek, "Das kurze Leben 'im Osten.' Jüdische Deutsche im Distrikt Lublin aus polnisch-jüdischer Sicht," in Kundrus and Meyer, *Deportation*, 112–134, here: 112–119.
19. Archive Centrum Judaicum, Berlin (hereafter ACJ): 2 B 1/1, Memo written by Eppstein, 19 February 1940, 3f.
20. Ibid., 4.
21. Bundesarchiv, Berlin (hereafter Barch): R 8150, 1.1., Minutes of the Board Meeting [Protokoll der Vorstandssitzung] of the Reichsvereinigung, 29 February 1940, No. 3; see also Archive of the Forschungsstelle für Zeitgeschichte, Hamburg: Schottelius on an Interview with Max Plaut, 11 July 1953, 4.
22. ACJ: 2 B 1/1, Memo written by Eppstein, 19 February 1940.
23. LBI, Jerusalem: D 52, 556/2, Memo written by Hirsch, 28 October 1940.
24. YVA: 01/53, Max Plaut, "Die Juden in Deutschland von 1939 bis 1941," 6.
25. See Hildesheimer, *Selbstverwaltung*, 200f., and Meyer, "Gratwanderung," 297–320.
26. Yedioth Hayom, 2 May 1941, "Das Nein der deutschen Juden. Hinter den Kulissen des Madagaskar-Plans," 11.
27. Ibid., 12; see also, Anonymous Report, compiled by the Jewish Agency, Geneva, February 1940, in *Archives of the Holocaust. An International Collection of Selected Documents*, ed. Francis Nicosia, Vol. 4 (New York/London: Taylor and Francis, 1990), Docs. 4, 9.

28. Archiv der Stadt Mannheim: 27/2002/7, Collection Paul Eppstein, Report Paula Eppstein, 1 July 1994, 9.
29. LBI, Jerusalem: 643, Berthold Simonsohn, Gedenkblatt für Paul Eppstein, 18 September 1959, 1f.
30. Archive of the AJDC, New York: Collection 33/44, File 631/2 of 2, Memorandum, 26 February 1941, Request from Dr. Meyerheim.
31. LBI, New York: AR 25033, Collection Rischkowsky, Memo written by Eppstein, 24 October 1941.
32. LAB: Rep. 235–07, MF 4170–4171, Martha Mosse, Erinnerungen, Attachment: Die Jüdische Gemeinde zu Berlin 1934–1943, 23/24 July 1958, 2.
33. Ibid. See also Leo Baeck, "A People Stands before its God," in *We survived. The Story of Fourteen of the Hidden and the Hunted of Nazi Germany*, ed. Eric H. Boehm (New Haven: Yale University Press, 1949), 288.
34. See Meyer, "Gratwanderung," and Meyer, "Handlungsspielräume regionaler jüdischer Repräsentanten (1941–1945). Die Reichsvereinigung der Juden in Deutschland und die Deportationen," in Kundrus and Meyer, *Deportation*, 63–85.
35. See Rivka Elkin, *"Das Jüdische Krankenhaus muss erhalten bleiben." Das Jüdische Krankenhaus in Berlin zwischen 1938 und 1945* (Berlin: Edition Hentrich, 1993), 46f.
36. See Guidelines in Alfred Gottwaldt and Diana Schulle, *Die "Judendeportationen" aus dem Deutschen Reich 1941–1945* (Wiesbaden: Marix Verlag, 2005), 56ff, 140ff, 148ff.
37. See Miroslav Kárný, "Theresienstadt 1941–1945," in *Theresienstädter Gedenkbuch. Die Opfer der Judentransporte aus Deutschland nach Theresienstadt 1942–1945*, ed. Theresienstädter Initiative (Prague: Academia, 2000), 15f.
38. See Elke Froehlich, ed., *Die Tagebücher von Joseph Goebbels*, Vol. 4 (Munich: Saur, 1987), Notice 24 May 1942, 351f.
39. See Meyer, "Gratwanderung," 309f.
40. Ibid. See also Meyer, "The Inevitable Dilemma: The Reich Association of Jews in Germany, the Deportations, and the Jews Who Went Underground," in *On Germans and Jews under the Nazi Regime: Essays by Three Generations of Historians*, ed. Moshe Zimmermann (Jerusalem: Hebrew University Press, 2006), 297–312.
41. Ibid., 303f.
42. See Wolf Gruner, *Widerstand in der Rosenstrasse. Die Fabrik-Aktion und die Verfolgung der "Mischehen" 1943* (Frankfurt: Fischer Verlag, 2005), 34–84.
43. There were 10,000 to 15,000 German Jews that went underground. This number includes 5,000 to 7,000 Berlin Jews. Of these, 1,400 survived in hiding. See Beate Kosmala, "Zwischen Ahnen und Wissen. Flucht vor der Deportation (1941–1943)," in Kundrus and Meyer, *Deportation*, 135–159.
44. Wiener Library, London: P.III.h. (Theresienstadt), Erich Simon, Theresienstadt als autarkes Stadtwesen, 13 April 1946, 3.
45. See Beate Meyer, "Altersghetto, Vorzugslager und Tätigkeitsfeld. Die Repräsentanten der Reichsvereinigung der Juden in Deutschland und Theresienstadt," in *Theresienstädter Studien und Dokumente 2006* (Prague: Sefer, 2006), 125–151.
46. See Meyer, "Altersghetto," 309f.
47. See Kárný, "Die Theresienstädter Herbsttransporte 1944," in *Theresienstädter Studien und Dokumente 1995* (Prague: Academia, 1995), 7–37.
48. Leonhard Baker, *Hirt der Verfolgten. Leo Baeck im Dritten Reich* (Stuttgart: Klett-Cotta, 1982), 415f.

49. YVA: 01/51, Moritz Henschel Vortrag (Lecture), "Die letzten Jahre der Jüdischen Gemeinde Berlin," given in Tel Aviv 13 September 1946, 3.
50. In 1933, ca. 35,000 German Jews lived in mixed marriages, in 1939, ca. 20,400, and in 1943, ca. 16,600. At the end of 1944, ca. 12,500 remained. See Beate Meyer, *"Jüdische Mischlinge." Rassenpolitik und Verfolgungserfahrung 1933–1945* (Hamburg: Dölling & Galitz Verlag, 1999), 24–95.
51. See Meyer, "Handlungsspielräume," 63ff.
52. For more on the Dresden intermediary Ernst Neumark, see Beate Meyer, "Der 'Eichmann von Dresden.' 'Justizielle Bewältigung' von NS-Verbrechen in der DDR am Beispiel des Verfahrens gegen Henry Schmidt," in *Deutsche, Juden, Völkermord. Der Holocaust in Geschichte und Gegenwart*, ed. Jürgen Matthäus and Klaus-Michael Mallmann (Darmstadt: Wissenschaftliche Buchgesellschaft, 2006), 275–292, here: 279–281.
53. See H.G. Adler, *Der verwaltete Mensch. Studien zur Deportation der Juden aus Deutschland* (Tübingen: Mohr/Siebeck, 1974), 354f.
54. See Raul Hilberg, *Täter, Opfer, Zuschauer. Die Vernichtung der Juden 1933–1945* (Frankfurt: Fischer-Verlag, 1992), 125.
55. See Hannah Arendt, *Eichmann in Jerusalem. Ein Bericht von der Banalität des Bösen* (Leipzig: Reclam, 1990), 220, 230f., 239f.
56. See also Doron Rabinovicis, *Instanzen der Ohnmacht. Wien 1938–1945. Der Weg zum Judenrat* (Frankfurt: Suhrkamp, 2000), 423, for the author's thesis on the Austrian Jewish Leadership.
57. See Kulka, *Reichsvereinigung*, 363.
58. See Michael Wildt, *Generation des Unbedingten. Das Führungskorps des Reichssicherheitshauptamtes* (Hamburg: Hamburger Edition, 2002), 858–861.
59. Wiener Library, London: P.III.h. (Theresienstadt), 894, Dr. Erich Simon Lecture, "Theresienstadt als autarkes Stadtwesen," 3.

Chapter Seven

JEWISH CULTURE IN A MODERN GHETTO

Theater and Scholarship Among the Jews of Nazi Germany

Michael Brenner

JUST A FEW WEEKS AFTER the Nazis had come to power, an impressive call for tolerance and an appeal to grant Jews equal rights could be heard on a Berlin stage. Those demands stemmed from the pen of a non-Jewish German, a true "Aryan" in the Nazi definition. He could hardly be dismissed, for he was one of Germany's greatest writers and philosophers—and he had been dead for 150 years. The capital of the new Nazi state must have been a rather awkward stage for Gotthold Ephraim Lessing's enlightened play *Nathan der Weise* (*Nathan the Wise*). It was hardly dangerous, however, to disseminate Enlightenment ideas among the audience at this play, for this audience did not have to be convinced of the equality of the Jews. It was an exclusively Jewish audience listening to exclusively Jewish voices. The performance of *Nathan the Wise* was the first major production of the Kulturbund deutscher Juden (Cultural League of German Jews), the organization founded to provide Jewish artists, musicians, and actors with work, and to provide Jewish audiences who could no longer attend regular theaters with entertainment.¹ In 1935, the Jewish leadership was obliged by the Gestapo to rename the Kulturbund deutscher Juden the Jüdischer Kulturbund (The Jewish Cultural League), as the Nuremberg Laws no longer recognized the existence of *German* Jews. By 1935, there were some thirty-six different branches of the Kulturbund (usually known in its abbreviated form as, simply, the "Kubu") throughout the German Reich, with over 70,000 members in total. Clearly, the Kubu was for many their only real possibility of attending cultural events.

The Kulturbund was perhaps the most blatant symbol of Nazi Germany's cultural ghettoization of Germany's Jewish community. Jews performed before exclusively Jewish audiences, with the exception of the notorious Gestapo spy in attendance at these performances. In addition to plays like Lessing's *Nathan the Wise*, there were concerts, operas, and recitals. Some of the musicians had been, or were to become, major figures in twentieth-century music. From 1934 to 1936, for instance, the director of music in the Berlin Kulturbund was Hans Wilhelm Steinberg. Steinberg emigrated from Germany to the United States in 1938 where, under the name William Steinberg, he later became the resident-conductor of the Pittsburgh Symphony Orchestra (1952–1976), and music director of the Boston Symphony Orchestra (1969–1973).

Of course, there were also other cultural enterprises that came into existence or were strengthened as a result of this ghettoization. In Nazi Germany, Jews expanded their adult education programs, strengthened their youth movements, and restructured their publishing activities. The Schocken publishing house, founded shortly before the Nazis came to power, launched its *Schocken Bücherei*, an innovative series of small paperbacks on essential Jewish topics. It was a kind of reader's digest of Judaism for a largely assimilated audience that had suddenly been confronted with its Jewishness after 1933. Jewish newspapers continued to be published in Nazi Germany, although censorship by the Nazi state obviously became an increasingly threatening reality.

While the writings of Jewish authors were, on 10 May 1933, burned publicly and increasingly purged from German libraries, Jewish publishing houses were allowed to print Kafka, and Jewish theaters in Nazi Germany were the only places where Lessing's *Nathan the Wise* could be performed. This last blossoming of Jewish cultural activities in times of persecution might seem a paradoxical development. It was, however, the logical consequence of the Nazi policy of separating Jews from non-Jews. Nazi authorities were willing to tolerate, and to some degree even support, Jewish culture, as long as it promoted the regime's goal of complete segregation of Jewish and non-Jewish Germans.

However, for those Jewish Germans who had been part and parcel of Jewish cultural life as it had developed in Germany over the century and a half following the Enlightenment, a flourishing period had clearly come to an end. Many of the artists, musicians, actors, and writers who had turned the 1920s into a golden age of cultural creativity left Germany in the 1930s. They include such prominent figures as

Kurt Weill, Bruno Walter, Otto Klemperer, Elisabeth Bergner, Lion Feuchtwanger, and others. Those who stayed behind were increasingly isolated. The most famous case was probably that of the painter Max Liebermann. As President of the Prussian Academy of Arts between 1920 and 1932, he was not only the most celebrated German painter of his time, but had also risen to a public position that no other Jew had ever achieved in Germany, with the possible exception of the ill-fated foreign minister, Walther Rathenau. In 1933, Liebermann resigned as honorary president of the Academy. He soon became a member of the honorary board of the Kulturbund and was active in the Berlin Jewish Museum, which opened its doors, ironically, a few days after Hitler had been appointed Chancellor. Liebermann became increasingly intrigued by the notion of Jewish art in his later years, and turned again to a biblical motif for one of his last paintings: *The Return of Tobias*. In a letter that Liebermann sent to the mayor of Tel Aviv, Meir Dizengoff, and to the Hebrew national poet, Haym Nahman Bialik, on 28 June 1933, he expressed the profound feeling of illusion that assimilated Jews, such as himself, had shared their whole lives: "Like a horrible nightmare the abrogation of equal rights weighs upon us all, but especially upon those Jews who, like me, had surrendered themselves to the dream of assimilation . . . As difficult as it has been for me, I have awakened from the dream that I dreamed my whole life long."[2]

Liebermann died in 1935. His funeral reflected the growing isolation of German Jewry. Only two non-Jewish friends, the physician Ferdinand Sauerbruch, whom Liebermann had portrayed in 1932, and the artist Käthe Kollwitz dared to attend the ceremony at the Schönhauser Allee Jewish cemetery. One might just imagine how the funeral of the former President of the Prussian Academy of Arts might have looked in better times. At least Max Liebermann died a peaceful death, unlike his widow Martha, who committed suicide when the deportation order reached her in 1943.

Much has been written in recent years about this unwanted revival of Jewish culture.[3] I would like to deal here very briefly with one aspect of this subject, the theater, which received considerable attention, and in more detail with another aspect much neglected so far, namely, the work of Jewish historians in the years between 1933 and 1939. There can be no doubt that the Kulturbund staged an impressive number of plays in the 1930s, provided unemployed actors with a chance to perform, and hungry audiences a way to enjoy culture within a society where they faced more and more restrictions. The Kulturbund's theater was confronted with the difficult task of satisfying the audience's need for German and European theatrical performances that they had been accustomed to seeing and, at the same time, of adding a Jewish experience for a community returned by force to its Jewish roots. The main dramaturge, Julius Bab, stressed this twofold task: "We will create a Jewish stage, which, at the same time, will be a German one."[4] In the beginning, this double function was still possible, but by 1938, no non-Jewish German or Austrian authors or composers could be staged or performed by a Jewish organization. More and more East European Jewish plays were produced, plays that were often translated from the Yiddish originals; moreover, under the leadership of Herbert Freeden, a more Zionist presentation of Jewish life was soon adopted. Still, the most successful play in the 1936–1937 season was neither a Yiddish classic nor a play about Zionist pioneers, but instead was Shakespeare's *A Midsummer Night's Dream*. Indeed, some 80 percent of all plays produced in the Berlin Kulturbund were by non-German authors.

The most intensely debated question surrounding the evaluation of the Kulturbund may be summarized in very simple terms: was the Kulturbund good or bad for the Jews? Opinions have been divided both among contemporaries as well as later historians. On the one hand, Herbert Freeden's judgment, both as a key player in and historian of the Kulturbund, stressed its positive function. He maintains that its activities were a means of spiritual resistance against increasing ghettoization. Most scholars have tended to agree with his position. Thus, Rebecca Rovit concluded her essay on the theatrical performances of the Kulturbund with the statement: "Such community cohesion appears to have strengthened the actors' resolve to use their art to provide both themselves and their audiences with insight and comfort amid extraordinary and extreme circumstances."[5] On the other hand, already occurring in the 1930s were German-Jewish critics making derogatory comments about the compliance with which the Kulturbund responded to the cultural ghettoization of the Jews. One critic observed: "The German Yids were ordered to found a ghetto theater and cultural associations—and they do it . . . The Kulturbund is truly an opportunity to say *nebbich*."[6] Modern historians, especially Eike Geisel and Henryk Broder, continued along this line in their 1992 exhibition on the Kulturbund. By continuing their cultural activities, the Kulturbund activists may have contributed to the notion that life under unacceptable conditions was possible, and thus may have discouraged more German Jews from emigrating.[7]

In many respects, 1933 was also a decisive turning point in German-Jewish scholarship, although it did not mark the end of cultural creativity of German Jewry. The first scholars of *Wissenschaft des Judentums* (Judaic Studies) had already left Germany well before 1933, either because they were Zionists or because they could not get or continue to hold a position at a German university. For example, Fritz Isaac Baer and Gershom Scholem went to Jerusalem, while Eugen Täubler moved to Switzerland and lived there for several years. In 1930, Ismar Elbogen rejected an attractive offer from Columbia University to become the first incumbent of the first chair of Jewish History at a western university. After 1933, Jewish academic institutions such as the Hochschule für die Wissenschaft des Judentums and, to a lesser extent, the orthodox Hildesheimer Rabbinerseminar in Berlin, as well as the Jüdisch-Theologisches Seminar in Breslau, not only lost but also gained faculty members. While some of their own faculty emigrated, others were drawn into those institutions after they had to quit their previous university positions. Thus, teaching continued at both institutions well into the Nazi period.[8]

Moreover, some of the first fruits of the modern Jewish research institutions were harvested in the years after 1933. The first volume of the *Germania Judaica*, which presented the earliest records of Jewish life in many parts of Germany in the Middle Ages, was completed at a time (in 1934) when attempts were underway to systematically eliminate Jews from German society. Just as Lessing's *Nathan the Wise* could be performed only on a Jewish stage in Germany after 1933, and the only critical media were the remaining Jewish newspapers, unbiased research on Jewish topics continued in the cultural ghetto of Jewish teaching and research institutions. In contrast to the two other areas, however, the university remained open to Jewish students, especially of non-German citizenship, until 1937.[9]

While the Jewish teaching institutions in this period have been covered by recent scholarship, less is known about those works of scholarship that were produced outside the "cultural ghetto," be it at German universities or in publicly accessible journals. I also will turn to the other side of scholarship on the Jews in this period, namely, that of the newly institutionalized research on the so-called Jewish Question, which was advanced at a few places in Germany after Hitler's assumption of power in 1933.

One year after Hitler's rise to power, three substantial volumes were completed that served as a unique epitaph of the German Jewish legacy. One of these volumes was the second and final part of volume one of the *Germania Judaica*, one of the most ambitious projects ever in German-Jewish scholarship. It records in meticulous detail the presence of Jews in

Germany from "the earliest beginnings until 1250." Reflecting the uncertainties for all German Jews at the time, as well as its own uncertain status, the preface concluded in a sober spirit: "It is, at the moment, too early to speak of continuing this work. We hope, in more auspicious times, to be able to resume our task, a task that, at present, exceeds the capacities of our society."[10]

While the *Germania Judaica* showed the deep roots of Jews in the German-speaking lands, the second of the three works concentrated on the Jewish contributions to German culture and society in the modern period. Edited by the publisher of the Jüdische Verlag, Siegmund Katznelson, it bore the title *Juden im deutschen Kulturbereich*. In fifty essays that covered more than a thousand pages, this study depicts Jewish involvement in almost all areas of life, from theater and film to geophysics and botany. There was even a separate essay on German Jews and chess. In 1934, however, the correct title for such an essay, as for all others in a similar vein, would have been "Jews in German Chess."

To remind Germans of what the Jews contributed to German culture was certainly not in the interest of state and party officials in 1934. Thus, it is not surprising that official institutions prevented the printing and circulation of the volume after the State Police (Staatspolizeiamt für den Landespolizeibezirk) in Berlin declared: "Upon reading the work, the unprejudiced reader will receive the impression that, until the National-Socialist revolution, the whole of German culture was carried by Jews alone."[11] Both volumes reached their readers only in postwar reprints: *Juden im deutschen Kulturbereich* in 1959, and the *Germania Judaica* in 1963.

The third book was Ismar Elbogen's *Die Geschichte der Juden in Deutschland*, first published in 1935, and republished in a different form after World War II by Eleonore Sterling. Although Elbogen did not or could not analyze the current situation of German Jewry, he offered enough hints that enabled his readers to understand what was happening. As Michael Meyer has pointed out recently, Elbogen's concentration on anti-Semitism in Imperial Germany could hardly be understood out of the context of the time in which it was written. One might add, however, that even Martin Philippson's *Modern History of the Jews*, written two decades earlier, viewed the Jewish experience in the *Kaiserreich* to a large degree as the history of anti-Semitism. Thus, there may have been this larger intent present in Elbogen's book. Be that as it may, Elbogen ended his book with a remark clear to any reader: "The upwards-spiraling welfare budgets of the Jewish communities bear witness to the desperate material situation of those who have remained in their homeland ... not to mention their spiritual suffering!"[12]

Those important works were only three among quite a few publications on Jewish history and culture appearing in Germany during the years after 1933. Dissertation topics ranged from biblical times through to the Middle Ages to modern regional and local Jewish and Polish, or Russian-Jewish, economic and political history. In some works, the influence of the *Zeitgeist* was apparent. A few authors of dissertations and scholarly articles were occupied with the specific status and protection of Jewish minorities in twentieth-century Europe. Thus, Willy Weichselbaum's 1935 dissertation was titled "Der Rechtsschutz der Juden in Deutsch-Oberschlesien nach dem Genfer Abkommen von 1922" (The Protection of the Rights of the Jews in German Upper Silesia after the Treaty of Geneva of 1922), while Kurt Stillschweig dedicated numerous articles in the journals *Zeitschrift für die Geschichte der Juden in Deutschland* (hereafter ZGJD) and *Monatsschrift für Geschichte und Wissenschaft des Judentums* (hereafter MGWJ) to the question of Jewish minority status.

This particular question, the status of Jews in Germany, was not a totally new one for German Jews, although it obviously gained new practical relevance in the years following World War I. With the revolution of 1918 and the end of the old order, the question of whether Jews should gain national minority status was discussed in the Reichstag, where it found a prominent advocate in the Social Democratic and Zionist deputy, Oskar Cohn. It was dismissed, however, by the vast majority of German Jews at the time and was never seriously considered. Only in the last years of the Weimar Republic were ideas of national autonomy, which had been implemented in Eastern Europe, taken up again in the German context. In 1932, the Stuttgart lawyer and writer Karl Lieblich published a "public question to Adolf Hitler" in a book with the title *Was geschieht mit den Juden? (What Shall Be Done with the Jews?)*, in which he tried to convince the Nazis, still an opposition party, to help establish a Jewish autonomy in Germany. Before this public appeal to Adolf Hitler,[13] Lieblich had published three lectures between 1928 and 1930 advocating the same idea, and he was not alone among German-Jewish intellectuals. The Social Democratic district attorney in Heidelberg, Hugo Marx, released a similar book in the same year, 1932: *Was wird werden? Das Schicksal der deutschen Juden in der sozialen Krise* (*What Will Be? The Fate of German Jews in the Social Crisis*). Following Carl Schmitt's thesis of the "total state," Marx predicted an authoritarian state with a new social and economic order, in which the old liberal principles of individual emancipation would lose

FIGURE 7.1.: Martin Buber speaking at the "Jüdisches Lehrhaus," Berlin, 17 January 1935. Photograph by Abraham Pisarek. *Courtesy*: Bildarchiv Preussischer Kulturbesitz, Berlin, and Art Resource, New York.

their relevance. Instead, he predicted the Jews would be able to survive only as an autonomous group with corporate rights.

The idea of Jewish autonomy was already being discussed among Jews on the eve of the Nazi rise to power, and it continued to occupy some Jewish historians in the years after 1933. The intellectual journal *Der Morgen* was occupied specifically with the discussion about cultural autonomy.[14] Moreover, Jewish intellectuals reacted to some Nazi ideologues such as Ernst Krieck (*Volk im Werden* 1/1, 1933), who suggested that German Jews build their own educational and cultural system within German society while at the same time retreating from the larger German institutions. Liberal commentators such as Fritz Friedländer rejected this ghettoization, but at the same time took it as an occasion to write about historical developments of minority rights. In a series of articles in the MGWJ, Kurt Stillschweig dealt with this question, which, from a variety of perspectives, now constituted a potential response to a dramatically changed situation. He analyzed emancipation in the context of the French definition of "nation," the non-recognition of nation-status for the Jews in the Habsburg monarchy, and the development of autonomy in the new states founded after World War I. When these articles were published in 1937 and 1938 respectively, the retreat to the idea of national autonomy for the Jews was already a rather optimistic vision for the future of German Jewry. In his last article, "On the Modern History of the Jewish Autonomy," Stillschweig had to include Israel as part of his name.

The 1939 volume of the MGWJ was the last endeavor of collective cultural creativity among the Jews in Nazi Germany; it was destroyed soon after it appeared. One article prepared for this volume was Selma Stern-Täubler's essay "On the Literary Struggle for Emancipation in the Years 1816–1819," an article that had special relevance for German Jews in 1939. Selma Stern-Täubler was mainly concerned with Jewish reactions to the resistance to Jewish emancipation, and, between the lines, German Jews could read arguments of a surprising and alarming actuality. She emphasized the dual world in which most German Jews lived: their rootedness both in Jewish and German culture and society, and the "unrequited love" of this "self-torturing and suffering" group that "endured the great Jewish grief" (*Judenschmerz*). In addition, she recalled the group of converts who became accepted in Christian society, and who—like Friedrich Julius Stahl—even became spokesmen for the Christian state. She also mentioned those representatives of *Wissenschaft des Judentums* who tried to advance Jewish emancipation by means of scholarship. Selma Stern-Täubler concluded her contribution with a sentence that expressed both the hope of those early generations and the disappointment of her own, when she spoke of the "time when, together with the demise of the Romantic movement and the victory of the Liberal idea, even the anti-Jewish feeling dwindled and one could believe that the end of the suffering had finally come."[15] German-Jewish readers, however, were not able to share her thoughts. This article, signed by Selma "Sara" Stern-Täubler, fell victim to censorship.

Most Jewish historians did not deal with possible reactions to the new situation, but were interested rather in analyzing the roots of modern German-Jewish history and its dilemmas. The age of emancipation, once hailed as the beginning of a new and glorious period in Jewish history, was now viewed rather critically. The two most important works published on this topic in Nazi Germany were Jacob Katz's 1934 Frankfurt dissertation "Die Entstehung der Judenassimilation in Deutschland und deren Ideologie," and Max Wiener's 1933 dissertation "Jüdische Religion im Zeitalter der Emanzipation." Katz came to Frankfurt from his native Hungary as a student at the Orthodox Breuer Yeshiva. At the university, he studied with the sociologist Karl Mannheim who, as a Jew, could teach him but was no longer in the position to evaluate him. Katz was left alone with professors unfamiliar with his topic, which was the origins of assimilation of German Jews. Professor Georg Küntzel, a German nationalist who took over from Mannheim, only insisted, according to Katz "that I write a preface to the effect that my scholarly treatment of the subject did not imply that the author regarded assimilation as the solution to the Jewish question." Küntzel did not have to fear that Katz's work would advocate assimilation. As Katz further recalls: "I grasped his point totally and immediately and merely remarked that anyone who read the work would see that my conclusions were scarcely a recommendation for assimilation."[16] Indeed, the preface of Katz's dissertation reads:

> The study arose from the need to pursue the causes of a historical process whose effects clearly extended into the present, effects which the author condemned from a non-scholarly point of view. The historical shift of 1933 subsequently lent a larger significance to the scholarly inquiry of the study, not only because the subject gained an unforeseen degree of relevance for our time, but also because the shift brought about the visible conclusion of the epoch whose origins the study sought to examine, thus allowing questions to be posed with much greater sharpness.[17]

Reflecting the spirit of the times in which he was living, Katz concludes his dissertation with a rather pessimistic tone. He explicitly refers to the resistance to assimilation: "Thus a new age was born that no longer wished to see assimilation as a certain solution to the basic dilemma that had driven it."[18] As a Zionist, Katz's skepticism toward assimilation is not surprising. He did not merely respond to the renewed ghettoization of German Jewry, but reflected a national Jewish spirit that had existed well before 1933.

More surprising perhaps was the growing estrangement of liberal Jewish thinkers from their traditional values of individualism and rational thought. A clear push away from rationalism was visible already in the Weimar period, for example, in the speeches held at the annual rabbinical associations by leading representatives such as Rabbis Max Dienemann and Max Wiener. Wiener, who once served as assistant rabbi to Leo Baeck in Düsseldorf, and after a short stay in Stettin became his colleague as Gemeinderabbiner of Berlin, published his magnum opus *Jüdische Religion im Zeitalter der Emanzipation* in 1933.[19] While Leo Baeck was still wavering between the more traditional rationalism of liberal Judaism and the adoption of non-rational elements, Wiener's break with nineteenth-century liberal traditions was complete. In his programmatic speech at the convention of liberal German rabbis in Berlin in January 1922, Wiener charged the transformation of Judaism into a rational *Weltanschauung* during the nineteenth century with the responsibility for the poor condition of modern Jewish religiosity. He demanded a religious renewal based on the integration of non-rational elements into modern Judaism: the "feeling" of belonging to the Jewish people and the self-consciousness of the particularity of the Jews as a chosen people. As Wiener's biographer, Robert S. Schine, has observed, Wiener's "historical-metaphysical irrationalism" constituted an assimilation of romantic *völkisch* ideas into liberal Judaism. For Wiener, religious acts based on revealed law, and not on rational doctrines, were the basis of Judaism. Wiener's critical position toward the development of German Judaism in the nineteenth century was also reflected in his book *Jüdische Religion im Zeitalter der Emanzipation*.

This preoccupation with the emancipation period was also evident in the contributions to the ZGJD after 1933. Numerous articles discussed representatives and contemporaries of the Berlin Haskalah, from Moses Mendelssohn to David Friedländer and Saul Ascher. The Heidelberg Rabbi Fritz Pinkuss, who wrote about Ascher, clearly expressed skepticism about liberal ideas. Referring to such ideas presented in Wiener's book, and referring to Ascher himself, Pinkuss wrote:

> Today especially both the struggle for rights and the apologetic will again have to take new paths, if they are to be understood. With the end of the liberal vision of the state in Germany, and perhaps in the entire world, they will have to redefine the proper sociological place of the Jews in the new [German] state. They will have to portray the Jewish cultural heritage in a way that corresponds to its essential content, and do it better than the generation of Saul Ascher and his subsequent followers could.[20]

The ZGJD was also a forum for one of the dirtiest attacks on Jewish historiography after 1933. While non-Jewish scholars mainly ignored Jewish historiography in the Weimar Republic, the Third Reich now began to develop a new interest in "research on the Jewish Question." Several research institutions were founded to advance a clearly anti-Semitic perspective toward Jewish history. The main protagonist of such a view was a young historian at the Munich Reichsinstitut für Geschichte des Neuen Deutschlands, Wilhelm Grau. In his dissertation, he dealt with the medieval Jewish community of Regensburg, and thus built on (some say he plagiarized) the work of the Jewish historian, Raphael Straus, the former editor of the ZGJD and cousin of its publisher, Ludwig Feuchtwanger. Obviously, the Nazi Grau came to quite different conclusions than did his Jewish colleague Straus. This is not the place to describe in detail the conflict between the two, which has been done by Christhard Hoffmann and Patricia von Papen in their work on the subject. It should suffice here to recall that in 1935 it was still possible for a Jewish historian who had emigrated from Germany to Palestine to publish very harsh words of criticism of the rising star of the Nazi historiography of the "Jewish Question." Thus, Straus writes about Grau: "The reasons why Grau's dissertation falls so completely on its face have already been suggested above. The young author, a doctoral student at the University of Munich, lamentably bit off more than he could chew."[21] Grau, in his reply, insists that Jewish historians do not possess the necessary objectivity to approach Jewish history. To use Grau's own words, which were published in the ZGJD in 1935:

> Jewish historical scholarship must come to terms with the fact that also German scholars will, in the future, systematically research and write about the Jewish problem, and will do so in the context of German National history. In Jewish circles, one will first and foremost have to face the fact that we Germans wish to write not about the history of the Jews or of Judaism, but rather the history of the Jewish Question. Moreover, we will accomplish this task with German scientific methods and German thoroughness, moved by our conscience.[22]

In the years that followed, German "thoroughness" was to characterize other tragic aspects of German-Jewish relations, aspects that included discrimination, persecution, and finally extermination. However, the scholarship around the "Jewish Question" would not stop. Historians in different parts of Germany were busy writing essays, dissertations, and source editions on the Jewish presence in Germany and other countries. Jews, however, were no longer among them.

In conclusion, we must ask ourselves what the meaning of this last breath of German Jewry means to historians of modern Germany and of German Jewry. First of all, we have to realize that some of the most remarkable publications on German-Jewish history, from the *Germania Judaica* to Max Wiener's *Jüdische Religion im Zeitalter der Emanzipation* to Ismar Elbogen's *Geschichte der Juden in Deutschland*, although often conceived before, were published in the years following 1933, as were dissertations on various Jewish topics and scholarly Jewish journals. Second, and perhaps more interesting, is the spirit of some of those works, a spirit that was already perceptible in the last years of the Weimar Republic and within an increasing climate of intolerance and exclusion. Criticism of enlightenment and individual emancipation, and a new interest in autonomist ideas, reflected an awareness of the crisis facing Jews in Germany as expressed in scholarly terms. Thus, those historical writings produced in Nazi Germany are unique documents of both history and historiography. Their scholarship stood in the tradition of *Wissenschaft des Judentums*, both reflecting and expanding on its new expression during the Weimar years; but it also began to pose the questions that occupied historians who would write about Jewish topics after 1945: why and how did emancipation and assimilation fail in the context of modern German-Jewish history?

Notes

1. The Viennese actor and director Fritz Wisten (1890–1962), engaged at the Württemberg Theater in Stuttgart, was dismissed in March 1933. He was summoned to Berlin by Julius Bab and given the position of director of theater at the Kubu, thus becoming one of the first members of the Berlin branch. Like almost all Jewish males of his age, he was summarily imprisoned following *Kristallnacht*, but later released. By dint of his marriage to a non-Jew, he survived the war in Berlin (partly in hiding), and then after the war was active in East Berlin, where, in 1946, he directed *Nathan der Weise*. See Martin Goldsmith, *The Inextinguishable Symphony: A True Story of Music and Love in Nazi Germany* (New York: John Wiley & Sons, 2000), 292.
2. Quoted in Chana C. Schütz, "Max Liebermann in Eretz Jisrael," in *Was vom Leben übrig bleibt, sind Bilder und Geschichten. Max Liebermann zum 150. Geburtstag*, ed. Hermann Simon (Berlin: Centrum Judaicum, 1997), 137.
3. This is especially true about the theater. See for example the two edited works which appeared in connection with the Kulturbund exhibit in Berlin in 1992: Walter Jens, ed., *Geschlossene Vorstellung: Der jüdische Kulturbund 1933–1941* (Berlin: Edition Hentrich, 1992), and Henryk M. Broder and Eike Geisel, eds., *Premiere und Pogrom: Der jüdische Kulturbund 1933–1941, Texte und Bilder* (Berlin: Siedler, 1992). See also the more recent works by Rebecca Rovit, such as her edited volume *Theatrical Performance during the Holocaust: Texts, Documents, Memoirs* (Baltimore: Johns Hopkins, 1999). Among the older standard works are Herbert Freeden, *Jüdisches Theater in Nazideutschland* (Tübingen: Mohr/Siebeck, 1964) and *Die jüdische Presse im Dritten Reich* (Frankfurt am Main: Jüdischer Verlag bei Athenäum, 1987), and Ernst Simon, *Aufbau im Untergang: Jüdische Erwachsenenbildung im nationalsozialistischen Deutschland als geistiger Widerstand* (Tübingen: Mohr/Siebeck,

1959). On publishing activities see Volker Dahm, *Das jüdische Buch im Dritten Reich* (Munich: C.H. Beck, 1993).
4. Quoted in Rebecca Rovit, "An Artistic Mission in Nazi Berlin: The Jewish Kulturbund Theatre as Sanctuary," *Theater Survey* (November 1994): 6–17, here: 6.
5. Ibid., 13.
6. Quoted in Volker Kühn, "'Zores haben wir genug ...' Gelächter am Abgrund," in Jens, *Geschlossene Vorstellung*, 95–112, here: 102.
7. See Eike Geisel's introduction to *Premiere und Pogrom*, 15.
8. On the latest chapters of the two Berlin institutions, see Christhard Hoffmann and Daniel R. Schwartz, "Early but Opposed—Supported but Late: Two Berlin Seminaries which Attempted to Move Abroad," *Leo Baeck Institute Year Book* 36 (1991): 267–304.
9. On the last case of a Jewish student submitting a doctoral dissertation in Cologne, see Frank Golczewski, *Kölner Universitätslehrer und die Nationalsozialisten* (Cologne: Böhlau, 1988), 347–349.
10. Ismar Elbogen, Aron Freimann, and Chaim Tykocinski, eds., *Germania Judaica* (Tübingen: Mohr/Siebeck, 1963), 14–15.
11. Robert Weltsch, "Vorbemerkung zur zweiten Auflage," in *Juden im deutschen Kulturbereich*, ed. Siegmund Katznelson (Berlin: Jüdischer Verlag, 1959), 16.
12. Ismar Elbogen, *Geschichte der Juden in Deutschland* (Berlin: Jüdische Buch-Vereinigung, 1931), 314.
13. Karl Lieblich, *Was geschieht mit den Juden? Öffentliche Frage an Adolf Hitler* (Stuttgart: Im Zonen Verlag, 1932). Here, Lieblich appealed to Hitler: "Nur von Ihrer Seite auch kann ich mir eine ernstliche und innerlich beteiligte Förderung meines Gedankens vorstellen, da Sie es unternommen haben, Neues und von Grund auf Erneuerndes zu versuchen. So lege ich denn diese Schrift und die Beantwortung ihrer Frage mit Vertrauen in Ihre Hände." ("I can envisage a serious and engaged advancement of my ideas coming only from you, because you have attempted to achieve something entirely new. Thus, with trust I put this booklet and the response to its question in your hands."), Ibid., 88. For more details, see my article "Zurück ins Ghetto? Jüdische Autonomiekonzepte in der Weimarer Republik," *Trumah: Jahrbuch der Hochschule für Jüdische Studien Heidelberg* 3 (1992): 101–127.
14. See for example Fritz Friedländer, "Grenzen der Kulturautonomie," *Der Morgen*, February 1935, 492–497, and "Der Jude im Wandel der Reichsidee," *Der Morgen*, August 1935, 197–202; and Rudolf Levy, "Der Stand des Minderheitenrechts," *Der Morgen*, August 1935, 203–207.
15. Selma Sara Täubler-Stern, "Der literarische Kampf um die Emanzipation in den Jahren 1816–1819," *Monatsschrift für Geschichte und Wissenschaft des Judentums* 83 (1939): 661.
16. Jacob Katz, *With My Own Eyes. The Autobiography of an Historian* (Hanover: University Press of New England, 1995), 93.
17. Jacob Katz, "Die Entstehung der Judenassimilation und deren Ideologie," in *Zur Assimilation und Emanzipation der Juden. Ausgewählte Schriften*, ed. Jacob Katz (Darmstadt: Wissenschaftliche Buchgesellschaft, 1982), 3.
18. Ibid., 79.
19. Max Wiener, *Jüdische Religion im Zeitalter der Emanzipation* (Berlin: Philo Verlag, 1933). See also, Max Wiener, "Was heißt religiöse Erneuerung?" *Liberales Judentum*,

vol. 14, 1–3 (January/March 1922): 5–9, and Robert S. Schine, *Jewish Thought Adrift: Max Wiener (1882–1950)* (Atlanta: Scholars Press, 1992), 109–120.
20. Fritz Pinkuss, "Saul Ascher, ein Historiker der Judenemanzipation," *Zeitschrift für die Geschichte der Juden in Deutschland* 6 (1935): 32.
21. Raphael Straus, "Antisemitismus im Mittelalter. Ein Wort pro domo," *Zeitschrift für die Geschichte der Juden in Deutschland* 6 (1935): 24.
22. Wilhelm Grau, "'Antisemitismus im Mittelalter'—Ein Wort contra Raphael Straus," *Zeitschrift für die Geschichte der Juden in Deutschland* 6 (1935): 198.

Appendix A

Law for the Restoration of the Professional Civil Service

7 April 1933

The Reich Government has enacted the following Law, promulgated herewith:

§ 1

1. To restore a national professional civil service and to simplify administration, civil servants may be dismissed from office in accordance with the following regulations, even where there would be no grounds for such action under the prevailing Law.
2. For the purposes of this Law the following are to be considered civil servants: direct and indirect officials of the Reich, direct and indirect officials of the *Länder*, officials of Local Councils, and of Federations of Local Councils, officials of Public Corporations as well as of Institutions and Enterprises of equivalent status . . . The provisions will apply also to officials of Social Insurance organizations having the status of civil servants . . .

§ 2

1. Civil servants who have entered the service since 9 November 1918, without possessing the required or customary educational background or other qualifications are to be dismissed from the service. Their previous salaries will continue to be paid for a period of three months following their dismissal.

2. They will have no claim to temporary pensions, full pensions or survivors' benefits, nor to retain designation of rank or titles, or to wear uniforms or emblems . . .

§ 3

1. Civil servants who are not of Aryan descent are to be retired (§ 8ff.); if they are honorary officials, they are to be dismissed from their official status.
2. Section 1 does not apply to civil servants in office from 1 August 1914, who fought at the Front for the German Reich or its Allies in the World War, or whose fathers or sons fell in the World War. Other exceptions may be permitted by the Reich Minister of the Interior in coordination with the Minister concerned or with the highest authorities with respect to civil servants working abroad.

§ 4

1. Civil servants whose previous political activities afford no assurance that they will at all times give their fullest support to the national State, can be dismissed from the service . . .

Reich Chancellor
Adolf Hitler

Reich Minister of the Interior
Frick

Reich Minister of Finance
Graf Schwerin von Krosigk

Source: Yitzhak Arad, Israel Gutman, and Abraham Margaliot, eds., *Documents on the Holocaust*, 8th ed. (Lincoln and London: University of Nebraska Press and Yad Vashem, 1999), 39–41.

Appendix B

Proclamation of the (New) Reichsvertretung der Deutschen Juden

At a time that is as hard and difficult as any in Jewish history, but also significant as few times have been, we have been entrusted with the leadership and representation of the German Jews by a joint decision of the State Association of the Jewish Communities (*Landesverbände*), the major Jewish organizations and the large Jewish communities of Germany.

There was no thought of party interests, no separate aims in this decision, but solely and wholly the realization that the lives and future of the German Jews today depend on their unity and cooperation. The first task is to make this unity live. There must be recognition of the vitality and aims of every organization and association, but in all major and decisive tasks there must only be one union, only the totality of the German Jews. Anyone who goes his own way today, who excludes himself today, has committed a wrong against the vital need of the German Jews.

In the new State the position of individual groups has changed, even of those which are far more numerous and stronger than we are. Legislation and economic policy have taken their own authorized road, including [some] and excluding [others]. We must understand this and not deceive ourselves. Only then will we be able to discover every honorable opportunity, and to struggle for every right, for every place, for every opportunity to continue to exist. The German Jews will be able to make their way in the new State as a working community that accepts work and gives work.

There is only one area in which we are permitted to carry out our own ideas, our own aims, but it is a decisive area, that of our Jewish life and Jewish future. This is where the most clearly defined tasks exist.

There are new duties in Jewish education, new areas of Jewish schooling must be created, and existing ones must be nurtured and protected, in order that the rising generation may find spiritual strength, inner resistance, and physical competence. There must be a thoughtful selection in order to develop and re-direct our youth towards professions which offer them a place in life and prospects of a future.

All there is now, all that has been begun, all that has been attempted must be joined together here to give aid and support. All that is destructive must be opposed, and all our strength devoted to reconstruction on the religious base of Judaism.

Much of our former economic security has been taken from us German Jews, or at least reduced. Within the area that remains to us the individual must be drawn away from his isolation. Occupational connections and associations, where permissible, can increase existing strength and give support to the weak, can make experience and contacts useful for all. There will be not a few who will be refused a place of work or the exercise of their profession on German soil. We are faced by the fact which can no longer be questioned or opposed, of a clear, historic necessity to give our youth new [living] space. It has become a great task to discover places and open roads, as on the sacred soil of Palestine, for which Providence has decreed a new era, as everywhere where the character, industry and ability of the German Jews can prove themselves, robbing none of their bread, but creating a livelihood for others.

For this and all else we hope for the understanding assistance of the Authorities, and the respect of our gentile fellow citizens, whom we join in love and loyalty to Germany.

We place our faith in the active sense of community and of responsibility of the German Jews, as also in the willingness to sacrifice of our Brothers everywhere.

We will stand united and, in confidence in our God, labor for the *honor of the Jewish Name*. May the nature of the German Jews arise anew from the tribulations of this time!

Appendix B

The Reichsvertretung der deutschen Juden

Leo Baeck

Otto Hirsch — Stuttgart	Siegfried Moses — Berlin
Rudolf Callmann — Cologne	Jacob Hoffmann — Frankfurt
Leopold Landenberger — Nuremberg	Franz Meyer — Breslau
Julius Seligsohn — Berlin	Heinrich Stahl — Berlin

Source: Yitzhak Arad, Israel Gutman, and Abraham Margaliot, eds., *Documents on the Holocaust*, 8th ed. (Lincoln and London: University of Nebraska Press and Yad Vashem, 1999), 57–59. This proclamation was published in the *Jüdische Rundschau*, 29 September 1933.

Appendix C

The American Jewish Committee
171 Madison Ave.
New York
1 March 1935

NOT FOR PUBLICATION

The Situation of the Jews in Germany

I. LEGAL STATUS

Although the depths of brutal discrimination against the Jews in Nazi Germany have been reached, there is no end to the rumors that the more radical members of the National Socialist Party are pressing forward for dis-enfranchisement of non-Aryans by forcing them to accept a formal second-class legal status. However, this question is considered under the present regime, of slight importance because in effect the Jews of Germany have already been relegated to a second-class position.

II. ECONOMIC POSITION

Opposed to the fanaticism of such men as Reichsminister of the Interior Frick, Streicher, Goebbels and Hitler, is Dr. Hjalmar Schacht, President of the Reichsbank and Minister of the Economy, who according to the latest reports has categorically demanded the cessation of violent Jew-baiting. It is well known that Dr. Schacht is more realistic than some of his colleagues and believes that the German economy will suffer if such a policy is continued. It will be remembered, also, that Dr. Schacht attempted to counteract the Nazi boycott activities during the Christmas season by pointing out the dangers that would result to the nation. However, despite his warning, there were in many towns boycotts which closely resembled that of April 1, 1933. In Frankfurt, Storm Troops stood as pickets outside Jewish shops during the last three days of the Christmas shopping rush, and prevented customers who did not openly state they were Jews from entering. According to reports which were never denied officially in Germany, in the town of Mainz, Nazis stormed a Jewish-owned department store which was thronged with customers and wanted to drive the customers out. A fight ensued when many insisted on buying their Christmas presents in this shop. Still, it is a fact not without significance that the anti-Jewish feeling of the German people must be stirred up by such means, and ordinarily does not exist openly or spontaneously.

III. ANTI-JEWISH PROPAGANDA

The press campaign continues to be led by the larger Nazi papers which are stressing with great vigor the "Protocols of the Elders of Zion" as proof of an international Jewish conspiracy. These papers seem to have been stimulated to activity by the growing independence and confidence of such "liberal" journals as the Frankfurter Zeitung, which in rather mild terms attempt to counter-balance propaganda by an effort of impartiality. For example, when some weeks ago a gathering of Nazi doctors in Nuremberg, after a speech by Herr Streicher, passed a unanimous resolution demanding the death penalty for any Jew having sexual relations with Aryan women, the Frankfurter Zeitung dared to raise a very careful protest. It was immediately attacked by Goebbel's "Angriff" and other Nazi journals. Despite this fact, the first protest against Streicher's rabid policy came forth on February 14th from health officials and the German Medical Society. The protest consisted of a letter to Chancellor Hitler, signed by the President of the Reich Health Office and the State Health Commissioners of Bavaria, Baden, Saxony, Thuringia and Wurtemberg, followed by a public statement from Dr. Gerhard Wagner, the leader of the German Medical Society. Although they expressed approval of Streicher's "fight against Judaism," they condemned his attempt to do away with vaccination and the use of other serums made by Jews.

But the patience of the Jews in Germany has been exhausted by the insults constantly disseminated in *Der Stuermer*, and circulating especially in the schools. A new feature of Streicher's newspaper is a section called "Jewish Want Ads," which contains such shameless vulgarities as advertisements for "a blond Aryan *shiksa* for a sexually ripe eleven year old boy." Another announces the sale of "good Jewish wine mixed with Jewish blood." A third advertises that an "unemployed rabbi wishes to give lessons in the Talmudic lore of homosexuality." As a result of the Saar plebiscite, also, the false allegation has been made that Max Braun, the Social Democratic Saarlander leader, is a Jew. The *Reichsvertretung* of German Jews issued an official statement signed by Rabbi Leo Baeck and Otto Hirsch repudiating this allegation. Meanwhile, the Jewish organizations in Germany are quietly attempting to combat some of the grosser libels cast upon their name. For example, the Central Verein für Deutschen Juden [sic] published a new edition of its pamphlet refuting the blood-ritual murder accusation.

IV. PUBLIC SCHOOLS

However, Jewish pupils in some public schools still are subjected to the most intense humiliation. At some institutions, they are required to have a students' card differing in color from those carried by non-Jewish students; in some they are required to sit apart from the other students; in many, they are excluded from student dining rooms and libraries. Happily this is true of only a small proportion of the public schools. But, Nazi "racial science" has now become a compulsory study in all schools throughout Germany. As a measure of mercy, classes in racial science are to be held on Saturdays, and Jewish children are to be allowed to remain at home.

V. LEGISLATION AND THE COURTS

Until the present, the Jews of Germany have had but one recourse — prevented as they were from retaining their professional positions and from emigrating, kept out of agriculture and the Labor Front. They have, despite the boycott, been permitted to begin new small businesses. However, a new decree has just prohibited the opening of new retail shops without a special license from the government. The Aryan clause will undoubtedly be applied in this connection also.

In the law courts Jews seem to have fared somewhat better, especially in the Higher Courts. The "Frankfurter Zeitung" was able to publish several cases where the rights of Jews were upheld by the judges. This seems to be evidence of a change of attitude among the members of the upper middle class, to which the judges belong, toward the Nazis. Apparently this class is beginning to realize the plebian manner and crude ways of so many of the Nazi leaders. The "Peoples' [sic] Court," also, meets with the resentment of those judges who still attempt to preserve certain principles of justice. Although the judges cannot openly express their political opposition to the Nazi party, they do so indirectly in this manner: by attempting to safeguard the rights of Jews whenever possible.

VI. THE CHURCH OPPOSITION

In a dictatorship political dissent must be expressed subtly and indirectly. Therefore, the Church struggle, the cultural battle between the Propaganda Ministry and the independent intellectuals and artists, and the conflict between the economic radicals and the economic conservatives in the Nazi camp, are symbolic of more fundamental political unrest. Now that the Saar plebiscite is over, the Catholics are taking the lead in expressing their indignation at certain developments in the Third Reich. It is probable that before the Saar vote was held, an agreement was made with the Catholic Church for support in that predominantly Catholic territory. The result has strengthened the hand of the Church and has given it a right to demand certain concessions. Cardinal Faulhaber delivered a stirring sermon in the Munich Cathedral protesting against paganism and the un-Christian nature of certain governmental policies. The Catholic Archbishop of Freiburg recently gave a striking address in which he rejected all Nazi racial theories. "We Catholics," he declared, "know of only one Father, who is also the Father of all peoples and races. We do not know of the German God and of a German National Church and we swear fidelity to our only leader, our Holy Father in Rome." A full and enthusiastic Protestant meeting in Hirschberg, Silesia, was addressed by Herr von Kirchbach, who for the last ten months has not been permitted to occupy his pulpit in Dresden Cathedral. "We welcomed the Nazi revolution with fervor," he said, "but when it began to meddle with the Church we rose against it. We reject the theory of Race and Blood. The Gospel is to all men, and those who spread it first were Jews." He gave as an example of the extremes to which racialism was leading, the governmental request that a sculptor in Saxony be asked to remove the figure of Moses from a marble altar piece, representing the Old and the New Testaments and transform the figure so that it would become St. Paul.

Despite the reactions of the religious and liberal elements to these extremes, the Jews of Germany are none too sanguine in their hopes for the future. The compliment paid by Chancellor Hitler to Julius Streicher in visiting him on the occasion of his recent birthday, seems to indicate that the anti-Semitic nature of the Hitler government is no less fundamental to it now than it was in March 1932.

POSTSCRIPT

In an important address before the American Chamber of Commerce in Berlin on February 26, Dr. Julius Lippert, State Commissar for Berlin, attributed the fall in German exports to the United States to the "so-called Jewish boycott movement in the commercial world center of New York." The boycott movement, he claimed, proceeded on the false assumption that the German government has destroyed the "economic existence of the Jews in Germany." According to Dr. Lippert, "not a single dispossession or destruction of the so-called Jewish enterprise has taken place." Then, he pleaded for increased trade with the United States. This statement, although a most authoritative pronouncement on the Jewish question by one of the highest Nazi officials, does not indicate any changed or more realistic policy with regard to the Jews of Germany. It is but another attempt to blame the boycott for all of the difficulties of German trade, to stir up resentment against the Jews in the United States, and to paint a false picture of the condition of the Jews in Germany.

Source: Central Zionist Archives, Jerusalem: S7–200, Central Bureau for the Settlement of German Jews in Palestine, Report of the American Jewish Committee, New York, 1 March 1935. The American Jewish Committee compiled this internal report in 1935 on the conditions of Jewish life in Germany. It was based on information that the Committee, in its own words, "is receiving periodically from authoritative sources."

Appendix D

Reich Citizenship Law

15 September 1935

The Reichstag has unanimously enacted the following law, which is promulgated herewith:

§ 1

1. A subject of the State is a person who enjoys the protection of the German Reich and who in consequence has specific obligations towards it.
2. The status of subject of the State is acquired in accordance with the provisions of the Reich and State Citizenship Law.

§ 2

1. A Reich citizen is a subject of the State who is of German or related blood, who proves by his conduct that he is willing and fit faithfully to serve the German people and Reich.
2. Reich citizenship is acquired through the granting of a Reich Citizenship Certificate.
3. The Reich citizen is the sole bearer of full political rights in accordance with the Law.

§ 3

The Reich Minister of the Interior, in coordination with the Deputy of the Führer, will issue the Legal and Administrative orders required to implement and complete this Law.

Appendix D

Nuremberg, 15 September 1935
at the Reich Party Congress of Freedom

The Führer and Reich Chancellor
Adolf Hitler

The Reich Minister of the Interior
Frick

Source: Yitzhak Arad, Israel Gutman, and Abraham Margaliot, eds., *Documents on the Holocaust*, 8th ed. (Lincoln and London: University of Nebraska Press and Yad Vashem, 1999), 77.

Appendix E

Law for the Protection of German Blood and German Honor

15 September 1935

Moved by the understanding that purity of the German Blood is the essential condition for the continued existence of the German people, and inspired by the inflexible determination to ensure the existence of the German Nation for all time, the Reichstag has unanimously adopted the following Law, which is promulgated herewith:

§ 1

1. Marriages between Jews and subjects of the state of German or related blood are forbidden. Marriages nevertheless concluded are invalid, even if concluded abroad to circumvent this law.
2. Annulment proceedings can be initiated only by the State Prosecutor.

§ 2

Extramarital intercourse between Jews and subjects of the state of German or related blood is forbidden.

§ 3

Jews may not employ in their households female subjects of the state of German or related blood who are under 45 years old.

§ 4

1. Jews are forbidden to fly the Reich or National flag or to display the Reich colors.
2. They are, on the other hand, permitted to display the Jewish colors. The exercise of this right is protected by the State.

§ 5

1. Any person who violates the prohibition under § 1 will be punished by a prison sentence with hard labor.
2. A male who violates the prohibition under § 2 will be punished with a prison sentence with or without hard labor.
3. Any person violating the provisions under §§ 3 or 4 will be punished with a prison sentence of up to one year and a fine, or with one or the other of these penalties.

§ 6

The Reich Minister of the Interior, in coordination with the Deputy Führer and the Reich Minister of Justice, will issue the Legal and Administrative regulations required to implement and complete this Law.

§ 7

This Law takes effect on the day following promulgations except for § 3, which goes into force on 1 January 1936.

Nuremberg, 15 September 1935
at the Reich Party Congress of Freedom

The Führer and Reich Chancellor
Adolf Hitler

The Reich Minister of the Interior
Frick

Appendix E

The Reich Minister of Justice
Dr. Gürtner

The Deputy Führer
R. Hess

Source: Yitzhak Arad, Israel Gutman, and Abraham Margaliot, eds., *Documents on the Holocaust*, 8th ed. (Lincoln and London: University of Nebraska Press and Yad Vashem, 1999), 78–79.

Appendix F

Issued by
American Jewish Committee
461 Fourth Avenue
New York, N.Y.

1 June 1937

The Jews in Germany Today

A Survey of the Current Anti-Jewish Campaign
Conducted by the National Socialists

The deadly monotony of relentless persecution that has characterized the plight of the German Jews in the past few months was smashed recently when the Nazi regime suddenly descended on the German branches of the B'nai B'rith, dissolved the organization, and took over its sanatoria and homes for the aged, flinging their Jewish inmates into the street.

The mass arrests and expropriations that followed marked another new twist in the tortuous Nazi policy toward the Jews in Germany. It ended the period of "cold pogrom," and brought home once again the day-to-day brutality in the life of the nearly 400,000 Jews still remaining in Germany.

La Guardia Incident Marks New Trend

The new and vigorous trend was made dramatic in typical Nazi fashion following the curious German press attack on New York's mayor Fiorello H. La Guardia for a remark no more vigorous than many others he has uttered. The acrimony that marked the Nazi attack on the American mayor was the signal for the renewed anti-Jewish outburst in the Reich. As has been their practice before, the Nazis insisted that they were insulted. They ended by revenging themselves—upon the Jews.

Appendix F

In recent months there has been a paucity of news concerning persecution of Jews in the Reich. It appeared as though the Hitler government was satisfied that the Nuremberg laws of 1935 had gone as far as any anti-Jewish program could go, short of physical terror, to accomplish the Nazis' aims—as though a *status quo* had been established under which the complete elimination of the Jews from German life was to become a routine affair.

But this routine, which had grown so commonplace that it no longer aroused special comment in the world outside, involved the continued boycott of those Jewish businesses which still existed in the German Reich; the continued stirring up of mob hatred against a tiny minority; the unceasing attacks on the morals of the German Jews; and the continuation and enforcement of all the systematic laws, decrees, regulations, and promulgations which have emanated from the Brown House in Munich.

Routine Persecution Too Slow For Nazis

The more recent events in Germany indicate, however, that the Nazis have decided to abandon this routine as too slow and that they will no longer abide even by their own laws in the conduct of their anti-Jewish campaign. Any law, no matter how harsh, the Nazis have apparently decided, offers some measure of protection to their victims; therefore the methods of "legal procedure" against the Jews are to be abandoned.

Thus, the recent raids on the B'nai B'rith lodges, the banning of Jewish meetings, the closing down of Jewish institutions, and the dissolution of Jewish clubs, all mark a new shift in Nazi tactics. The extermination of German Jews is to be speeded up. The job has been turned over to the Gestapo, the Secret State Police.

Secret Police Try Hand At Jew-Baiting

The Gestapo's major task is to eliminate all Jews from the economic life of Germany. Until now, Jewish business men have been afforded some measure of protection by the fact that no "Aryan clause" was even enacted in the economic field. But the Gestapo knows no law. Its activities are carried on without regard for legal procedure and there is no appeal from its decisions.

The method which the Gestapo has adopted to force Jewish firms out of business is exceedingly simple. The Jewish business man is notified that he must either sell or close up his business before a certain date. Failure to do so, he is warned, will result in his arrest on charges of violating the Reich currency laws. Since this is an offense which may be punished with death, there is usually little resistance.

Case Of The Scrap-Iron Dealer

There are occasions, however, when more direct methods are employed. The case of a Jewish scrap-iron dealer of Hagenow in Mecklenburg is typical of the Gestapo's tactics. The entire stock of scrap-metal belonging to this dealer was confiscated because, as the Nazi District Leader declared, there was ground for suspicion that this stock might be used for speculative purposes. This suspicion was considered ample justification not only for the expropriation of the Jew's property but also for the revoking of his trading license.

Under these new tactics, the list of Jewish firms which have passed into "Aryan" hands or have been liquidated entirely grows daily. Some of the oldest Jewish business houses in Germany have fallen under the Gestapo's assault. A recent victim was the firm of M. Kempinsky & Son, which operated a chain of restaurants and cafés, known the world over. Another was the firm of Loesser & Wolff of Elbing, whose cigar factory was one of the largest in Europe.

Gestapo Drive Is Systematic

The Gestapo appears to be following the rule of concentrating on one industry at a time. Thus, it announced recently that three hundred drug stores, formerly owned by Jews, are now under "Aryan" ownership. At present it is concentrating its attention on the textile and leather goods industries. Since these are commodities which may be needed for war purposes, the Gestapo officials have been particularly ruthless. They have announced that within a short time these industries will be "Judenfrei."

"Liquidations" Pauperize Wage-Earners

Even more disastrous than the plight of the Jewish business man is that of the Jewish wage-earner. Every liquidation or "Aryanization" of a Jewish enterprise automatically means the discharge of dozens and sometimes hundreds of Jewish employees. While the business man loses a major share of his property, his employee is reduced to the state of a pauper. He becomes dependent upon the relief agencies, which, because the government has refused any assistance, must rely solely upon Jewish support. Lately, the demands for relief have increased so tremendously that these agencies find it almost impossible to cope with the situation.

Recently, the German Labor Front, the government's gigantic company union, delivered a final blow to the Jewish worker. Under a new order issued by this organization, the Jewish labor exchanges have been dissolved. Both the Jewish employer and the Jewish job-seeker must now apply to general labor exchanges. Since it is dangerous for the Jewish business man to specify that he desires only Jewish help, this new regulation has resulted in the closing up of the last source of livelihood to the unemployed Jew. Last year the Jewish labor exchanges placed 18,000 Jews.

Emigration Becomes More Difficult

Slowly but surely, German Jewry is being reduced to a state of utter helplessness. The few avenues of escape open to them formerly are now gradually closing against them. Even emigration, the one solution to the Jewish problem of which the Nazi regime seemed to approve, is made increasingly difficult. The Gestapo has closed up a number of Hachscharah (training) colonies where hundreds of young Jewish men and women were being trained for new occupations before leaving Germany. They have also closed most of the schools where Jewish youth were learning the Hebrew language preparatory to emigration to Palestine.

There appears to be no logical explanation for the Gestapo's activities. Some of them are in fact directly contradictory to the expressed policy of the Nazi regime. Until now the Nazis have maintained that it is their purpose to exclude Jews from German life. On the other hand, the Jews were to be permitted and even required to develop their own cultural and communal life. The Gestapo, however, is utterly contemptuous of such legalistic attitudes. Its goal is the complete extermination of German Jewry, and its methods are not bound by any legal measures.

Thus, the Gestapo closed down, without warning, the only sanatorium in Germany for tubercular Jews. Since Jews are not admitted into "Aryan" institutions, this malicious action deprived Jewish sufferers of the only means of obtaining relief. Another recent measure was the eleventh-hour ban of the conference of the Reich Federation of Jewish Youth, which was scheduled to be held in Berlin. No reason was given for either of these two acts.

But Old-Line Jew-Baiting Continues

While the Gestapo has now taken the lead in the anti-Jewish campaign, other Nazi organizations have not slackened their activities. And, even before the Gestapo's ax of confiscation and expropriation finally falls, the Jewish merchant is harassed by boycott, by the cutting off of supplies, by frequent arrest without cause and by the stream of incessant anti-Jewish propaganda. The various sections of the Nazi party and individual government bureaus are vying with each other for first honors in the drive against the Jews. Daily, new restricting regulations are put into effect, new boycott proclamations published. Some of these new regulations are astonishing in their pettiness. Example: The recent order of the Reich Press Chamber instructing newspapers not to publish notices concerning Synagogue service. Other examples: An order prohibiting Jews from playing the music of Bach, Beethoven, Mozart and other "Aryan" composers; a Gestapo order permitting Jews to join the Jewish Automobile Club (the only motor club they may join at all) only if they sign a pledge promising to counteract anti-Nazi propaganda and promote German exports while travelling abroad in their cars.

Generally, however, these regulations fit well into the Nazi pattern. Most of them are aimed at those Jews who, while they own no property which can be expropriated or business which they can be forced to liquidate, still manage to eke out a livelihood. A recent order by the Minister of Education, Dr. Rust, prohibited "non-Aryans" from giving private lessons or teaching in private schools. The Reich Ministry of the Interior announced that an unemployed German will receive no financial assistance if he consults a Jewish physician or lawyer. At the same time it declared that medical certificates issued by Jewish physicians will not be considered valid. The same Ministry also ordered Jewish employers to discharge all Jewish employees of foreign citizenship.

Streicher On The Rampage

Meanwhile, Julius Streicher, publisher of the pornographic Stürmer and Germany's leading anti-Semite, has been increasing his activity. Shortly after the Nuremberg rally last September, Streicher summoned the tax collectors of Franconia and demanded that they rid the province of

Jews. He instructed them to institute a new system of business licenses which resulted in the elimination of all Jewish rag dealers in his district, more than 2000 food merchants, and about fifty corn dealers.

Streicher's special contribution to the 1936 Nuremberg rally was a special edition of his Stürmer, entitled "Jewish World Conspiracy," which contained a condensed version of the "Protocols of the Elders of Zion." This was followed by another special edition in which Streicher announced the "discovery" of a "ritual murder" case in Germany. The Stürmer had been reprinting stories of historical "ritual murder" trials and, as a climax, Streicher decided to produce a "living example." The case he trumped up involved the murder of a Christian girl in an East Prussian town more than eighteen years ago. Although the murderer, also a Gentile, had been apprehended and convicted immediately after the crime, Streicher presented "proof" that the real murderer was a Jewish butcher of that town. This "proof" consists of the statement of a young Storm-Trooper that when he confronted this Jewish butcher with the charge of having murdered a Christian girl eighteen years ago, the butcher's face "became deathly pale."

"Stürmer" Influence Increases

Streicher's influence in Germany is increasing. The circulation of his sheet has risen considerably, and recently he announced that 131 "display boxes" for the Stürmer have been established in various cities all over Germany. These boxes have been placed in hospitals, schools and other public buildings. The Thuringia authorities, who ordered that all illustrations depicting Old-Testament subjects be removed from the school-rooms, accompanied this order with a request that the Stürmer be used for the purpose of religious instruction as much as possible.

No Schooling For Jewish Children

The introduction of the Stürmer and other anti-Semitic literature into the public school system apparently serves a double purpose. The first is, of course, to instill Jew-hatred from early childhood. The other is far more subtle and is designed to pull the Nazis out of a dilemma.

In September, 1935, the Nazi government announced that in keeping with its plan to segregate the Jews it would establish special schools for Jewish children. This aroused the opposition of the extreme radicals among the Nazis who object to the building of permanent institutions for Jews, since that would imply permanence in the German Jewish status. This opposition has been strong enough to prevent the government from carrying out its original plan. At the same time, however, Nazi extremists insisted that Jewish children be removed from German schools. The introduction of anti-Jewish literature, causing the voluntary withdrawal of the Jewish children, accomplishes this purpose admirably. Today there are practically no Jews in the German elementary schools.

The Nazis have made remarkable progress in the field of juvenile anti-Semitic literature. A young Kindergarten teacher, Elvira Bauer, with the aid of the inevitable Stürmer, recently brought out a new Nazi fairy-tale book, with twenty-one brightly colored pictures showing horrible-visaged "non-Aryans," cheating, seducing and poisoning handsome "Aryans." Most interesting is the section depicting German children pointing a finger of scorn at these Jewish monsters and laughing joyously at their discomfiture.

The Gospel According to "St. Hitler"

No less an achievement than this new Mother Goose Book, is the new Nazi edition of the Gospel of St. John, brought out under the auspices of Dr. Weidemann, Bishop of Bremen and leader in the "German Christian" movement. Under the guidance of this Nazi churchman, a staff of expert Nazi propagandists have deleted from and added enough passages to the authorized version to make this a most effective piece of anti-Jewish propaganda.

Propaganda For All Tastes

The Nazis have overlooked nothing in their campaign against the Jews. The variety of propaganda they produced, designed to suit every taste, ranges from the gutter language of the Stürmer to the refinement of "scientific" treatises on the inferiority of the Jewish "race." The latest innovation is the establishment of a "Research Department for the Jewish Question" by the University of Munich to coordinate the production of the "scientific" anti-Jewish literature. The first achievement of this department was the publication of a list of books on economics and law written by Jews and therefore unfit for study by Nazis. Another new Nazi institution is a school of propaganda where one thousand young Nazis are being trained to become expert anti-Jewish agitators.

The decline of the Jewish communities in Germany under this constant pressure has been rapid. Following are outstanding facts:

Appendix F

Decrease—Since the advent of Hitler, the number of Jews in Germany has decreased from 500,000 to less than 380,000. 112,000 have emigrated during this time.

Population—55% of the Jewish population in Germany is over forty-five years old; 15% under twenty; 30% between twenty and forty-five.

Communities—Of the 1,400 Jewish communities in Germany, 276 are entirely dependent upon relief; 12 communities have been dissolved in the last six months.

Physicians—Of the 6,000 Jewish physicians in practice before 1933 only 3,000 remain. Of these 1,500 are in Berlin. More than two-thirds of the German Jewish physicians today are over 45 years old.

Lawyers—2,500 Jewish lawyers are now practicing in Germany. In 1933 there were 6,500.

Artists—Of 2,357 artists, including actors, musicians, painters and sculptors, in the pre-Hitler period, only 800 have managed to obtain temporary employment in Jewish cultural enterprises.

Ghetto—The Jewish population is concentrated in Berlin. Many cities and towns have lost the greater part of their Jewish population, while many others have become entirely "Judenfrei."

Charity—81,000 Jewish families are dependent upon charity—more than one-quarter of all German Jews.

Children—Of 42,000 Jewish children of school age, 22,000 are receiving education in Jewish schools; 20,000 are without adequate educational facilities.

Source: Central Zionist Archives, Jerusalem: S7–493, Central Bureau for the Settlement of Jews in Palestine, Report of the American Jewish Committee, New York, "The Jews in Germany Today," 1 June 1937.

Appendix G

8 February 1938

Herrn Dr. Martin Rosenblueth
London

Dear Rosenblueth,

The following remark may have no basis in fact. I would have sent this information to you sooner, but the recently reported upheavals in Germany have required a great deal of reflection.

Of course there is no relation between the sudden Nazi change in direction and the Jewish question, but the current situation gives the dark forces a free rein.

From a very reliable confidential source that is connected to the higher leadership of the SS, I have heard that there is much enthusiasm for an effective, genuine, and major pogrom in Germany in the near future. The fact that such information comes from such a source is something of which our friends in Germany should be aware.

Unfortunately, I am not aware of any additional details. I am also not asserting that this information is accurate. I do, however, vouch for the quality of the source.

With best wishes,

Dr. Georg Landauer

Source: Central Zionist Archives, Jerusalem: S7–689, Georg Landauer, Central Bureau for the Settlement of German Jews in Palestine, Jerusalem, to Martin Rosenblüth, Central Bureau for the Settlement of German Jews in Palestine, London, 8 February 1938. This letter was translated from the German by Francis R. Nicosia.

Appendix H

Law Concerning the Legal Status of the Jewish Religious Communities,

28 March 1938

The Reich Government has enacted the following law, which is promulgated herewith:

§ 1

1. Jewish religious communal organizations and their roof organizations obtain legal standing by means of registration in the Register of Associations.
2. At the end of 31 March 1938, Jewish religious organizations and their roof organizations will lose the status of Corporations under public law, insofar as they possessed such status up to the present time. From this date on they will be private Associations with legal status under civil law. Entry in the Register of Associations must be carried out . . .

Berlin, 28 March 1938

The Führer and Reich Chancellor
Adolf Hitler

The Reich Minister for Church Affairs
Kerrl

The Reich Minister of the Interior
Frick

Source: *Source*: Yitzhak Arad, Israel Gutman, and Abraham Margaliot, eds., *Documents on the Holocaust*, 8th ed. (Lincoln and London: University of Nebraska Press and Yad Vashem, 1999), 91.

APPENDIX I

REGULATION FOR THE ELIMINATION OF THE JEWS FROM THE ECONOMIC LIFE OF GERMANY
12 November 1938

On the basis of the regulation for the implementation of the Four Year Plan of 18 October 1936 (*Reichsgesetzblatt*, I, p. 887), the following is decreed:

§ 1

1. From 1 January 1939, Jews (§ 5 of the First Regulation of the Reich Citizenship Law of 14 November 1935, *Reichsgesetzblatt*, I, p. 1333) are forbidden to operate retail stores, mail-order houses, or sales agencies, or to carry on a trade [craft] independently.
2. They are further forbidden, from the same day on, to offer for sale goods or services, to advertise these, or to accept orders at markets of all sorts, fairs or exhibitions.
3. Jewish trade enterprises (Third Regulation to the Reich Citizenship Law of 14 June 1938—*Reichsgesetzblatt*, I, p. 627) which violate this decree will be closed by police.

§ 2

1. From 1 January 1939, a Jew can no longer be the head of an enterprise within the meaning of the Law of 20 January 1934, for the Regulation of National Work (*Reichsgesetzblatt*, I, p. 45).
2. Where a Jew is employed in an executive position in a commercial enterprise he may be given notice to leave in six weeks. At the expiration of the term of the notice all claims of the employee

based on his contract, especially those concerning pension and compensation rights, become invalid.

§ 3

1. A Jew cannot be a member of a cooperative.
2. The membership of Jews in cooperatives expires on 31 December 1938. No special notice is required.

§ 4

The Reich Minister of the Economy, in coordination with the Ministers concerned, is empowered to publish regulations for the implementation of this decree. He may permit exceptions under the Law if these are required as the result of the transfer of a Jewish enterprise to non-Jewish ownership, for the liquidation of a Jewish enterprise or, in special cases, to ensure essential supplies.

Berlin, 12 November 1938

Plenipotentiary for the Four Year Plan
Göring
Field Marshal General

Source: Yitzhak Arad, Israel Gutman, and Abraham Margaliot, eds., *Documents on the Holocaust*, 8th ed. (Lincoln and London: University of Nebraska Press and Yad Vashem, 1999), 115–116.

Appendix J

Establishment of the Reich Central Office for Jewish Emigration
January 1939

Berlin, 24 January 1939

Plenipotentiary for the Four Year Plan
To
The Reich Minister of the Interior
Berlin

The emigration of the Jews from Germany is to be furthered by all possible means.

A Reich Central Office for Jewish Emigration is being established in the Reich Ministry of the Interior from among representatives of the agencies concerned. The Reich Central Office will have the task to devise uniform policies as follows:

1. Measures for the *preparation* of increased emigration of Jews. This will include the creation of a Jewish organization* that can prepare uniform applications for emigration; the taking of all steps for the provision and efficient use of local and foreign funds; and a decision on suitable target countries for emigration, to be selected in coordination with the Reich Central Office for Emigration.
2. The *direction* of emigration, including, for instance, preference for the emigration of the poorer Jews.
3. The speeding up of emigration in *individual cases*, by means of speedy and smooth provision of the State documents and permits required by the individual emigrant, through central processing of applications for emigration.

Appendix J

The Reich Central Office for Jewish Emigration will be headed by the Chief of the Security Police. He will appoint a Responsible Manager and make rules for the operation of the Reich Central Office.

Regular reports on the work of the Reich Central Office will be forwarded to me. I will be consulted continuously on measures requiring decisions of principle.

In addition to representatives of other agencies involved, the Committee will include Ambassador Eisenlohr, who is responsible for local inter-state negotiations, and Ministerial Director Wohlthat, who is responsible for the negotiations in connection with the Rublee Plan.

Signed Göring

*The Jewish organization referred to here was to be the Reichsvereinigung der Juden in Deutschland (Reich Association of Jews in Germany), established in February 1939, to replace the defunct Reichsvertretung der Juden in Deutschland (Reich Representation of Jews in Germany).

Source: Yitzhak Arad, Israel Gutman, and Abraham Margaliot, eds., *Documents on the Holocaust*, 8th ed. (Lincoln and London: University of Nebraska Press and Yad Vashem, 1999), 125–126.

Appendix K

The Establishment of the Reichsvereinigung

Tenth Regulation to the Reich Citizenship Law

4 July 1939*

Pursuant to § 3 of the Reich Citizenship Law of 15 September 1935 (*Reichsgesetzblatt* I, p. 1146), the following Order is made:

Article I

Reichsvereinigung der Juden

§ 1

1. The Jews will be organized in a *Reichsvereinigung*.
2. The *Reichsvereinigung* is a legally recognized Association. Its name is "*Reichsvereinigung der Juden in Deutschland*," and it is located in Berlin.
3. The *Reichsvereinigung* will use the Jewish Communities as [its] local branches.

§ 2

1. The purpose of the *Reichsvereinigung* is to further the emigration of the Jews.
2. The *Reichsvereinigung* is also
    a. Responsible for the Jewish school system;
    b. Responsible for the independent Jewish welfare system.
3. The Reich Minister of the Interior is authorized to transfer further responsibilities to the *Reichsvereinigung*.

§ 3

1. All Jewish Subjects of the State as well as stateless Jews resident in the area of the Reich, or who normally live there, belong to the *Reichsvereinigung*.
2. In a mixed marriage the Jewish spouse is a member only if
    a. the husband is the Jewish spouse and there are no progeny from the marriage, or
    b. if the progeny are considered Jews.
3. Jews of foreign nationality and those maintaining a mixed marriage, who are not already members under section 2), may join the *Reichsvereinigung* voluntarily.

§ 4

The *Reichsvereinigung* is subject to the supervision of the Reich Minister of the Interior; its statutes require his approval.

§ 5

1. The Reich Minister of the Interior may disband Jewish Associations, Organizations, and Institutions or order them to be incorporated in the Reichsvereinigung.
2. In the event of disbandment the rules of Civil Law will apply . . . After the liquidation has been completed the funds of the disbanded Jewish organizations will be transferred to the Reichsvereinigung.
3. In the event of incorporation the property of the Jewish organizations concerned will be transferred to the *Reichsvereinigung*. There will be no liquidation in this case. The *Reichsvereinigung* will be fully liable with its entire property for the obligations of the incorporated organizations.
4. The Reich Minister of the Interior may revoke or amend statutes and decisions of Jewish Associations, Organizations, and Institutions, where they contain regulations not in accordance with the above Orders on the disposal of funds . . .

Article II

Jewish School System

§ 6

1. The *Reichsvereinigung* is obligated to provide schooling for Jews.
2. To this end the *Reichsvereinigung* will establish the required number of primary schools and maintain them. In addition it may maintain intermediate and high schools, as well as professional and technical schools and other schools or courses intended to assist the emigration of the Jews.
3. The *Reichsvereinigung* is responsible for the training and higher training of teachers at the schools which it maintains.
4. The schools maintained by the *Reichsvereinigung* are considered to be private schools.

§ 7

Jews may attend only the schools maintained by the *Reichsvereinigung*. They are obligated to attend these schools in accordance with the general regulations on compulsory education.

§ 8

1. Existing public and private Jewish schools and ... other Jewish educational establishments will be disbanded if the *Reichsvereinigung* fails to incorporate them by a date to be set by the Reich Minister for Science, Education and Popular Instruction.
2. The property of the Jews which had been used for Jewish educational establishments is to be ceded on request to the *Reichsvereinigung* in return for suitable compensation ...

§ 9

Teachers at Jewish schools who have Civil Service status will be retired as of June 30, 1939. They are obligated to accept employment at a Jewish school offered to them by the *Reichsvereinigung* ...

§ 10

The Regulations made in Reich and *Länder* Law concerning the education of Jews, in particular the admission of Jews to schools, the establishment and maintenance of public Jewish schools, as well as the provision of public funds for the purpose of instruction in the Jewish Religion are revoked.

§ 11

The Jewish school system is subject to the supervision of the Reich Minister for Science, Education and Popular Instruction.

Article III

Jewish Social Welfare

§ 12

The *Reichsvereinigung* as the body responsible for Jewish independent Welfare is obligated . . . to assist adequately Jews in need in accordance with its means, so that Public Welfare is not called upon. It is required to provide institutions intended solely for the use of Jews who are in need of institutional care.

Article IV

Final General Regulations

§ 13

No compensation will be provided for disadvantages occasioned by this regulation.

§ 14

1. The Reich Minister of the Interior will promulgate the Provisions required to carry out this Regulation.

2. Where the Jewish School System is concerned the Provisions will be made by the Reich Minister for Science, Education and Popular Instruction in coordination with the Reich Minister of the Interior . . .

Berlin, 4 July 1939

Reich Minister of the Interior—Frick
Deputy to the Führer—R. Hess
Reich Minister for Science, Education and Popular Instruction—Rust
Reich Minister for Church Affairs—Kerrl

*The Reichsvereinigung der Juden in Deutschland (Reich Association of Jews in Germany) was in fact established in February 1939 to replace the defunct Reichsvertretung der Juden in Deutschland (Reich Representation of Jews in Germany). However, the law formally granting the Reichsvereinigung official state recognition was not promulgated until July of that year.

Source: Yitzhak Arad, Israel Gutman, and Abraham Margaliot, eds., *Documents on the Holocaust*, 8th ed. (Lincoln and London: University of Nebraska Press and Yad Vashem, 1999), 139–143.

Contributors

Avraham Barkai was born in Berlin and emigrated from Germany to Palestine/Israel in 1938. He is a Research Fellow at the Leo Baeck Institute and at Yad Vashem in Jerusalem. His scholarly books include *From Boycott to Annihilation: The Economic Struggle of German Jews 1933–1943* (1989); *Nazi Economics, Ideology, Theory, and Policy* (1990); *Branching Out: German-Jewish Immigration to the United States, 1820–1914* (1994); (with Paul Mendes Flohr) *Renewal and Destruction 1918–1945*. Vol. IV: *German-Jewish History in Modern Times*, ed. Michael A. Meyer and Michael Brenner (1998); and *"Wehr Dich!" Der Centralverein deutscher Staatsbürger jüdischen Glaubens 1893–1938* (2002).

Michael Brenner is Professor of Jewish History and Culture at the University of Munich and International Vice President of the Leo Baeck Institute. Among his books are *A Short History of the Jews* (2010); *Prophets of the Past: Interpreters of Jewish History* (2010); *Zionism: A Concise History* (2002); *The Renaissance of Jewish Culture in Weimar Germany* (1996); and, *After the Holocaust: Rebuilding Jewish Lives in Postwar Germany* (1995).

Marion Kaplan is the Skirball Professor of Modern Jewish History at New York University. Among her many authored books are *Dominican Haven: The Jewish Refugee Settlement in Sosúa, 1940–1945* (2008); *Jewish Daily Life in Germany, 1618–1945* (2005); *Between Dignity and Despair: Jewish Life in Nazi Germany* (1998); and, *The Making of the Jewish Middle Class: Women, Family and Identity in Imperial Germany* (1991). She is also the editor or co-editor of several important volumes, including (with Renate Bridenthal and Atina Grossmann) *When Biology Became Destiny: Women in Weimar and Nazi Germany* (1984).

Konrad Kwiet is emeritus professor of German Studies at Macquarie University in Sydney, Australia. He was formerly chief historian of the

Australian war crimes commission, as well as a visiting professor and research fellow in Amsterdam, Oxford, Washington, DC, Heidelberg, Munich, Frankfurt am Main, and Berlin. He has published widely on Modern German and Jewish History, especially the Third Reich, Anti-Semitism, and the Holocaust. He is currently Adjunct Professor in Jewish Studies and Roth Lecturer in Holocaust Studies at the University of Sydney, and resident historian of the Sydney Jewish Museum.

Jürgen Matthäus is research director at the Center for Advanced Holocaust Studies of the United States Holocaust Memorial Museum, Washington, DC. He is co-author (with Mark Roseman) of *Jewish Responses to Persecution,* Vol. I: 1933–1938 (2010). He is co-editor (with Konrad Kwiet) of *Contemporary Responses to the Holocaust* (2005), and (with Klaus-Michael Mallmann and J. Böhler) of *Einsatzgruppen in Polen. Darstellung und Dokumentation* (2008).

Beate Meyer is senior researcher at the Institute for the History of German Jews in Hamburg. She is the author of *Jüdische Mischlinge. Rassenpolitik und Verfolgungserfahrung 1933–1945* (1999), and co-editor with Hermann Simon of *Juden in Berlin 1938 bis 1945* (2000) [English edition: *Jews in Nazi Berlin* (2009)], and with Birthe Kundrus of *Die Deportation der Juden aus Deutschland. Pläne-Praxis-Reaktionen, 1938 1945* (2004). She is currently doing research on "The Reichsvereinigung der Juden—a German 'Jewish Council'?"

Francis R. Nicosia is the Raul Hilberg Distinguished Professor of Holocaust Studies at the University of Vermont. He is the author of *Zionism and Anti-Semitism in Nazi Germany* (2008), and *The Third Reich and the Palestine Question* (1985, 2000), and co-author (with Donald Niewyk) of the *Columbia Guide to the Holocaust* (2000). He is also co-editor (with Jonathan Huener) of three books on medicine, business and industry, and the arts in Nazi Germany (2002, 2004, 2006), and (with Lawrence Stokes) of a book on the resistance against Hitler in Nazi Germany (1990).

David Scrase is Professor of German and the founding director of the Carolyn and Leonard Miller Center for Holocaust Studies at the University of Vermont (1993–2006). He is the author of *Wilhelm Lehmann. A Critical Biography* (1984), and *Understanding Johannes Bobrowski* (1995). He has edited and contributed to several books on the Holocaust and on German literature, and has translated from German multiple texts.

Selected Bibliography

Adam, Uwe Dietrich. *Judenpolitik im Dritten Reich*. Düsseldorf: Droste Verlag, 1972.
Adler-Rudel, Salomon. *Jüdische Selbsthilfe unter dem Naziregime 1933–1939. Im Spiegel der Berichte der Reichsvertretung der Juden in Deutschland*. Tübingen: Mohr/Siebeck, 1974.
Adler, H.G. *Der verwaltete Mensch. Studien zur Deportation der Juden aus Deutschland*. Tübingen: Mohr/Siebeck, 1974.
———. *Die Juden in Deutschland von der Aufklärung bis zum Nationalsozialismus*. Munich: Kösel, 1960.
American Jewish Congress. *The Economic Destruction of German Jewry by the Nazi Regime, 1933–1937*. New York: American Jewish Congress, November 1937.
Amkraut, Brian. *Between Home and Homeland: Youth Aliyah from Nazi Germany*. Tuscaloosa: University of Alabama Press, 2006.
Angress, Werner. *Between Fear and Hope: Jewish Youth in the Third Reich*. New York: Columbia University Press, 1988.
———. "Juden im politischen Leben der Revolutionszeit." In *Deutsches Judentum in Krieg und Revolution 1916–1923*, ed. Werner E. Mosse, 137–315. Tübingen: Mohr/Siebeck, 1971.
———. "Auswandererlehrgut Gross-Breesen." *Leo Baeck Institute Yearbook* 10 (1965): 168–187.
Arendt, Hanna. *The Origins of Totalitarianism*. Part I: *Antisemitism*. New York: Harcourt Brace Jovanovich, 1973.
Aschheim, Steven. *Beyond the Border: The German-Jewish Legacy Abroad*. Princeton: Princeton University Press, 2007.
———. *Scholem, Arendt, Klemperer: Intimate Chronicles in Turbulent Times*. Bloomington: Indiana University Press, 2001.
———. *Brothers and Strangers: The East European Jew in German and German Jewish Consciousness, 1800–1923*. Madison: University of Wisconsin Press, 1982.
Bajohr, Frank. "Die Deportation der Juden: Initiativen und Reaktionen aus Hamburg." In *Die Verfolgung und Ermordung der Hamburger Juden 1933–1945*.

Geschichte, Zeugnis, Erinnerung, ed. Beate Meyer, 33–42. Göttingen: Wallstein Verlag, 2006.

———. "'Nur deutsch will ich sein'. Jüdische Populärkünstler, antijüdische Stereotype und heutige Erinnerungskultur. Das Beispiel der Hamburger Volkssänger, Gebrüder Wolf." In *Jüdische Welten. Juden in Deutschland vom 18. Jahrhundert bis in die Gegenwart*, ed. Marion Kaplan, Beate Meyer, 373–396. Göttingen: Wallstein Verlag, 2005.

———. *"Unser Hotel ist judenfrei." Bäder-Antisemitismus im 19. und 20. Jahrhundert.* Frankfurt am Main: Fischer Verlag, 2003.

———. *Aryanization in Hamburg: The Economic Exclusion of Jews and the Confiscation of their Property in Nazi Germany.* New York: Berghahn Books, 2002.

Baker, Leonhard. *Hirt der Verfolgten. Leo Baeck im Dritten Reich.* Stuttgart: Klett-Cotta, 1982.

Ball-Kaduri, Kurt Jacob. *Das Leben der Juden in Deutschland im Jahre 1933.* Frankfurt am Main: Europäische Verlags-Anstalt, 1963.

Bankier, David, ed. *Probing the Depths of Antisemitism: German Society and the Persecution of the Jews, 1933–1941.* Oxford: Berghahn Books, 2000.

Barkai, Avraham. *"Wehr Dich!" Der Centralverein deutscher Staatsbürger jüdischen Glaubens 1893–1938.* Munich: C.H. Beck, 2002.

———. "Between Deutschtum and Judentum: Ideological Controversies within the Centralverein." In *In Search of Jewish Community: Jewish Identities in Germany and Austria, 1918–1933*, ed. Michael Brenner and Derek J. Penslar, 74–91. Bloomington: Indiana University Press, 1998.

———. *Hoffnung und Untergang. Studien zur deutsch-jüdischen Geschichte des 19. und 20. Jahrhunderts*, 141–165. Hamburg: Christians Verlag, 1998.

———. "Im mauerlosen Ghetto." In *Deutsch-jüdische Geschichte der Neuzeit. Aufbruch und Zerstörung 1918–1945.* Vol. 4, ed. Michael A. Meyer, 319–349. Munich: C.H. Beck, 1997.

———. "The Fateful Year 1938: The Continuation and Acceleration of Plunder." In *November 1938: From "Reichskristallnacht" to Genocide*, ed. Walter Pehle, 95–122. Oxford: Berg Publishers, 1991.

———. *From Boycott to Annihilation: The Economic Struggle of German Jews, 1933–1943.* Hanover and London: University Press of New England, 1989. In German as *Vom Boykott zur Entjudung. Der wirtschaftliche Existenzkampf der Juden im Dritten Reich 1933–1943* (Frankfurt am Main: Fischer Verlag, 1988).

Baumann, Angelika and Andreas Heusler, eds. *München arisiert. Entrechtung und Enteignung der Juden während des Nationalsozialismus.* Munich: C.H. Beck, 2004.

Benz, Wolfgang, ed. *Überleben im Dritten Reich. Juden im Untergrund und ihre Helfer*. Munich: C.H. Beck, 2003.

———, ed. *Die Juden in Deutschland 1933–1945. Leben unter nationalsozialistischer Herrschaft*. Munich: C.H. Beck, 1989.

Blumenfeld, Kurt. *Im Kampf um den Zionismus. Briefe aus fünf Jahrzehnten*. Stuttgart: Deutsche Verlags-Anstalt, 1976.

———. *Erlebte Judenfrage. Ein Vierteljahrhundert Deutscher Zionismus*. Stuttgart: Deutsche Verlags-Anstalt, 1962.

Boas, Jacob. "The Shrinking World of German Jewry, 1933–1938." *Leo Baeck Institute Year Book* 31 (1986): 241–266.

———. "German-Jewish Internal Politics under Hitler 1933–1938." *Leo Baeck Institute Yearbook* 29 (1984): 3–25.

Boehm, Eric. *We Survived. The Stories of Fourteen of the Hidden and the Hunted of Nazi Germany*. New Haven: Yale University Press, 1949.

Böhm, Adolf. *Die Zionistische Bewegung*. 2 vols. Berlin: Jüdischer Verlag, 1935–1937.

Botz, Gerhard. *Wohnungspolitik und Judendeportation in Wien 1938 bis 1945. Zur Funktion des Antisemitismus als Ersatz nationalsozialistischer Sozialpolitik*. Vienna: Geyer, 1975.

Brenner, Michael. *The Renaissance of Jewish Culture in Weimar Germany*. New Haven: Yale University Press, 1996.

Brodnitz, Friedrich. "Die Reichsvertretung der deutschen Juden." In *In Zwei Welten: Siegfried Moses Zum 75. Geburtstag*, ed. Hans Tramer, 106–113. Tel Aviv: Bitaon, 1962.

Browder, George. *Hitler's Enforcers: The Gestapo and the SS Security Service in the Nazi Revolution*. New York: Oxford University Press, 1996.

———. *Foundations of the Nazi Police State: The Formation of SIPO and the SD*. Lexington, KY: University Press of Kentucky, 1990.

Browning, Christopher. *The Origins of the Final Solution: The Evolution of Nazi Jewish Policy, September 1939–March 1942*. Lincoln: University of Nebraska Press and Yad Vashem, 2004.

———. *Nazi Policy, Jewish Workers, German Killers*. New York: Cambridge University Press, 2000.

———. *The Path to Genocide: Essays on Launching the Final Solution*. New York: Cambridge University Press, 1992.

———. *Fateful Months: Essays on the Emergence of the Final Solution*. New York: Holmes and Meier, 1985.

Brustein, William. *Roots of Hate: Anti-Semitism in Europe before the Holocaust*. New York: Cambridge University Pres, 2003.

Burrin, Philippe. *Nazi Anti-Semitism: From Prejudice to the Holocaust.* New York: The New Press, 2005.

Cochavi, Yehoyakim. "'The Hostile Alliance': The Relationship between the Reichsvereinigung of Jews in Germany and the Regime." *Yad Vashem Studies* 22 (1992): 237–272.

Dahn, Hugo. "Die Gründung der Reichsvertretung." In *In Zwei Welten: Siegfried Moses zum 75. Geburtstag,* ed. Hans Tramer, 97–105. Tel Aviv: Bitaon, 1962.

Dean, Martin. *Robbing the Jews: The Confiscation of Jewish Property in the Holocaust, 1933–1945.* New York: Cambridge University Press, 2008.

———. "The Development and Implementation of Nazi Denaturalization and Confiscation Policy up to the Eleventh Decree to the Reich Citizenship Law." *Holocaust and Genocide Studies* 16 (2002): 217–242.

Dunker, Ulrich. *Der Reichsbund jüdischer Frontsoldaten 1919–1938. Geschichte eines jüdischen Abwehrvereins.* Düsseldorf: Droste Verlag, 1977.

Efron, John. *Defenders of Race: Jewish Doctors and Race Science in Fin de Siècle Europe.* New Haven: Yale University Press, 1994.

Eisner, Ruth. *Nicht wir allein: Aus dem Tagebuch einer Berliner Jüdin.* Berlin: Arani Verlags-GmbH, 1971.

Elkin, Rivka. *"Das Jüdische Krankenhaus muss erhalten bleiben." Das Jüdische Krankenhaus in Berlin zwischen 1938 und 1945.* Berlin: Edition Hentrich, 1993.

Essner, Cornelia. *Die "Nürnberger Gesetze" oder die Verwaltung des Rassenwahns 1933–1945.* Paderborn: Schöningh, 2002.

Evans, Richard. *The Third Reich in Power, 1933–1939.* New York: Penguin Press, 2005.

Felstiner, Mary. *To Paint Her Life: Charlotte Salomon in the Nazi Era.* New York: HarperCollins, 1994.

Field, Geoffrey. *Evangelist of Race: The Germanic Vision of Houston Stewart Chamberlain.* New York: Columbia University Press, 1981.

Fleming, Gerald. *Hitler and the Final Solution.* Berkeley: University of California Press, 1984.

Foster, John, ed. *Community of Fate: Memoirs of German Jews in Melbourne.* Sydney, Boston: Allen & Unwin, 1986.

Freeden, Herbert. *Die jüdische Presse im Dritten Reich.* Frankfurt am Main: Jüdischer Verlag bei Athenäum, 1987.

Friedländer, Saul. *The Years of Extermination: Nazi Germany and the Jews, 1939–1945.* New York: HarperCollins, 2007.

———. *Nazi Germany and the Jews: The Years of Persecution, 1933–1939.* New York: Harper Collins, 1997.

Gaertner, Hans. "Problems of Jewish Schools during the Hitler Regime." *Leo Baeck Institute Year Book* 1 (1956): 123–141.

Gay, Peter. "Epilogue: The First Sex." In *Between Sorrow and Strength: Women Refugees of the Nazi Period*, ed. Sibylle Quack, 353–367. Cambridge: Cambridge University Press, 1995.

Gay, Ruth. *The Jews of Germany: A Historical Portrait*. New Haven: Yale University Press, 1992.

Gellately, Robert. *The Gestapo and German Society: Enforcing Racial Policy, 1933–1945*. New York: Oxford University Press, 1990.

Genschel, Helmut. *Die Verdrängung der Juden aus der Wirtschaft im Dritten Reich*. Göttingen: Musterschmidt Verlag, 1966.

Gillerman, Sharon. "The Crisis of the Jewish Family." In *In Search of Jewish Community: Jewish Identities in Germany and Austria, 1918–1933*, ed. Michael Brenner and Derek Penslar, 176–199. Bloomington: Indiana University Press, 1998.

Gottwaldt, Alfred and Diana Schulle. *Die "Judendeportationen" aus dem Deutschen Reich 1941–1945*. Wiesbaden: Marix Verlag, 2005.

Grubel, Fred and Frank Mecklenburg. "Leipzig: Profile of a Jewish Community during the First Years of Nazi Germany." *Leo Baeck Institute Yearbook* 42 (1997): 157–188.

Gruenewald, Max. "The Beginning of the 'Reichsvertretung'." *Leo Baeck Institute Yearbook* 1 (1956): 57–67.

Gruner, Wolf. *Widerstand in der Rosenstrasse. Die Fabrik-Aktion und die Verfolgung der "Mischehen" 1943*. Frankfurt am Main: Fischer Verlag, 2005.

———. "Von der Kollektivausweisung zur Deportation der Juden aus Deutschland (1938–1945): Neue Perspektiven und Dokumente." In *Die Deportation der Juden aus Deutschland: Pläne—Praxis—Reaktionen 1938–1945*, ed. Birthe Kundrus and Beate Meyer, 21–62. Göttingen: Wallstein Verlag, 2004.

———. *Öffentliche Wohlfahrt und Judenverfolgung. Wechselwirkungen lokaler and zentraler Politik im NS-Staat (1933–1942)*. Munich: Oldenbourg, 2002.

———. "Armut und Verfolgung. Die Reichsvereinigung, die jüdische Bevölkerung und die antijüdische Politik im NS-Staat 1939 bis 1945." In *Juden und Armut in Mittel- und Osteuropa*, ed. Stefi Jersch Wenzel, 405–433. Cologne/Weimar/Vienna: Böhlau, 2000.

———. *Zwangsarbeit und Verfolgung. Österreichische Juden im NS-Staat 1938–45*. Innsbruck: Studien Verlag, 2000.

———. *Der geschlossene Arbeitseinsatz deutscher Juden: Zur Zwangsarbeit als Element der Verfolgung 1938–1943*. Berlin: Metropol Verlag, 1997.

———. *Judenverfolgung in Berlin 1933–1945. Eine Chronologie der Behördenmaßnahmen in der Reichshauptstadt*. Berlin: Edition Hentrich, 1996.

———. "'Lesen brauchen sie nicht zu können…' Die Denkschrift über die Behandlung der Juden in der Reichshauptstadt auf allen Gebieten des öffentlichen Lebens vom Mai 1938." *Jahrbuch für Antisemitismusforschung* 4 (1995): 305–341.

Hambrock, Matthias. *Die Etablierung der Aussenseiter. Der Verband nationaldeutscher Juden 1921–1935*. Cologne: Böhlau Verlag, 2003.

Heim, Susanne and Götz Aly. "Staatliche Ordnung und 'organische Lösung'. Die Rede Görings über die Judenfrage vom 6. Dezember 1938." *Jahrbuch für Antisemitismusforschung* 2 (1993): 378–404.

Heims, Steven J., ed. *Passages from Berlin: Recollections of the Goldschmidt Schule, 1935–1939*. South Berwick, MA: Atlantic Printing, 1987.

Henry, Frances. *Victims and Neighbors: A Small Town in Nazi Germany Remembered*. South Hadley, MA: Bergin and Garvey, 1984.

Henschel, Hildegard. "Aus der Arbeit der jüdischen Gemeinde Berlin während der Jahre 1941–1943." *Zeitschrift für die Geschichte der Juden* 9 (1972): 33–52.

Herf, Jeffrey. *The Jewish Enemy: Nazi Propaganda during World War II and the Holocaust*. Cambridge, MA: Harvard University Press, 2006.

Herrmann, Klaus. *Das Dritte Reich und die deutsch-jüdischen Organisationen 1933–1934*. Cologne: Heymann, 1969.

Hertzberg, Arthur. *The French Enlightenment and the Jews: The Origins of Modern Antisemitism*. New York: Columbia University Press, 1990.

Heschel, Susannah. *Abraham Geiger and the Jewish Jesus*. Chicago: University of Chicago Press, 1998.

Heuberger, Georg, ed. *"Und keiner hat für uns Kaddisch gesagt". Deportationen aus Frankfurt am Main 1941 bis 1945*. Frankfurt am Main: Jüdisches Museum/Stroemfeld, 2004.

Hilberg, Raul. *The Destruction of the European Jews*. 3 vols. New Haven: Yale University Press, 2003.

———. *Perpetrators, Victims, Bystanders: The Jewish Catastrophe, 1933–1945*. New York: Aaron Asher Books, 1992.

Hildesheimer, Esriel. *Jüdische Selbstverwaltung unter dem NS-Regime. Der Existenzkampf der Reichsvertretung und Reichsvereinigung der Juden in Deutschland*. Tübingen: Mohr/Siebeck, 1994.

Hoffmann, Christhard, ed. *Preserving the Legacy of German Jewry: A History of the Leo Baeck Institute, 1955–2005*. Tübingen: Mohr/Siebeck, 2005.

Honigmann, Peter. *Die Austritte aus der jüdischen Gemeinde Berlin 1873–1941*. Frankfurt am Main: Peter Lang, 1988.

Selected Bibliography

Huerkamp, Claudia. "Jüdische Akademikerinnen in Deutschland, 1900–1938." *Geschichte und Gesellschaft*, 19 (1993): 311–331.

Johnson, Eric. *Nazi Terror: The Gestapo, Jews, and Ordinary Germans*. New York: Basic Books, 1999.

Kaplan, Marion, ed. *Jewish Daily Life in Germany, 1618–1945*. New York: Oxford University Press, 2005.

———. *Between Dignity and Despair: Jewish Life in Nazi Germany*. New York: Oxford University Press, 1998.

Kaplan, Marion and Beate Meyer, eds. *Jüdische Welten. Juden in Deutschland vom 18. Jahrhundert bis in die Gegenwart*. Göttingen: Wallstein Verlag, 2005.

Katz, Jacob. *From Prejudice to Destruction: Anti-Semitism, 1700–1933*. Cambridge: Harvard University Press, 1980.

Kershaw, Ian. *Hitler, 1889–1936: Hubris*. New York: W.W. Norton, 1998.

———. *Hitler, 1936–1945: Nemesis*. New York: W.W. Norton, 2000.

Klemperer, Victor. *I Will Bear Witness: A Diary of the Nazi Years, 1942–1945*. New York: Random House, 1999.

———. *I Will Bear Witness: A Diary of the Nazi Years, 1933–1941*. New York: Random House, 1998.

Klüger, Ruth. *Still Alive: A Holocaust Girlhood Remembered*. New York: Feminist Press, 2001.

Koonz, Claudia. "Courage and Choice among German-Jewish Women and Men." In *Die Juden im nationalsozialistischen Deutschland / The Jews in Nazi Germany, 1933–1945*, ed. Arnold Paucker, 283–293. Tübingen: Mohr/Siebeck, 1986.

Kosmala, Beate. "Zwischen Ahnen und Wissen. Flucht vor der Deportation (1941–1943)." In *Die Deportation der Juden aus Deutschland: Pläne-Praxis-Reaktionen 1938–1945*, ed. Birthe Kundrus and Beate Meyer, 135–159. Göttingen: Wallstein, 2004.

Kosmala, Beate and C. Schoppmann, eds. *Überleben im Untergrund: Hilfe für Juden in Deutschland 1941–1945*. Berlin: Metropol, 2002.

Krieger, Karsten, ed. *Der Berliner Antisemitismusstreit 1879–1881: Eine Kontroverse um die Zugehörigkeit der deutschen Juden zur Nation*. 2 vols. Munich: K.G. Saur, 2003.

Kulka, Otto Dov, ed. *Deutsches Judentum unter dem Nationalsozialismus: Dokumente zur Geschichte der Reichsvertretung der deutschen Juden 1933–1939*. Tübingen: Mohr/Siebeck, 1997.

———. "The Reichsvereinigung and the Fate of the German Jews, 1938/1939–1943: Continuity or Discontinuity in German-Jewish History in the Third Reich." In *Die Juden im nationalsozialistischen Deutschland/The Jews in Nazi*

Germany, 1933–1943, ed. Arnold Paucker, 353–363. Tübingen: Mohr/Siebeck, 1986.

Kwiet, Konrad. "Forced Labour of German Jews in Nazi Germany." *Leo Baeck Institute Yearbook* 36 (1991): 389–407.

———. "To Leave or Not to Leave. The German Jews at the Crossroads." In *November 1938: From Reichskristallnacht to Genocide*, ed. Walter Pehle, 139–153. Oxford: Berg, 1991.

———. "Nach dem Pogrom: Stufen der Ausgrenzung." In *Die Juden in Deutschland 1933–1945. Leben unter nationalsozialistischer Herrschaft*, ed. Wolfgang Benz, 614–631. Munich: C.H. Beck, 1989.

———. "The Ultimate Refuge: Suicide in the Jewish Community under the Nazis." *Leo Baeck Institute Yearbook* 29 (1984): 135–167.

Kwiet, Konrad and Helmut Eschwege. *Selbstbehauptung und Widerstand. Deutsche Juden im Kampf um Existenz und Menschenwürde 1933–1945*. Hamburg: Christians Verlag, 1986.

Lässig, Simone. *Jüdische Wege ins Bürgertum: Kulturelles Kapital und sozialer Aufstieg im 19. Jahrhundert*. Göttingen: Vandenhoeck und Ruprecht, 2004.

Lauber, Heinz. *Judenpogrom: Reichskristallnacht November 1938 in Grossdeutschland*. Gerlingen: Bleicher, 1981.

Lavski, Hagit. *Before Catastrophe: The Distinctive Path of German Zionism*. Detroit: Wayne State University Press, 1998.

Levenson, Alan. *Between Philosemitism and Antisemitism: Defenses of Jews and Judaism in Germany, 1871–1932*. Lincoln: University of Nebraska Press, 2004.

Levy, Richard. *The Downfall of the Anti-Semitic Political Parties in Imperial Germany*. New Haven: Yale University Press, 1975.

Lichtheim, Richard. *Rückkehr: Lebenserinnerungen aus der Frühzeit des deutschen Zionismus*. Stuttgart: Deutsche Verlags-Anstalt, 1970.

———. *Geschichte des deutschen Zionismus*. Jerusalem: R. Maas, 1954.

———. *Revision der zionistischen Politik*. Berlin: Kommissions-Verlag, 1939.

Limberg, Margarete and Hubert Rübsaat, eds. *Germans No More: Accounts of Jewish Everyday Life, 1933–1938*. New York: Berghahn Books, 2006.

Loewenstein, Kurt. "Die innerjüdische Reaktion auf die Krise der deutschen Demokratie." *Entscheidungsjahr 1932: Zur Judenfrage in der Endphase der Weimarer Republik*, ed. Werner Mosse, 349–403. Tübingen: Mohr/Siebeck, 1966.

Lösener, Bernhard. "Als Rassereferent im Reichsministerium des Innern." *Vierteljahrshefte für Zeitgeschichte* 9 (1961): 261–313.

Maierhof, Gudrun. *Selbstbehauptung im Chaos. Frauen in der jüdischen Selbsthilfe 1933–1943*. Frankfurt am Main: Campus, 2002.

Margaliot, Abraham. "The Dispute over the Leadership of German Jewry (1933–1938)." *Yad Vashem Studies* 10 (1974): 129–148.

Massing, Paul. *Rehearsal for Destruction: A Study of Political Antisemitism in Imperial Germany.* New York: Harper, 1949.

Matthäus, Jürgen. "Deutschtum and Judentum under Fire—The Impact of the First World War on the Strategies of the Centralverein and the Zionistische Vereinigung." *Leo Baeck Institute Yearbook* 33 (1988): 129–147.

Matthäus, Jürgen and Mark Roseman, *Jewish Responses to Persecution.* Vol. I: 1933–1938. Lanham, MD: Altamira Press, 2010.

Matthäus, Jürgen and Klaus-Michael Mallmann, eds. *Deutsche, Juden, Völkermord. Der Holocaust als Geschichte und Gegenwart.* Darmstadt: Wissenschaftliche Buchgemeinschaft, 2006.

Maurer, Trude. "From Everyday Life to a State of Emergency: Jews in Weimar and Nazi Germany." *Jewish Daily Life in Germany, 1618–1945*, ed. Marion Kaplan, 271–373. New York: Oxford University Press, 2005.

Meyer, Beate. "'Der 'Eichmann von Dresden.' 'Justizielle Bewältigung' von NS-Verbrechen in der DDR am Beispiel des Verfahrens gegen Henry Schmidt." In *Deutsche, Juden, Völkermord. Der Holocaust in Geschichte und Gegenwart*, ed. Jürgen Matthäus and Klaus-Michael Mallmann, 275–292. Darmstadt: Wissenschaftliche Buchgesellschaft, 2006.

———, ed. *Die Verfolgung und Ermordung der Hamburger Juden 1933–1945. Geschichte, Zeugnis, Erinnerung.* Göttingen: Wallstein Verlag, 2006.

———. "Geschichte im Film. Judenverfolgung, Mischehen und der Protest in der Rosenstrasse." *Zeitschrift für Geschichtswissenschaft* 52 (2004): 23–36.

———. "Handlungsspielräume regionaler jüdischer Repräsentanten (1941–1945): Die Reichsvereinigung der Juden in Deutschland und die Deportationen." In *Die Deportation der Juden aus Deutschland: Pläne—Praxis—Reaktionen 1938–1945*, ed. Birthe Kundrus and Beate Meyer, 63–85. Göttingen: Wallstein Verlag, 2004.

———. "Gratwanderung zwischen Verantwortung und Verstrickung—Die Reichsvereinigung der Juden in Deutschland und die jüdische Gemeinde zu Berlin 1938–1945." In *Juden in Berlin 1938–1945*, ed. Beate Meyer and Hermann Simon, 291–337. Berlin: Philo Verlagsgesellschaft, 2000.

———. *"Jüdische Mischlinge." Rassenpolitik und Verfolgungserfahrung 1933–1945.* Hamburg: Dölling und Galitz Verlag, 1999.

Meyer, Beate, Hermann Simon, and Chana Schütz, eds. *Jews in Nazi Berlin: From Kristallnacht to Liberation.* Chicago: University of Chicago Press, 2009.

Meyer, Michael A., ed. *Joachim Prinz, Rebellious Rabbi: An Autobiography—the German and early American Years.* Bloomington: Indiana University Press, 2008.

———. *Deutsch-Jüdische Geschichte in der Neuzeit*. 4 vols. Munich: C.H. Beck, 1996.

Milton, Sybil. "The Expulsion of Polish Jews from Germany: October 1938 to July 1939—A Documentation." *Leo Baeck Institute Yearbook* 29 (1984): 169–199.

Miron, Gai, Jacob Borut, and Rivka Elkin. *Aspects of Jewish Welfare in Nazi Germany*. Jerusalem: Yad Vashem, 2006.

Mommsen, Hans. "Dokumentation: Der nationalsozialistische Polizeistaat und die Judenverfolgung vor 1938." *Vierteljahrshefte für Zeitgeschichte* 10 (1962): 68–87.

Mosse, George. *Toward the Final Solution: A History of European Racism*. New York: Harper and Row, 1978.

———. *Germans and Jews: The Right, the Left, and the Search for a "Third Force" in Pre-Nazi Germany*. New York: Howard Fertig, 1970.

Nicosia, Francis R. *Zionism and Anti-Semitism in Nazi Germany*. New York: Cambridge University Press, 2008.

———. "Jewish Farmers in Hitler's Germany: Zionist Occupational Retraining and Nazi 'Jewish Policy.'" *Holocaust and Genocide Studies* 19 (2005): 365–389.

———. *The Third Reich and the Palestine Question*. New Brunswick, NJ: Transaction Publishers, 2000.

———. "Resistance and Self-Defence. Zionism and Antisemitism in Inter-War Germany." *Leo Baeck Institute Yearbook* 42 (1997): 123–134.

———. "Der Zionismus in Leipzig im Dritten Reich." *Judaica Lipsiensia: Zur Geschichte der Juden in Leipzig*, ed. Manfred Unger, 167–178. Leipzig: Edition Leipzig, 1994.

Niewyk, Donald. *The Jews in Weimar Germany*. New Brunswick, NJ: Transaction Publishers, 2001.

———. "Solving the 'Jewish Problem'—Continuity and Change in German Anti-semitism 1871–1945." *Leo Baeck Institute Yearbook* 35 (1990): 335–370.

Noakes, Jeremy. "The Development of Nazi Policy towards the German-Jewish 'Mischlinge' 1933–1945." *Leo Baeck Institute Yearbook* 34 (1989): 291–354.

Oberman, Heiko. *The Roots of Anti-Semitism in the Age of Renaissance and Reformation*. Philadelphia: Fortress Press, 1984.

Paucker, Arnold. "Changing Perceptions: Reflections on the Historiography of Jewish Self-Defense and Jewish Resistance, 1890–2000." In *Jüdische Welten. Juden in Deutschland vom 18. Jahrhundert bis in die Gegenwart*, ed. Marion Kaplan and Beate Meyer, 440–456. Göttingen: Wallstein Verlag, 2005.

———, ed. *Die Juden im Nationalsozialistischen Deutschland/The Jews in Nazi Germany 1933–1943*. Tübingen: Mohr/Siebeck, 1986.

———. *Der jüdische Abwehrkampf gegen Antisemitismus und Nationalsozialismus in den letzten Jahren der Weimarer Republik*. Hamburg: Leibnitz Verlag, 1969.

Pauley, Bruce. *From Prejudice to Destruction: A History of Austrian Anti-Semitism*. Chapel Hill: University of North Carolina Press, 1992.

Pegelow, Thomas. "Determining 'People of German Blood', 'Jews' and 'Mischlinge': The Reich Kinship Office and the Competing Discourses and Powers of Nazism, 1941–1943." *Contemporary European History* 15 (2006): 43–65.

Peukert, Detlev. *Inside Nazi Germany: Conformity, Opposition, and Racism in Everyday Life*. New Haven: Yale University Press, 1987.

Poliakov, Leon. *The Aryan Myth: A History of Racist and Nationalist Ideas in Europe*. New York: Basic Books, 1971.

Poppel, Stephen M. *Zionism in Germany 1897–1933: The Shaping of a Jewish Identity*. Philadelphia: Jewish Publication Society of America, 1977.

Prinz, Joachim. *Wir Juden*. Berlin: Erich Reiss, 1934.

Pulzer, Peter. *The Rise of Political Antisemitism in Germany and Austria*. Cambridge, MA: Harvard University Press, 1988.

Quack, Sibylle. *Zuflucht Amerika: Zur Sozialgeschichte der Emigration deutschjüdischer Frauen in die USA 1933–1945*. Bonn: Dietz, 1995.

Reinharz, Jehuda. "Hashomer Hazair in Germany I, 1928–1933." *Leo Baeck Institute Yearbook* 31 (1986): 173–208.

———. "Hashomer Hazair in Germany II: Under the Shadow of the Swastika, 1933–1938." *Leo Baeck Institute Yearbook* 32 (1987): 183–229.

———. "The Zionist Response to Antisemitism in Germany." *Leo Baeck Institute Yearbook* 30 (1985): 105–140.

———. "The Zionist Response to Antisemitism in the Weimar Republic." In *The Jewish Response to German Culture*, ed. Jehuda Reinharz and Walter Schatzberg, 266–293. Hanover: University Press of New England, 1985.

———, ed. *Dokumente zur Geschichte des deutschen Zionismus 1882–1933*. Tübingen: Mohr/Siebeck, 1981.

———. *Fatherland or Promised Land: The Dilemma of the German Jew, 1893–1914*. Ann Arbor: University of Michigan Press, 1975.

Richarz, Monika. "Der jüdische Weihnachtsbaum—Familie und Säkularisierung im deutschen Judentum des 19. Jahrhunderts." In *Geschichte und Emanzipation, Festschrift für Reinhard Rürup*, ed. Michael Grüttner, Rüdiger Hachtmann, and Heinz-Gerhard Haupt, 275–289. Frankfurt am Main: Campus, 1999.

———, ed. *Jewish Life in Germany: Memoirs from Three Centuries*. Bloomington: Indiana University Press, 1991.

———, ed. *Jüdisches Leben in Deutschland: Selbstzeugnisse zur Sozialgeschichte 1918–1945*. Stuttgart: Deutsche Verlags-Anstalt, 1982.

Rose, Paul Lawrence. *German Question—Jewish Question: Revolutionary Antisemitism from Kant to Wagner*. Princeton: Princeton University Press, 1992.

Roseman, Mark. *The Past in Hiding*. New York: Metropolitan Books, 2001.

Ruppin, Arthur. *Tagebücher, Briefe, Erinnerungen*. Königstein/Ts.: Jüdischer Verlag Athenäum, 1985.

Rürup, Reinhard. "Das Ende der Emanzipation. Die anti-jüdische Politik in Deutschland von der 'Machtergreifung' bis zum Zweiten Weltkrieg." In *Die Juden im nationalsozialistischen Deutschland / The Jews in Nazi Germany, 1933–1943*, ed. Arnold Paucker, 97–114. Tübingen: Mohr/Siebeck, 1986.

———. *Emanzipation und Antisemitismus. Studien zur "Judenfrage" der bürgerlichen Gesellschaft*. Göttingen: Vandenhoeck & Ruprecht, 1975.

Schatzker, Chaim. "The Jewish Youth Movement in Germany in the Holocaust Period II—The Relations Between the Youth Movement and Hechaluz." *Leo Baeck Institute Yearbook* 33 (1988): 301–325.

———. "The Jewish Youth Movement in Germany in the Holocaust Period I—Youth in Confrontation with a New Reality." *Leo Baeck Institute Yearbook* 32 (1987): 157–181.

Scheffler, Wolfgang. *Judenverfolgung im Dritten Reich*. Berlin: Colloquium Verlag, 1964.

Schleunes, Karl. *The Twisted Road to Auschwitz: Nazi Policy Toward German Jews 1933–1939*. Urbana: University of Illinois Press, 1970.

Scholem, Gershom. *From Berlin to Jerusalem: Memories of my Youth*. New York: Schocken Books, 1988.

Schorsch, Ismar. *Jewish Reactions to German Anti-Semitism, 1870–1914*. New York: Columbia University Press, 1972.

Schüler-Springorum, Stefanie. *Die jüdische Minderheit in Königsberg/Preussen, 1871–1945*. Göttingen: Vandenhoek & Ruprecht, 1996.

Schwarz, Mimi. *Good Neighbors Bad Times: Echoes of My Father's German Village*. Lincoln: University of Nebraska Press, 2008.

Steinweis, Alan. *Kristallnacht 1938*. Cambridge, MA: Harvard University Press, 2009.

———. *Art, Ideology, and Economics in Nazi Germany: The Reich Chambers of Music, Theater, and the Visual Arts, 1933–1945*. Chapel Hill: University of North Carolina Press, 1993.

Stoltzfus, Nathan. *Resistance of the Heart: Intermarrige and the Rosenstrasse Protest in Germany*. New York: W.W. Norton, 1996.

Strauss, Herbert. "Jewish Emigration from Germany—Nazi Policies and Jewish Responses II." *Leo Baeck Institute Yearbook* 26 (1981): 343–409.

———. "Jewish Emigration from Germany—Nazi Policies and Jewish Responses I." *Leo Baeck Institute Yearbook* 25 (1980): 313–361.

Tal, Uriel. *Christians and Jews in Germany: Religion, Politics, and Ideology in the Second Reich, 1870–1914*. Ithaca: Cornell University Press, 1975.

Volkov, Shulamit. *Germans, Jews, and Antisemites: Trials in Emancipation*. New York: Cambridge University Press, 2006.

———. *Jüdisches Leben und Antisemitismus im 19. und 20. Jahrhundert*. Munich: C.H. Beck, 1990.

———. "Kontinuität und Diskontinuität im deutschen Antisemitismus 1878–1945." *Vierteljahrshefte für Zeitgeschichte* 33 (1985): 221–243.

Walk, Joseph. *Jüdische Schule und Erziehung im Dritten Reich*. Frankfurt am Main: Verlag Anton Hain Meisenheim, 1991.

———, ed. *Das Sonderrecht für die Juden im NS-Staat: Eine Sammlung der gesetzlichen Massnahmen und Richtlinien—Inhalt und Bedeutung*. Heidelberg: Müller Juristischer Verlag, 1981.

———. "Das Deutsche Komitee Pro-Palästina, 1926–1933." *Bulletin des Leo Baeck Instituts* 15 (1976): 162–193.

Weiss, Ruth. *Wege im harten Gras: Erinnerungen an Deutschland, Südafrika und England*. Wuppertal: P. Hammer, 1995.

Weiss, Yfat. *Deutsche und polnische Juden vor dem Holocaust. Jüdische Identität zwischen Staatsbürgerschaft und Ethnizität 1933–1940*. Munich: Oldenbourg, 2000.

Weltsch, Robert. "Looking Back Over Sixty Years." *Leo Baeck Institute Yearbook* 27 (1982): 379–390.

———. "Entscheidungsjahr 1932." In *Entscheidungsjahr 1932: Zur Judenfrage in der Endphase der Weimarer Republik*, ed. Werner Mosse, 535–562. Tübingen: Mohr/Siebeck, 1966.

Wildt, Michael. *Generation des Unbedingten. Das Führungskorps des Reichssicherheitshauptamtes*. Hamburg: Hamburger Edition, 2002.

———. "Violence Against Jews in Germany, 1933–1939." In *Probing the Depths of Antisemitism: German Society and the Persecution of the Jews, 1933–1941*, ed. David Bankier, 181–209. Oxford: Berghahn Books, 2000.

———. "Before the 'Final Solution': The *Judenpolitik* of the SD, 1935–1938." *Leo Baeck Institute Yearbook* 43 (1998): 241–269.

———, ed. *Die Judenpolitik des SD 1935 bis 1938: Eine Dokumentation*. Munich: Oldenbourg, 1995.

Willems, Susanne. *Der entsiedelte Jude. Albert Speers Wohnungsmarktpolitik für den Berliner Hauptstadtbau*. Berlin: Edition Hentrich, 2000.

Zimmermann, Moshe. *Die deutschen Juden 1914–1945*. Munich: Oldenbourg, 1997.

———. *Wilhelm Marr: The Patriarch of Antisemitism*. New York: Oxford University Press, 1986.

———. "Two Generations of German Antisemitism—The Letters of Theodor Fritsch to Wilhelm Marr." *Leo Baeck Institute Yearbook* 23 (1978): 89–99.

INDEX

Abraham, Ruth, 19–20
Abstammungsbescheide (certificates of ancestry), 52
Adler, H.G., 142, 163
Adler-Rudel, Salomon, 87n6, 107, 115n67
Advisory Office for Jewish Economic Assistance (Beratungsstelle für jüdische Wirtschaftshilfe), 100
Ahlem, 131
Albersheim, Erna, 44n113
aliyah, 36, 45nn123–124, 91,
Allied Control Commission, 149
Altkarbe-Obermüle, 101
Altreich (Germany in its pre-1938 borders), 13n 24, 69n36, 86, 111
American Jewish Committee, 190–194
A Midsummer Night's Dream, 173
ancestry, 9, 51, 53, 56–59, 61, 64, 65
Anglo-Palestine Bank, 83
anti-Jewish measures, 5–6, 11, 48–50, 52–54, 56, 60, 92, 94, 106–7, 117–19, 121–123, 125, 127–129, 133, 145n27, 150, 178, 191, 200–204, 206
anti-Semitism,
German, 10, 14n 25, 21, 74, 80, 90–91, 94–96, 120, 122, 175, 180
legislation, 17
Anti-Soviet Exhibition, 159
Appel, Marta, 25
April Laws of 1933, 17, 21, 28
Arabs, 83, 98
Arbeitslager (work camps), 123
Arendt, Hannah, 47, 72, 87, 164, 169n55
"Armament Jews", 160
"Aryan," 4–6, 8–9, 20, 23, 26, 31–32, 42n96, 49, 51, 53–55, 58–64, 68n24, 70n46, 102, 122–123, 125, 134, 140, 170, 186, 190–193, 202–204, 206
"Aryan" paragraph, 49, 201

"Aryanization," 6, 106, 117, 125–126, 145n19, 202
Ascher, Saul, 180
assimilationist, 50, 74, 95, 97, 102, 103, 112n18
Auschwitz, 62, 86, 142, 147n75, 162
Australia, 30
Austria, 2
annexation of (*Anschluss*), 6, 7, 123
archives in, 69n33
artists, 173
conditions in, 2
Jews in, 7, 14n26, 43n107, 46n127, 46n131, 48, 54, 111, 112n17, 114n46, 120, 131, 152
Nazis, 126

Bab, Julius, 173, 182n1
Baden, 23, 42n96, 155, 185
Baden Württemberg, 44n113
Baeck, Rabbi Leo, 47, 71, 72, 76, 150, 156, 160, 162, 179
Baer, Fritz Isaac, 174
Baerwald, Alice, 44n113
Bajohr, Frank, 117, 135
Balfour Declaration, 95
Barkai, Avraham, 9–11, 43n108, 118, 134, 142
Bar Kochba, see Jüdische Turn- und Sportverein Bar Kochba
Baum, Herbert, 141, 159
Baum, Ulrich, 44
Baum Group, 141, 159
Belgium, 33
Benz, Wolfgang, 120
Bergner, Elisabeth, 172
Berlin, 1, 4, 7, 10, 21, 23, 27, 30, 38, 40n48, 40n59, 44n113, 45n123, 46n131, 53–62, 64–65, 68n28, 69n34, 69n36, 69n38, 76, 79, 83–84, 89–111,

Index

112nn13–14, 113n32, 118–119, 120–121, 122, 123–124, 128, 131, 134, 135–136, 137, 139, 141–142, 149, 152, 153, 155, 157–158, 159–160, 162–163, 168n43, 170, 171, 172, 173, 174, 175, 177, 189, 194, 204, 207, 209, 212, 213, 215, 219
Berliner, Cora, 150, 160
Berliner Illustrierte, 94
Berliner Jüdische Zeitung, 92
Berliner Tageblatt, 94
Bernheim, Hanna, 29, 40n48
Beth Chaluz, Hamburg, 100
Bialik, Haym Nahman, 172
Bick, Edith, 20
Bildung, 28
Birkenau, 142, 147
  gas chambers at, 86
  Sonderkommando revolt, 47
Black, Edwin, 88n18
Blau, Bruno, 46n127, 46nn130–131, 139
Bloch, Marie, 42n91
Blumenfeld, Kurt, 51, 95–96, 98, 105
Blut und Boden, 80
Board of Deputies of British Jews, 75
Boston Symphony Orchestra, 171
boycott (anti-German), 82–84, 85, 88n18, 194
boycott (anti-Jewish), 6, 26, 94, 129, 191, 192, 204
Brandenburg, 101
Breisach, 44n113
Brenner, Michael, 11–12
Breslau, 90, 101, 174, 189
Brith Chaluzim Datiim (Bachad) (Misrachi Youth Movement), 92
Broder, Henryk, 173
Brown House, 32, 195
Brunner, Alois, 160
Buber, Martin, 92, 177
Buchenwald, 6, 61

Callmann, Rudolf, 189
Caribbean, 151
Center for Research on Anti-Semitism, Berlin 120
Central Association of German Citizens of the Jewish Faith, see Centralverein deutscher Staatsbürger jüdischen Glaubens
Central Bureau for the Settlement of German Jews in Palestine, 1, 45n124, 106

Centralverein deutscher Staatsbürger jüdischen Glaubens (Central Association of German Citizens of the Jewish Faith), 14n25, 43n108, 74, 75, 77, 78, 91, 95, 97, 99
Chelmno, 142
Chug Halutzi (Pioneer Circle), 141
Cohn, Benno, 105, 106, 108, 111
Cohn, Conrad, 160
Cohn, Oskar, 176
Cologne, 90, 131, 189
communists, 3, 141, 159
concentration camps, 6, 34, 35, 37, 151–152, 155, 158, 159
Council for German Jewry, London, 26
CV-Zeitung, 17, 74, 99
Czechoslovakia
  dismemberment of, 6
  training camps in, 102, 114n46

Dachau, 6
death camps, see extermination camps
Decree for the Protection of the People and the State (28 February 1933)
Decree Regarding Physicians' Services with the National Health Service (22 April 1933), 4
Decree Regarding Registration of Jewish Property (16 April 1938), 6
Demnig, Gunter, 143
Denaturalization Law (14 July 1933), 5
Denmark, 33
denunciations, 119
Der jüdische Student, 92
Der junge Jude, 92
Der Morgen, 177
deutschblütig (of "Aryan" blood), 52, 55, 56
Deutscher, Isaac, 75
Die Geschichte der Juden in Deutschland, 175
Dienemann, Rabbi Max, 179
Diner, Dan, 11, 166
Dizengoff, Meir, 172
Dresden, 44n113, 129, 131, 133, 134, 163, 194
Dubitscher, Friedrich, 62–63
Düsseldorf, 19, 43n113, 135

East Frisia, 154
East Prussia, 44n113, 205
economic deterioration, Jewish, 73
education, Jewish, 5, 8, 10, 12, 18, 22–24, 28, 35, 77, 96, 109, 110, 111, 150,

– 238 –

Index

164, 171, 177, 185, 187, 204, 207, 217, 218–219
Eichmann, Adolf, 7, 80, 87n3, 115n63, 147n63, 169n52, 169n55
Eisner, Ruth, 24, 40n60, 41n81, 43n111
Elberstadt, 44n113
Elbogen, Ismar, 174, 175, 181
"enforced emigration", 151
England, 19, 26, 33, 34, 40n48, 42n96, 105
Enlightenment, 12, 28, 170, 171
Entfernung ("removal"), 117,
Entjudung ("de-Jewification"), 117, 125, 127, 134–135
entsiedelter Jude ("de-settlerd Jew"), 127
Eppstein, Paul, 150, 152–153, 154, 155–156, 160–161, 165
Erb- und Rassenbiologie, (Hereditary and Race Biology), 56
"evasion, Jewish, 9, 48, 49, 64–65
Evian Conference, 152
extermination camps, 3, 10, 55, 131, 161

Fabian, Erich, 162
Fabrik-Aktion (round-up for forced labor), 121, 147n75
family law novella, or the Law to Amend and Supplement Family-Related Regulations and to Regulate the Status of Stateless Persons (Gesetz über die Änderung und Ergänzung familienrechtlicher Vorschriften und über die Rechtstellung der Staatenlosen), 52–57, 59, 61, 64–66, 68n28, 69n33
Feuchtwanger, Lion, 172
"Final Solution," 2, 8, 11, 13n24, 49, 55, 57, 60, 64, 118, 119, 120, 121, 123, 124, 133, 135, 142, 143, 155, 165
France, 29, 30, 33, 44n113, 102, 114n46, 153, 155, 157
Frankfurt am Main, 95, 131
Freeden, Herbert, 173
Freier, Recha, 45n123
Freund, Elisabeth, 33–34, 37
Frick, Wilhelm, 186, 190, 196, 198, 209, 219
Friedländer, David, 180
Friedländer, Fritz, 177
Friedländer, Saul, 2, 118
Friedrich Wilhelm University, 21
Fuchs, Eugen, 75
Führerprinzip (leader principle), 76
"funtionalists", 85, 86

Fürst, Paula, 150, 160
Fürth, 44n113

Garsden, 120
Gay, Peter, 40n65, 89, 110
Gay Ruth, 89
Geisel, Eike, 173
General Government, 153
German Christian settlers in Palestine, 83
Germania Judaica, 174–175, 181
Gershom, Ezra Ben, 18
Gerstel, Else, 28, 30
Geschichte der Juden in Deutschland, 175–176
Gesellschaft für handwerkliche Arbeit (Society for Manual Labor), 101
Gestapo, 7, 19, 37, 58, 59–60, 64, 71, 76, 79, 80–81, 86, 123, 124, 127, 128, 131, 133, 137, 139, 140, 141, 151, 153–154, 156, 157–158, 160, 162–163, 170, 171, 201–204
ghetto, 10, 11, 55, 118, 120, 122, 123–124, 125, 126, 129, 132, 133, 143, 158, 164, 170, 173, 174, 207
Krankenhausghetto (hospital ghetto), 139
without walls, 140
ghettoization
of German Jews, 11, 12, 118, 123, 137, 142–143, 171, 173, 177
Ghettokultur, 121
Ghettomentalität, 121
Ginzburg, Pino, 1, 2
Glaser, Ruth, 36
Goebbels, Joseph, 82, 92, 112n13, 123, 159, 190
Göring, Hermann, 70n53, 124, 125, 126, 212, 214
Göring, Matthias H., 62–63, 70n53
Grau, Wilhelm, 180–181
Gruner, Wolf, 68n28, 127, 142
Grynszpan, Herschel, 6
Gurs, 153, 157
Gürtner, Franz, 199
gypsies, 3

Haavara Transfer Agreement, 77, 79, 82–85, 88n18
Habonim noar Chaluzi, 45n122, 97
Habsburg Monarchy, Jews in, 177
hachschara (vocational training), 10, 24–25, 34, 36 39n 30, 79–81, 88n13, 99–102, 109, 111, 114, 141, 152, 203

Hadassah, 45n123
Haganah (Jewish self-defense organization in Palestine), 1, 152
Halbjude ("half Jew"), 5, 59, 69n37, 133–134
Hamburg, 28, 38n4, 41n76, 61, 69n33, 69n38, 90, 100, 128, 133–134, 135, 138, 155
handicapped, 3
Hannover, 131, 138–139, 155
Hashomer Hazair, 97
Haskalah, Berlin 180
Hechaluz, 45n122, 81, 92, 97, 100, 101
Hed Bethar, 92
Heimeinkaufsverträge (home purchase contracts), 159, 162
Hellerberg, 131
Hellwig, Verena, 21, 31, 42n96
Henschel, Moritz, 160, 162
Hess, Rudolf, 199, 219
Heydrich, Reinhard, 96, 125, 129, 153–154, 159
Hilberg, Raul, 14n26, 45n125, 47–48, 71–72, 81, 87n2, 164
Hildebrand, Klaus, 86
Hildesheimer Rabbinerseminar, 174
Hilfsverein der deutschen Juden (Aid Association of German Jews), 36, 43n112, 45n121
Himmler, Heinrich, 57, 58
Hindenburg, Paul von, 3, 28, 41n79
Hirsch, Otto, 71, 150, 155, 189, 192
Hirschfeld, Gerhard, 86
Hirschfeld, Paul, 86, 153, 154
Hitler, Adolf, 3–4, 6–7, 13n24, 20, 22, 29, 37, 42n91, 50, 51, 52, 84–85, 92, 100, 103, 104, 109, 117, 124, 126, 132, 135, 172, 174, 176, 186, 190, 191, 194, 196, 198, 201, 207, 209
  Mein Kampf, 42
  Gospel according to "St. Hitler," 206
Hochschule für die Wissenschaft des Judentums, 174
Hoffmann, Christhard, 181
Hoffmann, Jacob, 189
Holland, 33, 102, 114nn45–46
Hollbeckshof, 131
Horn, Staatsanwalt Otto, 59–60, 61, 63
Housing Advisory Boards, 128
Hungary, 45n125

"intentionalists", 85, 86
Izbica, 142

Jedwabne, 117, 144n2
Jerusalem, 1, 45n124, 88n13, 105–106, 108, 174
Jewish Agency for Palestine, 45n121, 79, 82–83, 91, 92, 93, 99, 105, 106, 107, 108
Jewish Council, see *Judenrat*
Jewish Hospital, Berlin, 134
Jewish Joint Distribution Committee, 45n124, 156
Jews
  assimilation, 3, 9, 12, 50, 73, 74, 90, 95, 97–98, 102, 103, 104, 109, 112, 132, 172, 179
  blocked accounts, 42n89, 151
  brutality against, 2, 4, 5, 7, 8, 11, 12, 35, 37, 43n 111, 43–44n113, 92, 107, 110, 123, 135, 140, 165, 200
  children in Germany, 8, 15–37, 40n45, 43n88, 43n91, 44n113, 45n114, 45nn123–124, 54, 58–60, 62–64, 74, 91, 133, 136, 138–139, 140, 158, 192, 205, 206, 207
  civil service, 4, 49, 185, 217
  closure of businesses, 6, 17, 201–202
  communities (see also *yishuv*), 6, 43n108, 72, 73, 75, 76–77, 91–92, 94, 100, 107–108, 117–43, 149–152, 158–60, 175, 187, 206, 207, 209, 215
  concealment of, 48, 129
  converted, 8, 36, 49, 51, 74, 95, 178
  deportation, 4, 6, 7, 43n101, 55, 59, 60, 64, 72, 78, 81, 86, 118, 119, 121, 127, 128, 129, 130, 131, 133, 135, 137, 140, 151, 153–155, 157–166, 172
  divorce, 46, 61, 132–134, 136, 162
  domestics, 26, 36, 43
  emigration, 1, 4, 5, 7, 8, 9, 10, 13n24, 19, 24, 25–26, 27 29–30, 31–36, 45n121, 48, 77, 79, 81, 84–85, 91, 94, 96, 97–99, 101, 102–3, 105–111, 112n14, 123, 128, 150–151, 152–153, 157, 163, 203, 213–214, 215, 217
  employment, 17, 35 38n14, 38n18
  forced labor, 11, 35, 81, 118, 121, 123, 126, 128, 131–132, 140–143, 147n75,
  foreign securities, 74, 106, 108, 115n67, 159, 207, 217
  hiding (see also Jews, underground), 20, 48, 65, 134, 139, 142, 143, 160, 168n43, 182n1

– 240 –

Index

historians, 12, 50, 52, 66, 76, 89, 172–177
immigration, 1, 10, 34, 39, 80, 88n13, 99, 151–152
intimidation of, 2, 4, 7, 92
kosher meat problem, 17
language learning, 33, 80, 151, 197
lawyers, 4, 89, 94, 139, 162, 165, 207
legislation against, 4–8 ,11, 17, 21, 52–53, 106, 187, 192
loss of civil rights, 4–5, 89
marriage, 5, 30 36, 50, 60–61, 132–133, 159, 162–163, 169n50, 197, 216
newspapers, 5–6, 17, 23, 29, 92, 99, 171, 174, 204
organizations, 6–7, 10, 18, 34, 36, 71–81, 91–111, 112n18, 114n48, 128, 149–166, 185, 187, 192, 209, 216
orthodox, 8, 76, 90, 92, 100, 131, 142, 174
passports, 33 42n 89, 155–156
persecution of, 2–3, 8–12, 32, 47–66, 72, 76, 104, 117–143, 156–166, 171, 200–201
posing (or passing) as Christians, 9, 64
"privileged," 9, 48, 54, 60, 65, 132–133, 139, 158, 160
quotas, 5, 30, 99
rescue of, 10, 31, 42n96, 45n 123, 66, 111, 120, 163, 164
resistance, 12, 22, 47–48, 67n7, 140–141, 144n15, 173, 188
Rüstungs-Juden (Armament Jews), 131
schooling, 4, 15, 18, 21–24, 28, 34, 38n30, 40n45, 40n48, 40n59, 94, 99, 101, 109, 126, 136, 141, 159, 188, 192, 203–207, 215–219
segregation of, 2, 10, 49, 52, 117–143, 171
underground, 119, 120, 141, 160, 168n43
vegetarian menu, 17
violence against, 2–7, 11, 31, 44n113, 92, 107, 123, 135, 165
visas, 33, 119, 157
vocational training, see *hachschara*
war veterans, 28, 32, 41n81, 50, 59, 97, 103, 107
women in Germany, 8, 15–37, 39n38, 40n65, 41n72, 41n75, 41n81, 42n85, 43nn107–108, 43–45nn113–114, 45nn120–121, 45n123, 45n125, 46n127, 46n130, 64, 96–97, 138–139, 150
Jonas, Rabbi Regina, 141
Juden im deutschen Kulturbereich, 175

Judenbann (ostracism of Jews), 118, 126, 140, 142
Judenfreunde (friends of Jews), 120, 123
Judenhäuser (Jews' houses), 10, 11, 117–143, 158
Judenkarteien, (catalogue of Jewish registration cards), 127
Judenpolitik, 13n14, 47, 51–52, 55, 57, 59, 64, 65, 66n1, 85, 88n12, 117, 121
Judenrat (Jewish Council), 72, 76, 87n2, 164
Judensiedlungen (Jews' settlements), 10–11, 117–143
Judenstern (Jews' Star or Yellow Star/Badge), 49, 50, 118, 120, 121, 129, 140
Jüdisch-Theologisches Seminar, Berlin, 174
Jüdische Nachrichtenblatt, 151
Jüdische Rundschau, 50, 92, 95, 96, 99, 105, 146n52, 183
Jüdische Sportvereine (Jewish Sports Associations), 92
Jüdische Turn- und Sportverein Bar Kochba (Jewish Gymnastics and Sports Association Bar Kochba), 97, 99, 102
Jüdische Volkspartei (Jewish Peoples Party), 92
Jüdischer Frauenbund (League of Jewish Women), 17, 36, 39n38, 92
Jüdischer Kulturbund, 170
Jüdischer Verlag, 92, 175

Kafka, Franz, 171
Kaiser Wilhelm Institute for Anthropology, Genetics, and Eugenics, 54
Kaltenbrunner, Ernst, 57
Kaplan, Marion, 2, 8, 47, 48, 119, 121, 140, 142
Kareski, Georg, 104
Karminski, Hannah, 17, 45n120, 150
Kassel, 131
Katz, Jacob, 178–179
Katznelson, Siegmund, 175
Keren Hayesod (Palestine Foundation Fund), 107
Keren Tora Wa'awoda, Hamburg, 100
Kerrl, 209, 219
Kettenacker, Lothar, 86
kibbutzim, 34, 36
Kindertransporte, 34
Kitzingen, 131
Klemperer, Otto, 172
Klemperer, Victor, 129, 133

Index

Kluger, Ruth, 16, 138
Kollwitz, Käthe, 172
Kolmar, Gertrud, 136, 147n75
König, Joel (Ezra Ben-Gershom), 137
Kovno, 142
Krieck, Ernst, 177
Kristallnacht pogrom, 6, 31, 32–33, 35, 44nn113–114, 82, 105–106, 117, 119, 124, 125, 126, 129, 140, 150, 182n1, 200, 208
Krosigk, Graf Schwerin von, 186
Kubu, see Kulturbund der deutschen Juden
Kulka, Otto Dov, 164
Kulturbund der deutschen Juden (Cultural League of German Jews), 12, 94, 100, 159, 170–173, 182
Küntzel, Georg, 179
Kwiet, Konrad, 10, 11, 47

Landauer, Georg, 1, 2, 98, 105, 108–109, 208
Landenberger, Leopold, 189
Landesamt für Rassewesen (State Office for Race Affairs), 58
Landgericht (State Court), Berlin, 58, 68n28
Large, David Clay, 110
Law against Economic Sabotage (1 December 1936), 42n89
Law against Overcrowding of Schools (25 April 1933), 4
Law Concerning Admission to the Legal Profession (7 April 1933), 4
Law Concerning Tenant Relations with Jews (30 April 1939), 126
Law Concerning the Legal Status of the Jewish Religious Communities (29 March 1938), 209
Law Creating the Reich Chamber of Culture (29 September 1933), 5
Law for Removing the Distress of the People and the Reich (Enabling Act), 3
Law for the Elimination of Jews from the Economic Life of Germany (12 November 1938), 6
Law for the Protection of German Blood and German Honor (15 September 1935), 5, 50, 197
Law for the Restoration of the Professional Civil Service (7 April 1933), 4, 49, 185
Law to Amend and Supplement Family-Related Regulations and to Regulate the Status of Stateless Persons, 52–53
Leipzig, 90, 96
Lessing, Gotthold Ephraim, 170, 171, 174
Lessler, Toni, 23–24
Levi, Primo, 2
Levy Kurt, 160
Levy, Siegmund, 101
Lewis, Ann, 19
Liebermann, Martha, 172
Liebermann, Max, 172
Lieblich, Karl, 176, 183n13
Liebmann, Alexander, 137
Lippert, Julius, 194
Lithuania, 45n125, 120
Lodz, 142
Lösener, Bernhard, 58, 78n58
Löwenstein, Leo, 103
Lublin District, 153, 154
Lublin Reservation, 155
Lustig, Walter, 149, 162–163

Madagascar Plan, 155
Magdeburg, 38n14, 100
Maidanek, 142
Makkabi Hazair, Jüdischer Pfadfinderbund (Jewish Scouts' League Makkabi Hazair), 45n122, 92, 97, 99, 102
Mannheim, Karl, 178
Martyrs and Heroes Remembrance Authority, 120
Marx, Hugo, 176
Mason, Tim, 86
Matthäus, Jürgen, 9, 122, 125
Mauthausen, 155
Memel, 120
Mendelssohn, Moses, 180
Mengele, Josef, 54
mentally handicapped, 3
Mexico, 33
Meyer, Beate, 11, 52, 61, 69n33, 69n38, 76, 132, 133, 144n15, 148n97
Meyer, Franz, 51, 68n21, 106, 189
Meyer, Michael, 175
Milbertshofen, 132
Minsk, 142
Mischehe (mixed marriage; see also under Jews, marriage), 60, 61, 132–134, 139, 144n15, 162–163, 169, 216
Mischehenhäuser (mixed marriage houses), 133, 134

Mischlinge ("mixed breeds"), 5, 9, 21, 23, 31, 48, 49, 50–56, 58, 60, 65, 67n14, 68n24, 68n28, 69n35, 69n37–38, 132–134, 139, 169n50
Misrachi, 92
Modern History of the Jews, 175
Mommsen, Hans, 86, 125
Monatsschrift für Geschichte und Wissenschaft des Judentums (MGWJ), 176–178
Moses, Martha, 128
Moses, Siegfried, 98, 189
Mosse, Martha, 150
Mosse Verlag, 94
Mueller, Liselotte, 19
Müller, Heinrich, 7
Munich, 32, 117, 132, 134, 135, 137, 142, 163, 193, 201, 206

Nathan der Weise (*Nathan the Wise*), 170–171, 174
National Press Law (3 October, 1933), 5
National Socialist, 120, 121, 127, 142, 165, 175, 200
 assumption of power, 72, 73, 80, 94, 102, 118, 122
 party, 3, 132, 190
 party program, 86
Nationalsozialistische Volkswohlfahrt, or NSV (National Socialist People's Welfare Agency), 154
Nauen, Alice, 29, 35
Naumann, Max, 76
Nazi brutality, see Jews, brutality against
Nazis, 2, 3, 5, 6, 9, 10, 14, 19, 20, 22, 27, 29, 32, 34, 45, 49,72, 73, 73, 75, 78, 79, 80, 82, 84, 85, 89, 104, 110, 112, 117, 123, 125, 128–129, 132–133, 134–135, 141, 143, 150, 157, 160, 164–166, 170, 171, 176, 191, 193, 200–201, 203, 205–206
Nicosia, Francis, 10, 47, 79, 80, 81
"non-Jewish Jew," 75
North Hesse, 131
November pogrom, see *Kristallnacht* pogrom
Nuremberg, 43–44n113, 131, 191, 204–205
Nuremberg Race Laws, 5, 17, 42n91, 50, 51, 53, 58–60, 67n14, 71, 107, 118, 122, 170, 195–199, 201

Oberstotzingen, 131
occupational retraining, see *hachscharah*
Offenberg, Mario, 131

Oldenburg, 154
Oppenheim, Moritz, 16
ORT (Obshchestvo Rasprostraneiia Truda—Organization for the Distribution of Artisanal and Agricultural skills for the Jews of Russia), 101
Ostjuden, 5, 87n6, 90, 91, 92

Palatinate, 155
Palästina-Amt (Palestine Office of the Jewish Agency for Palestine), 45n121, 79, 82, 83, 91, 92, 93, 99, 105–108
Palestine, 1–2, 9, 10, 18, 19, 34, 36, 45nn123–124, 77, 79, 80, 82–85, 88n13, 88n18, 90–92, 93, 94–103, 104, 105–111, 114n46, 141, 152–153, 155, 188, 203
Palestine Foundation Fund, 107
Panama, 33
Papen, Patricia von, 181
Philippson, Martin, 175
Pinkuss, Rabbi Fritz, 180
Pittsburgh Symphony Orchestra, 171
Poliklinik für Erb- und Rassenpflege (Polyclinic for Hereditary and Race Care), 81
Polish Jews, 6, 11, 45n125, 74, 153
Portugal, 33
Prague, 1, 83, 159
Preussischer Landesverband jüdischer Gemeinden (Prussian State Association of Jewish Communities), 91
Prinz, Rabbi Joachim, 89, 98, 118, 119, 143
prisoners of war, Russian, 131
Property Utilization Office (Vermögensverwertungsstelle), 128
"Protocols of the Elders of Zion," 185, 199
Prussian Academy of Arts, 172

Quakers, 34
quotas, 5, 99, 30

racial policy, 53, 56, 64
racial status or classification, 8, 9, 49, 52, 53, 54, 55, 58, 65, 150
Rassenschande (race defilement), 5, 20,
Rath, Ernst vom, 6
Rathenau, Walther, 172
Reche Otto, 56
Regulation for the Elimination of the Jews from the Economic Life of Germany (12 November 1938), 211

Reich Chamber of Culture, 3, 5
Reich Citizenship Law, 5, 50, 195–196, 211, 215
Reich Foreign Ministry, 79, 84
Reich Ministry of the Interior, 50, 52, 58, 70, 204, 213
Reich Ministry of Justice, 53, 56, 57
Reich Press Chamber, 198
Reichsausschuss der jüdischen Jugendverbände (Reich Committee of Jewish Youth Associations), 78
Reichsbank, 84, 184
Reichsbund jüdischer Frontsoldaten, or RjF (Reich League of Jewish War Veterans), 97, 101, 103–104
Reichsfluchtsteuer (Reich flight tax), 42n89
Reichsinstitut für Forschung und Psychotherapie (German/Reich Institute for Research and Psychotherapy), 62
Reichsinstitut für die Geschichte des Neuen Deutschlands (Reich Institute for the History of the New Germany), 180
Reichsjugendführung (Reich Youth Leadership), 78
Reichsnährstand (Reich Farmers' Bureau), 101
Reichssicherheitshauptamt, see RSHA
Reichssippenamt (Reich Kinship Office), 51, 52, 57
Reichstag fire, 3
Reichsstelle für Sippenforschung (Reich Office for Kinship Research), 52
Reichsvereinigung der Juden in Deutschland (Reich Association of Jews in Germany), 7, 11, 71–72, 76, 99, 128, 139, 149–60, 162–165, 214, 215–219
Reichsvertretung der Juden in Deutschland (Reich Representation of Jews in Germany), 6, 23, 45n121, 68n21, 71, 72, 75–78, 81, 91, 96, 99, 101, 103–105, 107, 108, 114n46, 115n67, 149, 150, 156, 187, 189, 192, 214, 219
Reichszentrale für jüdische Auswanderung (Reich Central Office for Jewish Emigration), 7, 213–214
Reinhard, Johanna, 44n113
The Return of Tobias, 172
Revisionist Zionist movement, 96, 104
Rexroth, Staatsanwalt, 53

Richarz, Monika, 43n107
Riesenburger, Martin, 139, 141–142
Riga, 60, 138, 142
Righteous Among the Nations, 120
Röhm purge, 29
Rosenblüth, Martin, 105, 106, 107, 109
Rosenfeld, Else Behrend, 142
Rosenstrasse, Berlin, 121, 144n15
Rovit, Rebecca, 173
RSHA or Reichssicherheitshauptamt (Reich Security Main Office), 150–151, 153–155, 158–160, 162–163, 165
Ruppin, Arthur, 1, 108
Rust, Bernhard, 204, 219

SA (Sturmabteilung), 20, 44
Sachsenhausen 6, 43n100, 61, 155, 159
Salomon, Charlotte, 30
Sammellager (collective camps), 131, 158
Sammelstellen (collective points), 121, 121, 132
Sammelunterkünfte (collective accommodations), 131
Sauerbruch, Ferdinand, 172
Schine, Robert S., 180
Schmitt, Carl, 176
Schneidemühl, 154
Schocken Publishers 171
Scholem, Gershom, 174
Schwede-Coburg, Franz, 153
SD or Security Service (Sicherheitsdienst—SD), 57, 80, 150, 214
Seligsohn, Julius, 150, 155, 189
Shakespeare, William, 173
Shanghai, emigration to, 32, 41n72, 151
Simon, Erich, 160, 166
Sippenforscher (certified genealogist), 82
Sobibor, 142
"social death," 9, 47, 64, 66, 121, 142
Social Democrats, 3, 4, 74, 176, 192
Sonderrecht (special law), 126–127, 132
South America, 151
Speer, Albert, 124, 134
SS (Schutzstaffel), 6, 7, 20, 30, 80, 150
Staatszionistische Organisation (State Zionist Organization), 96, 104
Stahl, Friedrich Julius, 178, 189
Stahl, Heinrich, 71
Steckelsdorf, 81–82
Steinberg, Hans Wilhelm (later Willam Steinberg), 171
Stein-Pick, Charlotte, 30, 31, 32, 33

Index

Sterling, Eleonore, 175
Stern-Täubler, Selma, 174, 178
Stettin, 153–154
Stillschweig, Kurt, 176, 177–178
Straus, Rafael, 181
Der Stürmer, 123, 204, 205–206
Sudetenland, 46n127, 46n131

Talmud-Torah School, 100
Täubler, Eugen, 174
Theresienstadt, 59, 132, 133, 141, 142, 158, 160, 161–162, 164, 165
Thuringia, 58–59, 191, 205
"total state," 176
Traub, Michael, 107
Treblinka, 142
Trunk, Isaiah, 72
Tuch, Theodor, 138

Ullstein Verlag, 94
Ulm, 131
Unger, Karl, 62–63
United States, 19, 42n91, 45n123, 73, 114n46, 155, 163, 171, 194
Unser Werk, 92
Usingen, 44n113

Verband jüdischer Frauen für Palästina-Arbeit (Association of Jewish Women for Palestine Work), 97, 113n32
Verband nationaldeutscher Juden (Association of National German Jews), 76, 97
Verschuer, Otmar Freiherr von, 54, 63
Vertrauensmänner (intermediaries) 162–163, 164
Volksgemeinschaft (people's community), 9, 64, 65, 127
Volljuden ("full-blooded" Jews), 5, 55, 69n38
Vorzugslager (camp for the "privileged"), 158
Vossische Zeitung, 94

Walter, Bruno, 172
Wannsee Conference, 124
Warsaw, 47, 142
Warsaw Ghetto Uprising, 47
war veterans, Jewish, 28, 50, 97, 107
Was geschieht mit den Juden? ("What Shall be Done with the Jews?"), 176

Was wird werden? Das Schicksal der deutschen Juden in der sozialen Krise ("What Lies Ahead? The Fate of the Jews in the Social Crisis"), 176
Weichselbaum, Willy, 176
Weill, Kurt, 172
Weimar Republic, 4, 38n4, 74, 75, 121, 122, 176
Weizmann, Chaim, 95
Weltsch, Robert, 50, 105, 129, 146n52
Wertheimer, Martha, 34
Wiener, Rabbi Max, 178, 179–180, 181
Wildt, Michael, 165
winter relief, Jewish, 39n18
Wissenschaft des Judentums (The Study of Jewry), 174, 176, 178
Wisten, Fritz, 182n1
World Zionist Congress, 83
World Zionist Organization, London, 83, 91, 94, 95
Würzburg, 131
Wyden, Peter, 27

Yad Vashem (Martyrs' and Heroes' Remembrance Authority), 120
yellow star, see *Judenstern*
yishuv (Jewish community in Palestine), 82, 85, 98
Youth Aliyah, see *aliyah*
Yugoslavia, 110

Zeiss Ikon, 131
Zeitschrift für die Geschichte der Juden in Deutschland (ZGJD), 176, 180, 181
Zentralausschuss der deutschen Juden für Hilfe und Aufbau, or ZJHA (Central Committee of German Jews for Assistance and Construction), 77–78, 91, 100
Zentralwohlfahrtsstelle der deutschen Juden (Central Welfare Organization of German Jews), 73, 77, 78, 91, 100
Zion (monthly journal), 92
Zionism, 1, 8, 9, 10, 34, 51, 89–111
Zionistische Vereinigung für Deutschland or ZVfD (Zionist Federation for Germany), 68n21, 74, 79, 91, 92, 93, 95–96, 98, 102–106, 107, 108, 109, 111, 130n24

www.ingramcontent.com/pod-product-compliance
Lightning Source LLC
Chambersburg PA
CBHW071957290426
44109CB0001B/2056